Practical Data Privacy
Enhancing Privacy and Security in Data

Katharine Jarmul

Beijing · Boston · Farnham · Sebastopol · Tokyo

Practical Data Privacy

by Katharine Jarmul

Copyright © 2023 Kjamistan, Inc. All rights reserved.

Published by O'Reilly Media, Inc., 1005 Gravenstein Highway North, Sebastopol, CA 95472.

O'Reilly books may be purchased for educational, business, or sales promotional use. Online editions are also available for most titles (*http://oreilly.com*). For more information, contact our corporate/institutional sales department: 800-998-9938 or *corporate@oreilly.com*.

Acquisitions Editor: Andy Kwan
Development Editor: Rita Fernando
Production Editor: Kristen Brown
Copyeditor: Kim Wimpsett
Proofreader: Piper Editorial Consulting, LLC

Indexer: WordCo Indexing Services, Inc.
Interior Designer: David Futato
Cover Designer: Karen Montgomery
Illustrator: Kate Dullea

April 2023:   First Edition

Revision History for the First Edition
2023-04-19:   First Release

See *http://oreilly.com/catalog/errata.csp?isbn=9781098129460* for release details.

978-1-098-12946-0

[LSI]

Praise for *Practical Data Privacy*

Practical Data Privacy is exactly what it claims to be—a practical exploration of the approaches to data privacy. The book carefully balances, and makes the case for, the business benefits of protecting our users' data.

—*Rebecca Parsons, Chief Technology Officer, Thoughtworks*

Finally, a book on practical privacy for some of the most important actors of data protection in practice: data scientists and engineers! From pseudonymization to differential privacy all the way to data provenance, *Practical Data Privacy* introduces fundamental concepts in clear terms, with examples and code snippets, giving data practitioners the information they need to start thinking about how to implement privacy in practice, using the tools at their disposal.

—*Damien Desfontaines, Staff Scientist, Tumult Labs*

Gone are the days of saying "data is the new oil"; if data and oil have kinship today, it is that both are at risk to leak and make a huge, expensive mess for you and your stakeholders. The data landscape is increasing in complexity year over year. Regulatory pressures for data privacy and data sovereignty, not to mention algorithmic transparency, explainability, and fairness, are emerging worldwide. It's harder than ever to smartly manage data. Yet the tools for addressing these challenges are also better than ever, and this book is one of those tools. Katharine's practical, pragmatic, and wide-reaching treatment of data privacy is exactly the treatise needed for the challenges of the 2020s and beyond. She balances a deep technical perspective with plain-language overviews of the latest technology approaches and architectures. This book has something for everyone, from the CDO to the data analyst and everyone in between.

—*Emily F. Gorcenski, Principal Data Scientist,*
Data & AI Service Line Lead, Thoughtworks

Consumer privacy protection will define the next decade of internet technology platforms. Jarmul has written the definitive book on this topic, capturing a decade of learnings on building privacy-first systems.

—*Clarence Chio, CTO, Unit21 and coauthor of*
Machine Learning and Security *(O'Reilly)*

Some data scientists see privacy as something that gets in their way. If you're not one of them, if you believe privacy is morally and commercially desirable, if you appreciate the rigor and wonder in engineering privacy, if you want to understand the state of the art of the field, then Katharine Jarmul's book is for you.

—*Chris Ford, Head of Technology, Thoughtworks Spain*

I finally have a book to point people to when they avoid the topic of data privacy.

—*Vincent Warmerdam, Creator of Calm Code;*
Machine Learning Engineer, Explosion

Practical Data Privacy lives totally up to its promises—it is very practical! You will learn a lot about privacy in the context of machine learning with examples from big companies and many packages that will help you solve typical problems. I learned a lot while reading this book and recommend it to people who are working with data.

—*Natalie Beyer, Cofounder, LAVRIO.solutions*

Table of Contents

Foreword

Given the multitude of benefits that come with digital connectivity, it is not always apparent that waves of futuristic tech have also brought an undertow of drawbacks. Instant messaging, biometric scanning, real-time motion-tracking, digital payments, and more, were, after all, the stuff of sci-fi fantasies.

For those of us who work in technology (or just consume it), the "cool factor" of integrating digital tools into our daily routines is difficult to deny. But the other side of digitally connected living is the right to unplug. To hear some first-generation tech millionaires tell it, preventing their kids from going online at home and at school is highly desirable. That may sound strange, especially if you're used to hearing about the digital divide as a chasm between people with multiple Apple products versus have-nots who lack 24/7 high-speed internet. In fact, with so many of our everyday interactions having gone digital, it's a challenge for most of us to function without unlimited online access.

Using digital tools and accessing online spaces is sold to us today the same way it was at the dawn of the internet: as a drop-in experience that's completely voluntary and fun. But nothing is fun about an internet experience that feels like a stay at the Hotel California—"you can check out any time you want, but you can never leave." Nothing is fair about an online world that restricts your offline life in terms of what you can see, what you can do, and how you might be treated. The idea that we are choosing to "drop in" on the internet world for a casual set of interactions is no longer true: if anything, we're often obliged to navigate a highway jam-packed with data about ourselves and others.

Many of us incorrectly assume that our data is uninteresting to anyone else. But that's when we don't see the full picture of how today's apps and algorithms hoard our data to connect where we live, what we earn, who we date, and whether we've had mental health problems or a sexually transmitted infection. That's when we don't realize that the predictive function of algorithms is usually used to "profile" us using data that we've willingly and also unknowingly provided, so as to sell us (or prevent us from accessing) financial products, insurance coverage, jobs, homes, or potential romantic partners.

Digital connectivity is supposed to be fun, not reminiscent of being criminally tracked. But near-criminal tracking is the shopping experience that I've had in the real world since I was a child in New York City: it was typically anything but pleasant to shop or find a taxi as a visible minority then. I know very well the feeling of being scanned, surveilled, and singled out from a group. This is what one tech exposé after another shows us: that having our private, personal, and permanent data being hoovered up into "profiles" and passed to data brokers, governments, and law enforcement destroys our privacy. Just as it does for convicted criminals.

For those who haven't considered it much, privacy is—like access to good credit or a good lawyer—something better to have and not need than to need and not have. It should not take a biometric data shakedown while boarding an airplane (which I had to protest recently in San Francisco) to recognize that our personal data is too often collected without our consent or understanding. It should not require a person from a racial minority group to flag a data-driven health or financial algorithm as being discriminatory. For those of us working in tech, it shouldn't require lawsuits, corporate fines, and government regulation to see that systems that all but forcibly extract our data leave us without privacy or choice. And as for adopting "neo-Luddite" measures to protect one's privacy by staying offline? Much like having good credit and a good lawyer, preserving personal data privacy has become the new privilege of the wealthy.

That divide may be the most glaring problem of our digitally connected lives. If we ever want to return to a digital world that we can choose to "drop in" on, we will need to limit the degree to which digital systems extend their tentacles to us offline. Giving people back the right to browse anonymously or to announce themselves online means reining in the data-collection mechanisms that currently drive most digital systems. With *Practical Data Privacy*, Ms. Jarmul offers tested techniques for building an online world very different from what we have today. Her real-life examples prove that you do not need to be a privacy engineer to meaningfully engineer privacy.

I hope everyone who worries about algorithmic discrimination and "ethical technology" will read this book. Moreover, I encourage anyone who designs, engineers, or tests digital systems to decide for themselves if privacy is the component that separates the online experiences that we have from the ones we want and need.

> — *Dr. Nakeema Damali Stefflbauer*
> *CEO, FrauenLoop and Global AI Ethics lecturer,*
> *Stanford University*

Preface

Welcome to the wonderful world of data privacy! You might have some preconceived notions around privacy—that it is a nuisance, that it is administrative and therefore boring, or that it's a topic that interests only lawyers. What this book will show you is just how technically challenging and interesting data privacy problems are and will continue to be for years to come. If you entered the field of data science because you liked challenging mathematical and statistical problems, you will love exploring data privacy in data science. The topics you'll learn in this book will expand your understanding of probability theory, modeling, and even cryptography.

Learning how to solve data privacy problems is increasingly critical for data science practitioners today. You'll be able to solve real-world problems in fields like cybersecurity, healthcare, and finance, and you'll be able to advance your career in a patchwork world of privacy regulations, policies, and frameworks. Since 2018 when the General Data Protection Regulation (GDPR) went into effect in Europe, the global landscape has become more complicated, and that complexity will increase as regulatory agencies and lawmakers continue to change the rules about how, where, why, and when you store data. Building up your data privacy and data security skill set now is an investment in your career.

Additionally, taking the time to learn new privacy skills means you are contributing to the field of data science—enhancing trust, accountability, understanding, and social responsibility. Currently, there is fear and backlash against the use of machine learning to solve real-world problems. This response is based on real issues and actual deployments, where data, models, and systems were not used in a trustworthy manner and where justice and fairness come into question. For example, Clearview AI scrapes faces from social media sites and sells the facial recognition model built from those faces to law enforcement (*https://oreil.ly/PE6u1*),[1] raising questions regarding data ownership, privacy, and accountability. To help counter this

---

1 For a full URL list without shorteners, please see *https://practicaldataprivacybook.com*.

reputational damage and to create pathways for responsible and trustworthy data, the industry needs data scientists and machine learning engineers who understand the tasks at hand, the risks involved, and who can competently address these issue when designing systems. Privacy can help guide you to fairer, more ethical, and more responsible systems, where the user has power and input and is at the center of your design. Use this book as you navigate these challenges, finding ways forward with practical, hands-on guidance.

I hope this book can contribute to new data science by expanding familiarity with how to appropriately implement privacy for sensitive data. Worldwide, apprehension around digitizing personal data—even for responsible government use—is so prevalent that it obstructs the use of data to provide assistance with social problems such as climate change, financial auditing, and global health crises. Building privacy into data science creates new pathways for data use in critical decisions for our societies and for our world.

What Is Data Privacy?

In a simple sense, data privacy protects data and people by enabling and guaranteeing more privacy for data via access, use, processing, and storage controls. Usually this data is people-related, but it applies to all types of processing. This definition, however, doesn't fully cover the world of data privacy.

Data privacy is a complex concept—with aspects from many different areas of our world: legal, technical, social, cultural, and individual. Let's explore these aspects and how they overlap so you get an idea of the vast implications of the topics and practices you will learn in this book.

In Figure P-1, you can see the different categories of definitions of privacy, and I've tried to represent their respective size in the figure. Let's walk through them, starting with legal definitions.

In a legal context, data privacy involves the regulations, case law, and policies that declare what efforts are needed and what constitutes data privacy in a particular state or jurisdiction. As you'll learn in Chapters 1 and 9, this is an ever-changing understanding and landscape that in recent years has changed dramatically. It is important to familiarize yourself with the legal aspects of data privacy because they can directly impact your work. For example, what happens when your organization is subject to an audit, data breach, or consumer complaint? These legal definitions also impact your personal life: what rights do you have as a data citizen?

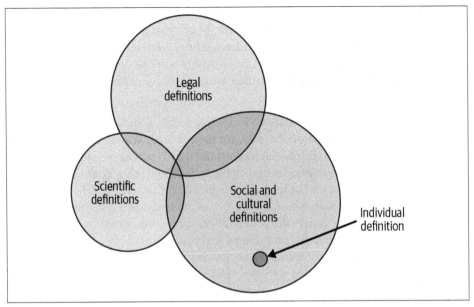

Figure P-1. Privacy definitions

The scientific or technical definitions of privacy and their implementations in your daily work are the focus of this book. You will learn these definitions, how to deploy scientific privacy technologies at scale, and how to make technical decisions about privacy. With the tools in this book, you will learn state-of-the-art best practices that might not yet be well-known at your organization as they are only recently available in production systems. Staying up-to-date on these practices will be part of your job—should you decide to focus on this area. As a technical expert on the topic, you will be asked to support business and legal decisions on privacy and translate them into working software and systems. This is a significant role as many of the other stakeholders will not have a technical and up-to-date understanding of privacy.

The social and cultural aspects of privacy are best explained by danah boyd's work in data privacy (*http://www.danah.org*). She studied teenage girls and their interaction with social media to understand how technology impacted their understanding of concepts like privacy. Her definition is as follows:

> Privacy is not about control over data nor is it a property of data. It's about a collective understanding of a social situation's boundaries and knowing how to operate within them. In other words, it's about having control over a situation. It's about understanding the audience and knowing how far information will flow. It's about trusting the people, the situating, and the context.
>
> —danah boyd, "Privacy and Publicity in the Context of Big Data" (*https://oreil.ly/ThnPz*)

boyd shows us a new aspect of privacy in this definition that poses significant changes in how to design privacy into systems. In contrast to technical and legal definitions, boyd puts social and cultural understanding, context, and individual choice and understanding in the center. When you read her work or see her speak, you hear truths you have often felt but never clarified around how we as humans and as society understand privacy and information.

For example, when I lower my voice to a whisper and lean in to tell you something, you understand that information is not meant to be shared. When I shout it in a public square and ask people to listen, you understand that I want as many people to hear it as possible. How a person decides and changes the people they communicate with, and the way in which they communicate, are greatly influenced by how that person defines and views privacy, shown in Figure P-1 as the individual definition. The ability for someone to experiment with and shift their communication with others has significantly changed over time. Technology and the internet have allowed everyone to expand their communication and resulting privacy choices to contexts that are not physical. In doing so, you have new possibilities for connection, community, and information sharing—which are wonderful!

What this shift from the physical world to the online world has also done, however, is obfuscated our ability to reason about what context we are operating in. What are the rules of this space? Who can see me and hear me? Am I talking to you or to a group, and how big is that group? Helen Nissenbaum's work on contextual integrity (*https://oreil.ly/SZ0iF*) demonstrates that technology has changed how perceptible and transparent these lines are—not only via user interfaces but in the fundamental ways systems and software are designed. Choices for application defaults end up affecting privacy for potentially millions of people at once. Decisions on security and encryption make private conversations open for law enforcement and state surveillance. Data warehouses can take sensitive information meant for only one person and create access paths for employees and third-party data services. When the context is lost or obfuscated and the system design does not take the social and cultural definitions of privacy into account, the technology has essentially ignored the human aspect of privacy.

This book will show you opportunities to take these social understandings and build them into practical systems. There will be many difficult decisions you'll need to make—but giving users ways to navigate their privacy context in digital spaces and safe defaults are invaluable gifts that the world needs more of. As you read through this book and learn more about the technical aspects of privacy, keep the social and legal definitions in mind—they are and will be forever entwined.

Who Should Read This Book

This book is for data scientists who want to upskill themselves with a focus on data privacy and security. You could have many reasons, such as:

- You'd like to pursue a specialization (data privacy) that you care about, which has a long future in the industry.

- You want to move into a more regulated industry like finance or healthcare, and these skills will set you up as a promising candidate in these sectors.

- You work with research data, and you'd like to get faster approval from ethics board reviews and publications.

- You are a data science freelancer or consultant and want to expand your customer base by ensuring that you know how to manage sensitive data.

- You manage a data team and want to be able to design products and architect solutions with attention to data privacy.

- You would like to use "AI for good" and think privacy is an important human right.

- Your team has been told that privacy is important, but you aren't sure of what that means or how to go about implementing it.

- You work with sensitive data and want to ensure you are following best practices.

- You'd like to become a privacy engineer and focus on engineering privacy into data products.

- Privacy and security are neat topics, and you just enjoy learning more about them.

I could go on and on, actually, and I have met different folks from all of these backgrounds. One thing I can tell you with certainty is that demand for these skills is increasing rapidly, driven by much more than new regulations. Companies are investing in these skills so they can build a secure future for data management. By investing in privacy, companies not only avoid expensive incidents but also create a trusted brand and company culture when managing data, benefiting their recruitment, marketing, and liability.

Familiarity with Python, Jupyter notebooks, math, and statistics will help you follow along with all sections, but this book can also be read without those deeper theoretical and implementation-focused sections as long as you understand the overarching concepts.

Don't worry if you haven't worked on math in a while. I've included information about each of the examples to help explain them—and reading through slowly will help.

In writing this book, I've gotten feedback from software engineers, security specialists, and even privacy lawyers who found this book useful. Although these people are not my target audience, I do hope this book can help anyone who has an interest in privacy and technology and their intersection in data systems.

As you read this book and work through exercises, you'll see how aspects of data privacy highlight the wonders of data science you already know and love. As with other challenging areas of data science, this book will take you from simple methods for solving privacy into more difficult ones, some of which aren't completely solved yet. Just like when linear regression "just works," you want to start with simple and obvious solutions. But when you need something more than the simple solution, you will need to ask deeper questions that have technical and ethical implications. Finding these questions and exploring them and their answers will make you a better data scientist, technologist, statistician, and mathematician.

This book may be all you require to become a technologist with some extra skills around data privacy. That's fine! You might also decide this book is the first of several in a path that takes you farther into the field. In case that's enticing to you, let me introduce you to the concept of privacy engineering.

Privacy Engineering

In the next 10 years,[2] I foresee that the field of privacy engineering (*https://oreil.ly/XENvQ*) will continue to grow in importance. The skills you gain in this book by working through the exercises and applying this new knowledge to your work will prepare you for this role.

At companies where data science is an important product, a privacy engineer is part data scientist and part engineer. This means that, unlike some roles in data science, you are actively engineering and architecting solutions rather than exploring data or testing an idea in a lab setting. This could mean working directly with the data engineering teams, the software or applications teams, or even the architects at your

---

2 Disclaimer: I generally avoid predictions, as they are often wrong; however, I am offering this one, based on hard-won experience in the industry for the past 6 years.

company to ensure privacy is built into the product as well as the internal applications. This covers all consumer and employee data flows, software used in data management, and internal and external data use cases. You'll need to understand engineering and architecture basics as part of this work, especially as it pertains to designing systems and integrating systems with one another. Some related titles you can pick up on these topics are:

- *Software Architecture in Practice*, 4th Edition (*https://oreil.ly/5M2Zt*)
- *Fundamentals of Software Architecture* (*https://oreil.ly/Ti01n*)
- *Head First: Design Patterns* (*https://oreil.ly/5PG_R*)
- *Designing Data-Intensive Applications* (*https://oreil.ly/xIyh9*)
- *Practical MLOps* (*https://oreil.ly/tXioO*)

Determining what tooling and software works for an organization requires a sophisticated architecture, so simply implementing privacy policy via plug-and-play vendors is often too naive to address these problems. That said, the growing space of privacy technology companies means that you become a decision maker for evaluating technologies to build, or buy, and use for data privacy management. In doing so, you'll be using concepts learned from this book to put together evaluation criteria, ask probing questions on the implementation, and analyze the flexibility, support, and product features. In this role, you will determine how well potential vendors can meet your company needs as the dependence on private, sensitive, and confidential data grows.

A privacy engineer is not just another data scientist or architect who cares about privacy but is given no authority, time, or budget to make decisions about privacy. Although it is great that advocacy has become part of the data science role, privacy engineering is about building and applying privacy techniques as data is ingested, collected, transformed, stored, and then used in data science applications. Advocacy is a nice side job, but implementation proves these technologies work.

Nor is a privacy engineer just a data engineer who thinks about privacy. While privacy engineers can work alongside data engineers and often might embed in a team for a project or a proof of concept, they must work with different parts of the organization and will be pulled into many projects where their expertise is relevant. They are specialists and are not locked into a single project or use case for too long. Instead, their knowledge is a tremendously valuable resource that should be applied to the most pressing business problems affected by data privacy.

The position of a privacy engineer is still being defined and continues to evolve. Although larger technology companies are actively hiring actively hire for these roles now, its emergence reminds me of the rise of the term *machine learning engineer* in 2018. Privacy engineering as a practice is a relatively new skill set in data science that is emerging because of industry needs and demands. I am excited to see how privacy engineers shift 2 or 10 years from now—and hope that this book inspires a few new people in the field.

Why I Wrote This Book

When I first became interested in data privacy, it felt like a maze. Most of the material was beyond my comprehension, and introductory guides were often written by folks trying to sell me software. Luckily, I knew a few folks in the data privacy community who helped shepherd me to a deeper and broader understanding of privacy. It took many hours of study and several helping hands to get me from curious data scientist to someone who had command of the topics you'll find in this book—and I continue learning new things and diving deeper into the field every year.

I am convinced the skills you will learn in this book are essential for data scientists today and in the future. The steep learning curve I experienced is unnecessary, and that's what this book will help you avoid. I wrote this book to provide a welcoming, fast-paced, and practical environment for you to learn, ask questions, find helpful advice, and begin to dive deeper into the challenging topics.

This book is meant to be a useful overview—leading you from zero knowledge to actively integrating data privacy into your work. You'll learn popular strategies, like pseudonymization and anonymization methods, and newer approaches, like encrypted computation and federated data science. If this book acts as a springboard for your academic career or leads you to a research role, that would be terrific. The field needs intelligent and curious folks working on the unsolved problems in this space. But at its core, this book is a practical-minded overview providing pointers along the way should you want to learn more.

Data scientists and technologists who need to integrate data privacy and security topics as part of their daily work will find this book helpful. There are several chapters that work as quick references for you as you navigate data privacy. While a cover-to-cover read will help you create your knowledge base and teach you how to solve new and unknown data privacy challenges, a quick search provides straightforward advice on how to manage specific data privacy emergencies that come up in your day-to-day work.

Navigating This Book

This book is organized into chapters with a practical approach to data privacy and a mixture of theory, exercises, and use cases:

- Chapter 1, "Data Governance and Simple Privacy Approaches", focuses on data governance and simple privacy approaches, answering questions you might have about how to manage data, track consent, and pseudonymize data for internal use.

- Chapter 2, "Anonymization", dives into anonymization, covering state-of-the-art approaches that you can use today and exploring the rise of differential privacy as a tool for data scientists at the US Census Bureau.

- Chapter 3, "Building Privacy into Data Pipelines", covers how to begin automating privacy in data pipelines and workflows, documenting several use cases around consent, anonymization, and data engineering.

- Chapter 4, "Privacy Attacks", outlines well-known privacy attacks, including the de-anonymization of the Netflix prize dataset, and introduces ways you can reason about potential breaches and attacks when working with sensitive data.

- Chapter 5, "Privacy-Aware Machine Learning and Data Science", explores privacy-aware data science and machine learning, introducing how to integrate data privacy into data science projects. This chapter should be used as a quick reference for exploring particular approaches in a project- or product-based data science team.

- Chapter 6, "Federated Learning and Data Science", describes how federated techniques work in machine learning and data science and compares those approaches to other privacy-preserving and data minimization techniques.

- Chapter 7, "Encrypted Computation", covers encrypted learning and encrypted computation for data privacy in data science, diving into multiparty computation and homomorphic encryption protocols and libraries.

- Chapter 8, "Navigating the Legal Side of Privacy", navigates how to read and apply data privacy regulation and policies, looking at the GDPR, the California Consumer Privacy Act (CCPA), and internal policy examples to support your path through the legal side of privacy.

- Chapter 9, "Privacy and Practicality Considerations", helps you apply what you have learned to design secure and private data systems with real-world use cases. This is another chapter that serves as a quick reference for architects and data science management.

- Chapter 10, "Frequently Asked Questions (and Their Answers!)", summarizes frequently asked questions and use cases as a handy reference for data privacy emergencies, allowing you to confidently move forward and ensure data privacy is baked into each project and your normal workflow. It also opens up the social and personal aspects of privacy to integrate them into your life outside of work.

- Chapter 11, "Go Forth and Engineer Privacy!", is the book's conclusion, and provides support and motivation for using your newly acquired data privacy skills to push the field and your own path forward!

Links in this book are shortened for your convenience to O'Reilly URLs. These URLs have minimal tracking and have been reviewed for GDPR compliance and privacy. Should you want to opt out of this minimal tracking, you can find the full list of URLs at *https://practicaldataprivacybook.com*.

Conventions Used in This Book

The following typographical conventions are used in this book:

Italic
Indicates new terms, URLs, email addresses, filenames, and file extensions.

`Constant width`
Used for program listings, as well as within paragraphs, to refer to program elements such as variable or function names, databases, data types, environment variables, statements, and keywords.

`Constant width bold`
Shows commands or other text that should be typed literally by the user.

`Constant width italic`
Shows text that should be replaced with user-supplied values or by values determined by context.

 This element signifies a tip or suggestion.

 This element signifies a general note.

This element indicates a warning or caution.

Using Code Examples

Supplemental material (code examples, exercises, etc.) is available for download at *https://github.com/kjam/practical-data-privacy*.

If you have a technical question or a problem using the code examples, please send email to *bookquestions@oreilly.com*.

This book is here to help you get your job done. In general, if example code is offered with this book, you may use it in your programs and documentation. You do not need to contact us for permission unless you're reproducing a significant portion of the code. For example, writing a program that uses several chunks of code from this book does not require permission. Selling or distributing examples from O'Reilly books does require permission. Answering a question by citing this book and quoting example code does not require permission. Incorporating a significant amount of example code from this book into your product's documentation does require permission.

We appreciate, but generally do not require, attribution. An attribution usually includes the title, author, publisher, and ISBN. For example: "*Practical Data Privacy* by Katharine Jarmul (O'Reilly). Copyright 2023 Kjamistan, Inc., 978-1-098-12946-0."

If you feel your use of code examples falls outside fair use or the permission given above, feel free to contact us at *permissions@oreilly.com*.

O'Reilly Online Learning

For more than 40 years, *O'Reilly Media* has provided technology and business training, knowledge, and insight to help companies succeed.

Our unique network of experts and innovators share their knowledge and expertise through books, articles, and our online learning platform. O'Reilly's online learning platform gives you on-demand access to live training courses, in-depth learning paths, interactive coding environments, and a vast collection of text and video from O'Reilly and 200+ other publishers. For more information, visit *https://oreilly.com*.

Please address comments and questions concerning this book to the publisher:

O'Reilly Media, Inc.
1005 Gravenstein Highway North
Sebastopol, CA 95472
800-998-9938 (in the United States or Canada)
707-829-0515 (international or local)
707-829-0104 (fax)

We have a web page for this book, where we list errata, examples, and any additional information. You can access this page at *https://oreil.ly/practicalDataPrivacy*.

Email *bookquestions@oreilly.com* to comment or ask technical questions about this book.

For news and information about our books and courses, visit *https://oreilly.com*.

Find us on LinkedIn: *https://linkedin.com/company/oreilly-media*

Follow us on Twitter: *https://twitter.com/oreillymedia*

Watch us on YouTube: *https://youtube.com/oreillymedia*

Acknowledgments

I would like to first thank my partner, Aaron Glenn, for the long coffee walks, discussions, and daily support that led to the creation and writing of this book. If you want to learn about open source, community-driven, and software-defined computer networking, or you are just curious about how the internet actually works, please find his work at Predicted Paths (*https://predictedpaths.com*).

My experience in privacy technology has exposed me to people who taught me more than I can imagine. Most prominently, not only was my time with the "PETs" team at Dropout Labs/Cape Privacy: (Morten Dahl (*https://oreil.ly/WjCQt*), Jason Mancuso (*https://oreil.ly/jZUgU*), and Yann Dupis (*https://oreil.ly/d9myd*)) one of the best working experiences of my life, but I also learned everything I know about encrypted computation. Morten, thank you for your articles that inspired new thinking around encryption and machine learning, the countless hours of Jamboarding and answering questions, and generally being the best non-professor-but-actually-could-be-a-professor I've had a chance to learn from in my life. Jason, I miss hearing your thoughts about new breakthroughs in multitask learning and what is on your mind that will revolutionize Privacy Preserving Machine Learning (PPML) next. Yann, your pragmatic let's-build-it-and-see and countless explanations showed me and our customers how these technologies can lead not only to better outcomes but also to true privacy guarantees. My time with you all is something I will always cherish.

My journey in building privacy technology started with cofounding KIProtect (*https://kiprotect.com*) with Dr. Andreas Dewes. Andreas, thank you for being my sparring partner, business partner, and thinking partner in those years! I would not be where I am today without everything we built and learned.

A special thank-you to Damien Desfontaines, who put me through differential privacy boot camp when I started this book. Damien, thank you for the many conversations, for your contributions to the field, and for being a humble and awesome human. Your openness to share your knowledge, your work to make open source differential privacy usable in the field, and your amazing blog (*https://desfontain.es/*) are invaluable. Keep up the good fight!

To the woman technologists and good friends in my life who help keep me sane, motivated, and happy: Dr. Nakeema Stefflbauer (*https://www.nakeema.net*), Dr. Carma Lüdtke (*https://oreil.ly/t91bF*), Ellen König (*https://www.ellenkoenig.de*), Christine Cheung (*https://www.xtine.net*), and Sandy Strong (*https://oreil.ly/Zs85P*). I am so lucky to know you all—thank you for being there with me through all the peaks and valleys of life in this crazy world. I wouldn't have the chutzpah to write such a book if it weren't for being inspired by your work.

To my mom and tireless unpaid editor, thank you for muddling through my words and spending your retirement time correcting my passive voice. I bet you never thought you'd still be correcting that 30 years later! Learning German didn't really help; sorry about that. I could never put into words all the things I am thankful for, but here I can at least thank you for the book edits.

To my dad and Cathy, thank you for cheering me on and believing in my work. Sitting on the porch watching the river go by helped clear my mind while writing some of the most challenging sections of this book. Taking the appropriate breaks to play with the puppies, go for a walk, and have a glass of wine helped too!

To Dai and Rhys, you always are there to pump me up—both on social media and in real life! It's so nice to have the positive energy during the times when projects like this book seem daunting.

To my editors at O'Reilly: Rita Fernando and Andy Kwan. Rita, thank you for so much input, guidance, and patience as I learned how to write this book and what this book was about. I will miss our check-ins, and I hope to get a chance to say hello sometime in real life. Andy, you were the first believer in this book—thank you for taking the chance on it!

To my technical reviewers: Natalie Beyer (*https://www.lavrio.solutions*), Clarence Chio (*https://cchio.org*), and Timothy Yim (*https://oreil.ly/XkAgF*). Natalie, thank you so much for giving me the data science lens and feedback. Your feedback helped make the unclear parts of this book easier and ideally will help many data scientists along the way. Clarence, I've been such a fan of your work on adversarial ML; it was an honor to have your thoughtful input and years of expertise in this book as well. Timothy, your expertise helped clarify early chapters' advice on governance and consent workflows, thank you!

To my fellow Thoughtworkers, who supported me by listening to me think out loud, kept me thinking via interesting questions and new ideas, helped me keep learning and working by giving me encouragement and feedback along the way, and helped me evolve my ideas into what they are in this book. Special thanks to Chris Ford (*https://oreil.ly/eJOEG*), who was also a technical reviewer, and Enrico Massi (*https://oreil.ly/nNNny*) and Lisa Junger (*https://oreil.ly/EKQn5*), whose regular chats and expertise helped make the security concerns in this book real and accurate. Additional kudos to Clara Brünn (*https://oreil.ly/xmgYP*), for such helpful feedback and interesting insights from your own data science work and experience, and Mitchell Lisle (*https://oreil.ly/16N7v*) and Menghong Li (*https://oreil.ly/oqe4z*), whose interest in privacy engineering sparked new ideas and led to the book repository's database reconstruction attack—thank you! To my "nonboss" Emily Gorcenski (*https://oreil.ly/ViIc5*), who gave me support and time to write and encouraged my thinking in how privacy and strategy intertwine. And the warmest of thanks to Sowmya Ganapathi Krishnan (*https://oreil.ly/rMA6q*), Nimisha Asthagiri (*https://oreil.ly/l8trh*), and Erin Nicholson (*https://oreil.ly/sVZmW*)—whose own passion for security and privacy technology and truly amazing new friendships helped me on the long road to get this book from idea to print.

To my technical writers group, for motivating me and sharing your ideas, feedback, and own journeys—thank you! Although our crazy schedules meant that the group met only a few times, it helped me through the initial growing pains to get back into a normal writing flow.

To Freddie Hubbard and Beyoncé, whose tracks helped me through the early mornings and late nights.

To my niece Charlotte, to my godson Neorth, to Ragnar and Horik, I hope this book is one small drop in the wave of change. I hope you grow up to see a world where privacy is a fundamental right for everyone, no matter who they are or where they live.

## CHAPTER 1

Data Governance and Simple Privacy Approaches

Data privacy is a large and long-lived field. I want you to picture it like an old road, packed with interesting side streets and diversions but hard to navigate if you don't know the way. This chapter is your initial orientation to this road. In this chapter and throughout this book, I'll help you map important parts of the privacy landscape, and you'll find areas where you want to learn more and deviate from the original path. Applying this map within your organization means uncovering who is doing what, what their responsibilities are, and what data privacy needs exist in your organization.[1]

You might have heard the phrase *data governance* only once or hundreds of times, but it is often left unexplained or open for interpretation. In this chapter, you'll learn where data governance overlaps with data privacy for practical data science purposes and learn simpler approaches for solving privacy problems with data, such as pseudonymization. You'll also learn how governance techniques like documentation and lineage tracking can help identify privacy problems or ways to implement privacy techniques at the appropriate step.

---

1 Throughout this book, I'll use the term *organization* as a word to describe your workplace. If you are at a small agile data science consultancy, a massive corporation, or a midsize nonprofit, you will have a vastly different experience. This book should be useful for all groups—take the advice and learnings and use your own knowledge of your work to fit them to your size and culture.

If you already know or work in data governance, I recommend skimming or skipping this chapter. If governance and data management are new to you, this chapter will show you the foundations needed to apply the advanced techniques you'll learn in later chapters.

This chapter will help give you tools and systems to identify, track, and manage sensitive data. Without this foundation, it will be difficult to assess privacy risk and mitigate those concerns. Starting with governance makes sense, because privacy fits well into the governance frameworks and paradigms, and these areas of work support one another in data systems.

Data Governance: What Is It?

Data governance is often used as an "all-encompassing" way to think about our data decisions, like whether to opt in to allowing a service to contact you or determining who has access rights to a given database. But what does the phrase really refer to, and how can you make it actionable?

Data governance is literally governing data. One way to govern happens via a transfer of rights people individually and communally possess. Those rights are passed onto elected officials who manage tasks and responsibilities for individuals who have no time, expertise, or interest. In data governance, individuals transfer rights when data is given to an organization. When you use a website, service, or application, you agree to whatever privacy policy, terms, and conditions or contract is presented by those data processors or collectors at that time. This is similar to living in a particular state and implicitly agreeing to follow the laws of that land.

Data governance helps manage whose data you collect, how you collect and enhance it, and what you do with it after collection. Figure 1-1 illustrates how privacy and security relate to data governance, via an imaginary island where users and their data are properly protected by both privacy and security initiatives. In this diagram, you can see the sensitive data inside a tower. Security initiatives are supported by Privacy by Design.[2] Regulations and compliance provide a moat that keeps sensitive data separate. Privacy technologies you will learn in this book are bridges for users and data stakeholders, allowing them to gather insights and make decisions with sensitive data without violating individual privacy.

---

2 Privacy by Design is a set of principles developed by Ann Cavoukian outlining measures technologists can use to ensure systems are architected and software is designed with privacy in mind from the beginning. You will hear it used quite often in conversations with experienced governance experts. I recommend taking time to read and explore these principles and determine how they fit your data work. These principles are included in Chapter 11.

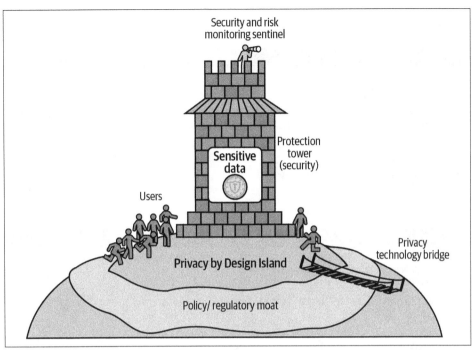

Figure 1-1. Mapping data governance

Data governance can be described as a mixture of people, process, and technology. Regardless of your organization size, there is always some amount of data governance work to be done. If you are at a large organization, there is probably a large team or committee creating standards, which turn into policies and procedures; those then need to be implemented in the organization's technology. If your organization is small, this might be the job of your technical or legal leader. Let's zoom into the technology section, as this is likely where you'll be asked to help take these policies and procedures and ensure they are actually part of regular data processing.

What elements of taking governance standards and policies and implementing them in technology are important for data scientists? Table 1-1 outlines significant areas and related questions within data governance that you will grapple with as a data scientist.

Table 1-1. Data governance in data science

Data lineage/Origin	Policies and controls
Where did the data come from?	What laws or internal policies apply to this data?
Whose data is it? Is it possible to contact them?	Where, when, and how was it collected?
Was this data acquired from someone else, and if so, did they document how it was processed and who it belongs to?	What privacy or security concerns do you need to address when using this data?
How did the processing change the data?	What was the privacy policy and terms at collection time?
Is the metadata for lineage information easily accessible and queryable?	Did the data come from a third party? If so, what are the restrictions and obligations, contractual or otherwise, for this data?

Data reliability/Knowledge	Data privacy and security
What are the concerns around understanding the data and systems (i.e., including collection, transformation, and downstream systems)?	How is access to sensitive data managed and monitored?
Does the data have an understandable documentation trail from the moment it was collected?	Does the organization know if and when data has been breached? How?
When there are data quality problems, do you know how to diagnose and resolve them?	Who is responsible for managing privacy controls? Security controls?
Are there data storage infrastructure or old data stores that are undocumented or even unknown?	When someone invokes their data rights (i.e., GDPR), is there a system that is well documented and understood to apply these rights?
Is the data well documented and understood? (Know your data.)	What data loss prevention technologies and privacy technologies do you use and how?

You are likely already focused on many of these questions since data is a major part of your job. You might have personally suffered from a lack of data documentation, incomplete understanding of how a certain database came to be, and issues with data labeling and quality. Now you have a new word to use to describe these qualities: *governance*!

Working on the governance side of data administration or management is really about focusing on how to collect and update information about the data throughout its lifecycle. The regulatory, privacy, and security concerns shape that information and ensure governance decisions and frameworks expedite measures like individual data rights and appropriate usage of data. If your data does not come from individuals, there may be other concerns with regard to proprietary data or related security issues that guide governance initiatives.

When you think about governing data in a concrete way, you begin to look at tasks such as documenting the ever-changing data flows at your organization. It seems obvious and easy, but on closer look it is anything but.

Let's say you have a huge data lake that gets fed from 10 different sources, some external, some internal. How can you actually begin to govern that data? What would a scalable and easy-to-use solution look like? What happens when those data flows change? It may be enough just to document the code or the workflows that are actively running and in use and to leave the rest for future work. But what do you do with data from partners or other external data collection systems? You'll need to coordinate this documentation so the legal, privacy, and risk departments can use it for auditing and assessment. This process should not be solved with piecemeal and temporary solutions but instead addressed as holistically as possible.

To begin, let's identify which data is the most important to protect for the purpose of practical data privacy. How can you identify sensitive data? What exactly is sensitive data?

Identifying Sensitive Data

In the context of privacy, sensitive data is normally defined as person-related data or even just personally identifiable data.[3] It includes your full name, your email address, your gender, your mailing address, your IP address, your social media profile, your phone number, your Social Security number or other national identification number, your credit card number, your birthday, your health records or biometric data (i.e., fingerprints, iris scan, or even your gait (*https://oreil.ly/-ykxk*)!).

All of these fall under the category of personally identifiable data, or what many refer to as *personally identifiable information* (PII). This data is specific to you; it can be used alone or in combination with other sources of information about you to directly identify, indirectly identify, or re-identify you. This is the most sensitive and frequently regulated data because it provides a nearly or completely unique identifier.

As defined in this book, sensitive data includes:

PII
> Data that is unique or close to unique for a particular individual. This is usually defined in policy and regulations and can include things that you might not expect, such as your IP address, date of birth, and workplace.

Person-related data
> Data that relates to a person but doesn't fall under PII. This could be anything related to their personhood, including interests, beliefs, locations, and online and offline behaviors and activities.

---

3 Your organization might have their own definition of sensitive data that varies from the one used in this book. Ensure you use appropriate terms internally when bringing up these topics.

Proprietary and confidential data
> Data deemed sensitive for contractual or business-related purposes. Its release would endanger a business or other legal relationship or agreement.

One thing I hope this book will do is expand your definition of sensitive data to include a broader range. For example, do you think your phone location is sensitive? Or does it depend on where you are? If you are sitting at home, your phone location also reveals your mailing address or residence, which again is personally identifiable. What about if you are at work? Or in a movie theater? Or at a close friend's house?

What about your political affiliation and areas of interest? Voting history? Religious beliefs and practices? Your friendships, partnerships, and who you connect with? What about your daily routines, the news you consume, your music and entertainment choices, the devices you own?

These questions begin to reveal the range of privacy preferences. Some individuals might be comfortable sharing their location at work or might even be required to do so. Others might see this as an invasion of privacy. Whereas one person might be quite open about their personal relationships, political choices, and religion, another person might see these topics as deeply personal and sensitive. This echoes the notion of contextual privacy and social privacy as discussed in the Preface. Here, regulations step in, giving individuals more choice regarding their privacy preferences and the ability to communicate that sensitivity to data collectors via changes in privacy policies and consent choices.

It also means, however, that when you work with data, you recognize the range of what is considered *sensitive*. You should be aware of the additional privacy risk created when person-related data is combined in a new way that inadvertently exposes the individuals. For example, if I track your location throughout the day, I would likely learn where you work, where you eat, your daily personal activities, and where you live. Even if I were to collect data just while you were moving (i.e., driving data), I would be able to identify some of those attributes. Even if I collected data only when you were in the presence of others, I could likely still infer things about you, such as if you travel with family or a friend or if you like to shop at a particular store or commute along a particular route and at what times.

Similarly, it's been shown by researchers that a series of Facebook likes can be used to infer things such as gender, sexual orientation, and political beliefs—even the marital status of your parents.[4] These are inferences, not necessarily fact—but it is clear that online behavior and social network behavior create unique breadcrumbs and reveal patterns that expose personal and private traits of an individual. This proves any person-generated data is potentially identifiable.

The power of inference combined with vast quantities of information can identify individuals even when that is not the intention. In targeted advertising, sensitive attributes are often inferred and combined without consent, leading to recommendations that might leak sensitive information such as sexual orientation or political views. When an advertiser is choosing targeted groups, the more factors they specify, the more easily they could erroneously target a particular individual or very small target group. If an advertiser is acting maliciously, they can use the information they have to figure out how to target that exact person or get fairly close.

For these reasons, the term *sensitive data* could mean any person-related data, regardless of if it is directly personally identifiable or not. Person-related data, particularly in large quantities or in aggregate, is identifiable. In this book, when I say sensitive data, I am referring not only to PII but also to a broader range of person-related data, which could be used in combination with other information to identify a person or small group of people.

A final category of sensitive data is data that is proprietary or confidential for non-person-related reasons. This can be trade secrets, proprietary information about the business, or a particular product or information that falls under confidentiality clauses. This could be data shared between parent companies and their subsidiaries, which must be kept secret due to internal policies or confidentiality agreements. Or it could be sensitive internal data that, if leaked, would give competitors an edge or compromise the company in another manner. This type of sensitive information also benefits from approaches and technologies you'll learn in this book.

 I am a supporter of whistleblowing. If you have data you believe should be publicly known but is considered sensitive, think about the techniques you will learn in this book as ways to release that data publicly or to the appropriate authorities in a responsible and thoughtful way.

---

4 This work was published by some of the researchers who later worked on Cambridge Analytica. See: Kosinki et al., "Private traits and attributes are predictable from digital records of human behavior" (*https://oreil.ly/ZZCnR*), 2013.

The first step toward protecting sensitive data is reliably identifying it. Once data is identified and documented as sensitive, you can then figure out how best to protect it.

Identifying PII

PII falls under a particular legal category in most data protection regulations, which requires close attention when data governance is implemented at an organization. If your organization collects any personal data—even for employees—then this data often has special governance requirements. Frequently, there is a lack of documentation or categorization of PII because it often shows up in text files, log files, or other unstructured data, which are all notoriously poorly documented.

There are several tools built explicitly for PII discovery in unstructured data using a variety of methods. I've also seen teams successfully build their own tools and systems for PII discovery. Many tools use fairly brittle methods like regular expressions (which are strings used to match patterns) or string entropy (for finding things like application programming interface [API] keys, cryptographic keys, or passwords). I have also successfully built deep learning models to identify PII in message text. Your results with these approaches will vary and should be evaluated depending on your use cases.

PII discovery is never perfect and never will be. It's important to talk with your risk teams (privacy, legal, security) about this fact, whether you purchase a PII discovery toolkit or build your own. It's safest to treat human-input data as extremely sensitive (e.g., as PII), regardless of the "cleaning processes." If you would like to use human-input data without extra protections associated with PII, you need to properly identify risks and ensure they are addressed and appropriately tested.

If you are working with a backlog of undocumented data and you fear there is a lot of PII contained therein, take a look at an easy-to-use open source tool. After you see how far that will take you, determine whether you need to invest in a more advanced or expensive approach. I can recommend Microsoft's Presidio (*https://oreil.ly/Tao7Z*), which also includes some basic pseudonymization techniques covered later in this chapter.

The best approach to manage and track PII is to actually track the data as it comes in and to label and manage this data as it traverses the system so you don't need to aggressively search or discover it later. One of the ways you can start the habit and culture of detecting PII early and often is to build a culture of documentation around data collection and data use. Table 1-1 gives you a good start. To develop a comprehensive approach, you might involve numerous parts of your organization, including the security team, the information and data stakeholders, and the infrastructure and IT departments.

Documenting Data for Use

Documenting your data—sensitive or otherwise—is an essential part of data governance. At larger organizations, you may also have a classification system for your data: where particular policies are applied to different categories or classes of data. For example, you might need to tag and label PII so that you ensure access to it is restricted. In this case, you can use privacy classification as an initial step for your documentation.

But documentation goes way beyond sensitive data categories. In this section, I'll walk you through ways to think about data documentation, including how to begin basic data documentation; how to find undocumented data; how to add lineage, collection, and processing information; and finally when to implement data version control. Many of these systems are necessary to create the baseline for how sensitive data is used and managed around the organization—allowing you to identify use cases that lend themselves to advanced privacy technologies you'll learn later in this book.

Basic Data Documentation

Data needs to be documented based on how it will be consumed. When you document data, think of your readers, as you would if you were documenting code. What is this reader going to understand? How will they find and access the documentation in their normal workflow? How will they search through the documentation? What words will they use? What is the most important information? How can you make it concise and helpful enough so they will actually read it? How do you make data more self-documenting and easy to update?

Although the topic of data documentation is not new, it's also not a widely used practice, especially within data science teams. Data science practices have shifted from research-oriented teams and analysis-driven dashboards to experimentation, failures, agile development, and deployment standards. This makes it even more important that others understand what is happening in data workflows and experiments via well-written documentation.

Like data and experiment version control, documenting data enables other teams to discover and utilize data sources that might have been obtuse or hard to find if not properly documented. In many organizations, data sources are often split or duplicated across teams in different parts of the organization. It can be challenging to get even the basic access and interoperability right, and producing documentation can often fall by the wayside.

It doesn't have to be that way if documentation is seen as an essential part of data work. Here are some ways to convince data management or business units that data documentation is worth the extra time and effort. Data documentation:

- Speeds up data experiments, which can lead to new data-driven insights and discoveries
- Enables cross-department and team collaboration
- Accelerates data access and use for all stakeholders
- Helps eliminate unknown or undocumented data
- Empowers data teams when deciding which data to use for new ventures, products, and models
- Signals to product teams what data is available for new ideas
- Shows analysts disparate datasets that could be used for new insights and reports
- Gives compliance and audit teams proper oversight and assists in new data security and privacy controls
- Reduces compliance and data security risk

Data governance within your organization will work only if there is functional and effective data documentation. Proper documentation can even integrate into identity management and access systems to give data administrators, data owners, and data managers easy ways to grant and revoke access based on documentation.

To empower a responsible AI-driven organization, you'll need some extra documentation to communicate any stereotypes or known biases in the data itself. In this case, I recommend taking time to read about data cards (*https://oreil.ly/zPPZu*), which is a way to document data for consumption by nontechnical users. If your team is focused on consumer-facing machine learning systems, I recommend using both data cards and model cards (*https://oreil.ly/_5NL5*) to ensure you are providing accurate, fair, and reliable systems!

The documentation can collect information on any or all of the following sections and can expand beyond what is discussed in this chapter. If you are setting up new documentation, figure out what will work best given your constraints. Prioritize the most valuable sections for your organization and expand from there.

Data Collection

Explanation and related questions

Who, where, when, why, and how was data collected? A description of when each dataset was collected, what team or software managed the collection, any post-collection processing that was performed, and why the collection happened (i.e., under what circumstances and legality).

Example

A diagram showing the data flow, with documentation on when it was implemented, by whom, and a data snapshot of the data at that point in time. The diagram should also contain consent information for legal, privacy, and compliance stakeholders—or other legitimate interest reasons for data collection, should no consent be given.

Data Quality

Explanation and related questions

What standardization has the data undergone (if any)? What quality controls were established? How many null values or extreme values are present in the data? Has the data been checked or processed for duplicates or inconsistencies? Here you can also document schema or unit changes.

Example

An analysis of the data quality in a particular time frame, including the frequency of null values, the standardization and harmonization of values (i.e., values that are changed to percentages or that are converted to a standard unit), and the data bias and variance. A deeper investigation could show histograms across numerous dimensions, show covariance or correlation between attributes, and provide information on outliers or extreme values. Should the data shift significantly in a short period of time, you could employ monitoring and alerting.

 Each of these aspects needs to be taken care of individually and then also as a complete picture. Applying only data quality tests without data privacy or security can end up inadvertently exposing sensitive data. Ensure you apply these governance mechanisms holistically and integrate the different measures thoroughly and completely.

Data Security

Explanation and related questions

What level of security risk applies to this data? What measures should be taken in use or access of this data? Perform a risk analysis on the sensitivity of the data and its infrastructure, architecture, and storage details. Provide information to help other teams (i.e., security and operations) accurately model and assess risk and make decisions on access restrictions. Here you can also document security and privacy technologies used to mitigate risk. These mitigations should also be documented so data consumers—people who will use, analyze, or further process the data—know how to work with the data intelligently. You'll learn more about how to assess, mitigate, and document security risk in Chapter 4.

Example

An evaluation of how a particular mitigation reduces the data security risk and a recommendation should this mitigation successfully address assessed risk. Implementation details should be included along with the required decision records if this mitigation is implemented.

Data Privacy

Explanation and related questions

Does the data contain person-related information? If so, what Privacy by Design (*https://oreil.ly/S13mS*) for legal or data protection requirements have been performed to ensure the data is properly handled? If PII or person-related data is stored, the documentation should include information about the jurisdiction of the data and what privacy policies and consent options were shared with the users at collection time. There should also be clear documentation on all privacy-preserving mechanisms performed with linked code and even commit hashes if possible. Ensure all person-related data is treated as sensitive data and that protection measures are adequately documented.

Example

A list of columns that contain person-related data along with a timestamp column declaring when data should be deleted based on the policy and jurisdiction when data was collected. Even better if the deletion has been automated.

Data Definitions

Explanation and related questions

What is the organization of the data? If tabular, what do the column names mean? What data types are there? What units of measurement are used? Clarify the meaning of jargon or codes in the data (i.e., shorthand or internal mappings). A description of the data fields, column names (if any), keys and values, codes, units of measure, and other details that help a new consumer of the data understand what they are using. If particular formatting standards are chosen, such as ISO date representations, 24-hour time, or other standard units, please include details on how this processing is done in case others need to find potential errors or if processing changes.

A queryable and easily accessible list of columns, their descriptions, and data types including categorical column codes listed in a searchable tabular format for easy reference.

Descriptive Statistics

Explanation and related questions

What are the standard descriptive statistics of the dataset, such as variance, distribution, mean, and so forth? How is the data distributed across particular features of importance? Is there concern that the data has particular biases or unequal classes? Summarized statistical descriptions of the data can be included in written or graphical form to allow others to quickly assess if the data fits their needs. Here, an interactive experience goes a long way. These properties can be quite sensitive, so you should expose them only after assessing the security and privacy risks of granting access. One great tool to look at for inspiration is Google's Facets (*https://oreil.ly/tV1PK*).

Example

A chart showing the percentiles of numerical columns (using box charts with outliers removed, for example). These could be selectable and dynamic based on other features, which allows you to analyze correlations and biases in the dataset itself.

This list is not all-encompassing, but it can guide you as you begin to address data documentation at your organization. Remember, this documentation is not for you but instead for the data consumers. Figure out language, visualizations, and descriptions that work for teams across the organization so end users are able to properly find what they are looking for and easily use it.

Rolling Out Data Documentation

When first rolling out your data documentation, you should experiment with what works by doing smaller tests and documentation and getting feedback. Here are a few other useful tips to help you along the way:

User experience

If you can, pair with user experience or product experts for help. Run interviews with your users and determine if the documentation is useful. Iterate and improve with this feedback.

Standardize only after success

Standardize and roll out full data documentation only when you have a system that is working and one that you can maintain and improve over time.

Maintain accuracy

Inaccurate documentation is often worse than no documentation at all, because your users will think they understand the data, but they don't. If they end up building models or making decisions based on this misunderstanding, it can end in disaster. This means you need to build something sustainable that is as easy to maintain as possible.

Just like with code and architecture documentation, your organization and data users will reap the rewards of well-documented data. This will expedite projects, standardize how the organization works with data, and help clarify data lineage and quality for easier decision-making. It will also bring up privacy and security questions at the beginning of the data lifecycle and at the start of new projects, where they are most effective!

You may already have a good grip on documentation but one nagging problem, the presence of undocumented data, that is unknown to you. It's important to tackle this problem, as undocumented data is often sensitive in nature.

Finding and Documenting Unknown Data

Unknown data are gaps in data documentation or even basic knowledge and understanding of the data. These occur at large organizations due to lack of best practices, usually over the course of many years. Data from past applications or sunsetted products, data amassed via acquisitions and partnerships, or data purchased long ago accumulate in undocumented databases or files. Sometimes this data is in active use, but no one knows how it got there or when it was collected. Other times the data is newly discovered, and the company is unclear on its origin. These types of undocumented data can also be the result of knowledge loss—where data was not documented before key people left.

When dealing with unknown data, it's important to establish a process and routine so as to prevent the data from sitting around even longer without documentation. Unknown, unmanaged, and untracked data presents large privacy and security risks, which you'll learn later in this chapter as well as in Chapter 4. Here is a suggested process you can use to investigate, document, and determine a decision when you find unknown data. Feel free to modify it to fit your needs by adding steps or clearer requirements for each stage, such as the specific location and technology that should be used.

1. Investigate potential provenance.

Does the data look like any already documented data at the company? Is the data easily found by searching a search engine (i.e., publicly available data)? Does anyone on a related team know where it came from?

---

2. Dive into discovery.

Investigate all potential sources and connect with other teams and departments. Someone might know the origin of the data or might see similarities with data they have used. Look at the contents of the data for potential clues and document your findings as you go.

3. Determine sensitivity.

Does the data have person-related or personally identifiable information? Can you determine the date it was collected by looking at any related dates in the database or document? If person-related, what would your company's privacy policy say regarding the data you found? Is there a particular data privacy or sensitivity classification that should be noted and maintained?

4. Start documentation for consumption.

How can you build documentation people will read and use? To start, document where the data was found, what it includes, and what you were able to find when asking about provenance and the sensitivity levels. Documentation should follow organizational standards and should be discoverable and accessible. At this point, you may want to involve data management decision makers to determine next steps.

5. Delete, archive, or maintain?

What are the next steps for the "now known" data? To decide, involve interested parties, including compliance and audit departments if they exist at your organization. If the data isn't sensitive, doesn't relate to any proprietary details or people, and is useful, you can likely just integrate it. Ensure the documentation is shared and updated and move on. Otherwise, you might choose to archive the data until more details become available. This is also a good option if the data isn't useful, but you would like to wait a given time before deleting it. Data minimization standards for data privacy recommend deleting the data, particularly if it contains personal details and you were not able to ascertain under what circumstances it was acquired. You should still document this decision and the investigation before you delete it so there is an audit trail. I would almost always suggest deletion if the data appears too old to be valuable for data science or business purposes.

There are several products that help teams find unknown data, if you are particularly concerned about its existence at your company. These services often provide scanning software that looks at servers and attempts to find data where you expect none. That said, if you are properly documenting your data processes and are working closely with other data teams, it's unlikely that data will just sit around unused and undiscovered.

One common issue with unknown data is that it is historical reporting data, often collected and used by business decisions makers before data science was established at the company. If the data science team or focus at your company is fairly new, then it might be worth investigating reporting data used by business units that falls outside your normal data collection mechanisms. For example, there could be many spreadsheets or other types of document-based reports that were used for years before there was better data available on customers or products. There could also be integrations with tools like employee or customer management systems or other software that pull data and place it onto internal servers or filesystems. Familiarize yourself with these if you join a new team concerned about undocumented data sources.

Sometimes these practices have developed due to *shadow IT*, where sensitive data is copied to many locations because of access restrictions. Shadow IT is a term used to describe processes outside of IT leadership or purview—often created as helpful shortcuts—that frequently lead to security and auditing nightmares. Sadly, this process is commonplace, because humans spend lots of hours, days, and weeks waiting for access to be granted. Once access is granted, users immediately copy the data or develop automation to do so, so they don't have to wait again. Part of your job as a privacy-focused data person will be to identify these practices and build better privacy technologies to expedite future access. Replace shadow IT with transparent, easy-to-use, well-documented, and privacy-preserving access systems!

 You may encounter a variety of reactions to your search for unknown data as well as your recommendations to delete it. Some folks might be defensive, afraid, or resistant to the approach; however, it's important for the business to ensure data rights are reliably and verifiably respected—regardless of good intentions. Some data teams have an idea that data should be saved, no matter what, and this type of data hoarding presents significant privacy challenges.

Rather than tackle the cultural and communication problem alone, educate decision makers about the risks of harboring unknown data. Spreadsheets full of customer or employee information are valuable assets, which either should be documented and managed by capable data and security teams following best practices or should be deleted so as to not become a target for internal or external security threats. If these reports are useful for answering questions, move the data into the light and keep it documented and audited. You will also get better insights and high-quality decisions by doing so!

Undocumented data is often orphaned data in systems with no or little lineage tracking. Similar to the basic documentation you've learned thus far, data lineage is an essential tool for data governance.

Tracking Data Lineage

Data lineage (sometimes called *data provenance*) is a way of tracking where the data came from, how it got there, and what actions have been performed on the data since entering the system. As you can imagine, this information is extremely useful for data scientists to clarify data quality, data content, and data utility.

Lineage information helps you answer questions like these:

- When was this data collected? From where?
- How am I allowed to use this data? What consent was given at collection?
- What processing, cleaning, and preparation has this data undergone (i.e., removal of nulls, standardization of units, etc.)?
- Where else is this data processed, and where is related data stored?
- What should I keep in mind about the quality and origin of the data?

Unfortunately, when companies originally developed their data infrastructure, adequate systems to track data lineage were often not available. The focus tended to be on ingesting the data and storing it away as efficiently as possible—not on tracing it and determining how it was processed. Technological debt builds up around data systems. If you find there is no lineage data, you can always start now.

Depending on how advanced your data infrastructure and engineering systems are, there might already be great places to begin documenting lineage. This information can be pulled from systems like Apache Spark (or Beam, Flink, Kafka, Airflow) or other pipeline automation systems and integrated into whatever documentation or tracking systems you are using. If you aren't sure what's already being done, it's a good idea to connect with the teams who manage data catalogs and data schema. A data catalog is an index with documentation on data sources managed and made available across the company, often including data documentation, access requirements, and even processing, storage, and quality information. If your company doesn't currently catalog data or track lineage information, then you should coordinate a group of data folks and determine the most lightweight approach to getting started.

As a data scientist, you've probably investigated a dataset that makes you question its validity. Only via proper lineage or provenance tracking can you ascertain if errors were made in collection or processing. Knowing when and where the error occurred can help you and other team members determine what might have caused it and whether there's a bug involved. Tracking origin and processing is essential when maintaining streaming or near real-time systems, as errors in the data collection and transformation can quickly propagate into models and other downstream products.

There are now many tools around data documentation, lineage, and version control. Ideally, you can find a good set of tools or even a single tool to help manage the governance concerns you have. There are always newcomers, but some tools I've seen teams enjoy are DBT (*https://oreil.ly/gBfKh*), CKAN (*https://ckan.org*), AWS Glue (*https://aws.amazon.com/glue*), and Tableau (with their Data Catalog (*https://oreil.ly/rQzle*)).

To monitor changes in data flows, I recommend using tools like Great Expectations (*https://oreil.ly/F-SPq*), which can be used to test data midstream and determine if anything has markedly changed. Great Expectations allows you to write what I call *data unit tests*, to assert that the data meets your expectations. For example, you may want to test if a particular value is not null, that a value is above or below a certain number, that a date string has been properly standardized, or even that a value is a string or an integer. These tests, when used properly by data teams, can immediately alert you of aforementioned bugs.

There are also clear wins for privacy when implementing lineage data. You'll learn more about consent tracking in Chapter 3, but a lineage and consent tracking pipeline could look like Figure 1-2. First, the user is presented with an interface with fine-grained privacy preferences explained in clear language. As the data is collected, provenance details like where, when, and how the data was collected are inserted into the data structure at the same level as the data as database fields, instead of being attached in a separate JSON document that no one uses.[5] The data enters the normal cleaning and transformation pipelines. That data is then analyzed for quality and other governance standards. Data sensitivity or the presence of PII is also analyzed in a semi-automated manner. This step may need to occur as the initial step depending on the data source and the logging included in the transformation steps. Please make sure to not log sensitive data! The data will then be stored, and the additional information is saved in linkable data structures. This process ensures additional governance data is easily referable and remains current and attached to the user data until the data is removed from the system.

---

5 Ideally this is either a separate easily linkable table or the rows themselves have extra columns or attributes, making lookup easy. You will see a concrete example of this in Chapter 3.

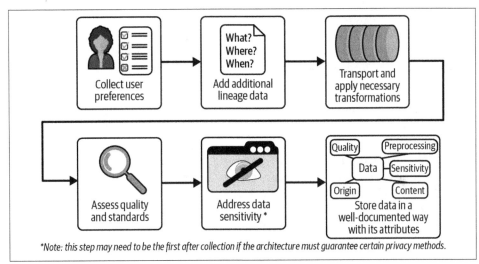

Note: this step may need to be the first after collection if the architecture must guarantee certain privacy methods.

Figure 1-2. Lineage and consent tracking pipeline

Lineage also addresses data sovereignty legislation and policies, which seem to be increasing over time. These laws focus on keeping residents' data inside a particular jurisdiction, such as keeping EU resident data hosted on infrastructure in the EU. Ensuring sovereignty controls are in place can assist your legal, compliance, and security teams in validating that the data infrastructure is following the law.

Tracking data lineage and consent adds overhead now but helps debugging and speeds up access to data later. If you work closely with a data engineering or infrastructure team, talk with them about sharing the workload for setting up and maintaining lineage information. Just like your data documentation, ensure it's readable, interpretable, and usable for the data consumers. If it sits in a file that no one ever looks at, it's not worth producing and maintaining in the first place!

Data Version Control

When you work with data daily, you understand incremental data changes occur. If you have a very large dataset, these changes are not noticeable. These incremental changes have a larger effect and impact workflows, analytics, and modeling when the data collection and transformations significantly shift or when external forces impact the incoming data, like during a global pandemic.

This is when data versioning comes into play. Data versioning is the ability to create versions or checkpoints for your data tied to a particular time. Similar to code version control systems like git, data version control allows you to monitor changes by creating a snapshot or "commit" at a particular point in time. This can then be compared with earlier or later versions to understand how the data changed.

Similar to agile software development practices such as testing, continuous integration (CI), continuous delivery (CD), and software version control, data version control benefits data science. Imagine being able to pinpoint when a change or bug happened in order to diagnose why a model isn't performing as expected or why a particular report or analytics tool stopped working.

Knowing how data you collect changes over time can be a superpower for understanding the behavior or systems you are modeling. How are the users of your application changing over time? How are your experiment results shifting? What assumptions did you have about the data originally, and how have they held up? Many questions you ask about the data can benefit from a periodic review to understand the data itself and its changes over time. Changes in software, pipelines, or other processing can significantly shift and introduce errors into the data. This is important to monitor with the potential to roll back the data and software as it might negatively affect other data models, analysis, and systems.

Data versioning also helps data privacy and trustworthy AI practices. When you can determine what data was used for a particular model, when you can pin a before and after point when someone requested their data be removed, and when you can transparently demonstrate the changes you have made to preserve privacy, you can ensure and audit responsible data use in the system. Data versioning supports each of these actions and helps ensure that you are clear about the outcomes of the data privacy measures. Then you can debug them should anything go wrong.

So how do you start versioning data? There are several tools available. Here are some evaluation questions to find what versioning tools are appropriate for you:

- How does the tool manage snapshots and checkpoints for the data? This should be done in a way that is both programmable and well understood. You don't want to be reading through documentation when you need to recover data immediately!

- Are the snapshots or versions memory efficient? How will you manage space? A fairly naive way to manage data would be to copy your entire database every day and save an old copy. This is great if you have unlimited memory and space and only a few hundred rows, but that's fairly abnormal. You'll want to evaluate how many snapshots you save, how much extra space and processing power those will take, and when to delete old snapshots.

- Will this integrate well with other teams and their workflows? As with all software choices, you should ensure that what works for your team also helps other teams working with the data. Check with the data engineers and software engineers to ensure they also know how to "recover" data. You should ensure that they understand both the API and programming language and how the tool is used.

- Can you imagine how this tool would be used? Have your team play with the tools and write up a few example stories to see if you can pre-program relevant use cases. How would a data recovery after a schema change work? How could you answer what data was used for a particular model that was trained and deployed? What if a GDPR deletion request comes in and you want to prove the data was properly removed? Spend time with the data team to make a comprehensive list and ensure the use cases you want to use it for are well understood and maybe even programmed!
- Can this be used in conjunction with data lineage efforts to better select data for particular use cases? As you learned earlier in this chapter, understanding lineage can help determine if a particular dataset is well suited for the task at hand. This information, combined with version control, can speed up the type of modeling and experimentation by increasing the data understanding and finding shifts or changes best as soon as possible.

Data versioning is closely related to model versioning. The prior questions can also be asked in relation to model versioning tools, and several open source libraries today do both. Whatever your plan is and however your team works best, think about incorporating versioning for data and models into normal workflows. These practices are well understood in software and can help make the data science work in your organization more predictable, error-free, and better understood. Setting them up now and having them evolve with data governance usage is something I would recommend for every team, even if the first few years are a learning process.

There is also growing support for version control of datasets directly in data lake and data warehousing tools. If your organization is already using large data management tools, it'd be a good idea to first check if there is some support or integration before introducing another library.[6]

As you are likely aware, the data tooling landscape changes quickly. Having a look around at what new tools are available and evaluating several before deciding what is best is always a good idea! Use these questions to guide your evaluation and selection criteria and don't be afraid to do a few proof-of-concept implementations before setting up one as the standard.

---

6 If the organization is on an older on-premise setup without these features, you might think about a low-tech solution like regular snapshots of data used for particular tasks and some tools to easily load or exchange snapshots as required. There is also expanded support for self-hosted and on-premise setups from many of the versioning tools, including DVC.

Basic Privacy: Pseudonymization for Privacy by Design

You've learned about what data governance is, how to find and evaluate sensitive data, how to document data with regard to its sensitivity, and how to figure out when things change via governance tracking and version control. With this command of data governance, you can now begin to apply privacy techniques for person-related data in well-documented and repeatable ways.

To begin, start with the basics. Sometimes the simplest approach can solve your problems and address numerous internal and external concerns. You'll be evaluating which privacy technologies and techniques are appropriate for the risks at hand and what are the rewards (for example, granting expanded access to the data).

Pseudonymization is a great match for basic privacy needs, like when you are dealing with a data use case where the data will never be exposed to someone outside of a trusted group of employees. Pseudonymization is a technique that allows you to use "pseudonyms" instead of real names and data. There are several approaches to pseudonymization, outlined in Table 1-2.

Table 1-2. Approaches to pseudonymization

Pseudonymization approach	Description	Example
Masking	Applying a "mask" to the data that often replaces values with a standard series of values.	888-23-5322 → <ID-NUMBER> or <XXX-XX-5322>
Tokenization (table-based)	Replacing identifiable tokens via a lookup table that allows a one-to-one replacement.	Mondo Bamber → Fiona Molyn
Hashing	Using a hash mechanism to make the data less interpretable but still linkable.	*foo@bar.com* → 32dz22945nzow
Format-preserving encryption	Using a cipher or other cryptographic technique to replace the data with similar data. Often this is also linkable.	(0)30 4344 3333 → (0)44 4627 1111

As you may already notice in Table 1-2, these approaches can significantly vary the quality of your data as well as the privacy of the individuals. For example, the hashing mechanism takes what is easily interpreted as an email address and turns it into something that is no longer interpretable. This provides minimal privacy but also destroys our ability to extract useful information (such as linking email accounts based on domain). Depending on the implementation, masking can either remove all identifying information or leave too much information where it is easily linked with other datasets to reveal personal information. Table-based tokenization means maintaining a solution that may not scale with your data but that allows appropriate and human-readable linking if you need to connect disparate datasets.

As you'll explore further in Chapter 4, linking is a primary attack vector to determine the identity of an individual. The more data you are able to link, the easier it is to use that linked information to infer who the person is or to learn enough about them to make a good guess. Format-preserving encryption retains linkability but is more scalable due to using a standard two-way mechanism based in cryptographic techniques. The linkability can often be destroyed at arranged time intervals by changing the secret key material. This can provide enough security for internal use cases as long as reasonable defaults are used. If linkability is what you are after, you should also consider varied techniques in the field of Privacy-Preserving Record Linkage (PPRL) (*https://oreil.ly/wjU2i*), which covers these pseudonymization methods along with several probabilistic hash methods.

Table 1-3 summarizes the benefits and drawbacks of pseudonymization.

Table 1-3. Benefits and drawbacks of pseudonymization

Benefit	Drawback
Linkable: Pseudonymization techniques often retain the ability to link data, which helps when you are connecting datasets using personal identifiers or other sensitive columns.	Pseudonymization is not anonymization. Re-identification of pseudonymized data via linkage attacks are a prominent and consistent threat to privacy protection and become easier the more data is available (more on these in Chapter 4).
Format-preserving utility: Several pseudonymization methods allow you to preserve format or learn the original intention for that data (i.e., is it an email?). This can be helpful if you have questions about the original data source and makeup.	Any information included in the pseudonymized data is already more information and more risk should the data get released or accidentally exposed. Would data documentation be a better way to understand the underlying schema?
Privacy by Design technique: Pseudonymization is a technique proposed by frameworks like Privacy by Design to provide useful alternatives to using the raw data, especially when this data is sensitive.	Basic techniques like pseudonymization can create a false sense of security, making people more likely to share the data more widely or to claim it is "anonymized" because personal identifiers are removed or pseudonymized.

In my experience, the biggest argument against using pseudonymization would be that it creates a false sense of security and privacy. I have seen teams struggle with privacy solutions and determine that pseudonymization is good enough because it "anonymizes" the data. This is unfortunately a widespread myth. You'll learn what anonymization is and isn't in Chapter 2, but I can guarantee you that no amount of pseudonymization will bring you the anonymization you seek, should that be the recommended method.

However, if you can guarantee the data will be used only internally by a small group of individuals who may require privileged access, then pseudonymization might be a good fit. One use case might be for internal sales or customer support teams, who need to see customer details but likely don't need access to all of the information. Another could be for internal business intelligence (BI) and analytics dashboards, which need to link data but should not have direct access to the sensitive values.

In both of these cases, however, there are clear alternatives to pseudonymization. You could imagine the BI Dashboard reporting orders across geographies would only need aggregated queries for large-enough geographies to ensure some privacy is preserved. Or you can imagine a customer support system that doesn't expose fields that are not necessary to perform the task at hand.

I've often seen pseudonymization used as a mechanism to extract data from production systems and use it in testing environments (for software development and analytics tools) or to log potential errors in a secure system. This has the benefit that the data is "close" to the data seen in production but is not the actual raw production data. As you can imagine, having this production data in a testing environment is extremely risky and should not happen, since the data is only weakly protected and test environments are often insecure. If production-data properties are required for a test to pass (for example, for model testing), I recommend that you find a way to synthetically generate those properties in your testing data rather than use real production data with minimal privacy protections.

If pseudonymization is recommended by your internal stakeholders and you have also deemed the risk low enough for its use, there are several tools and libraries to evaluate. I also have a notebook in the book's repository (*https://github.com/kjam/practical-data-privacy*) where I walk through some silly and fun examples of pseudonymization.

Here, I'll present an example workflow using Hashicorp Vault (*https://oreil.ly/xvvlt*). Hashicorp Vault is a service used by infrastructure teams to manage secrets across applications. This is a common pattern for microservice setups, where many applications and services are deployed in containers and need to access sensitive data such as API keys, encryption keys, or identity details in a scalable and secure way.

To use the format-preserving mechanism, you would first build a regular expression pattern for the format you need. Here is an example of a regular expression for a credit card number:

```
\d{4}-\d{2}(\d{2})-(\d{4})-(\d{4})
```

You register this pattern as a template for a particular transformation in Hashicorp with a set of roles attached (i.e., who is allowed to use this transformation). Hashicorp already supports certain types of format-preserving encryption. Note: some of these methods are reversible, and some are not!

You can test your transformation by using the command-line interface (CLI) and seeing that a fake generated number comes back as a different but still valid credit card number:

```
$ vault write transform/encode/payments value=1111-2222-3333-4444

Key              Value
---              -----
encoded_value    1111-2200-1452-4879
```

If you chose a method that is reversible, you can also check that you can properly decode with the proper role and permissions:

```
$ vault write transform/decode/payments value=1111-2200-1452-4879

Key              Value
---              -----
decoded_value    1111-2222-3333-4444
```

 The API calls may change and need to be cleared with the infrastructure support running Hashicorp for your organization. I recommend taking a look at the latest Hashicorp documentation to see if they are the right solution for your pseudonymization needs.

There are also several open source libraries with format-preserving encryption support as well as other pseudonymization methods (such as hashing, masking, or tokenization). Here are a few with useful documentation and functionality at the writing of this book:

- KIProtect's Kodex (*https://heykodex.com*) provides an open source community edition that has several pseudonymization methods.[7]
- Format-Preserving Encryption Python library by Mysto (*https://oreil.ly/RKvpV*) allows you to set up several format-preserving algorithms with an easy-to-use Python interface.
- Microsoft's Presidio (*https://oreil.ly/Tao7Z*) allows for several masking and tokenization options as well as measures to discover PII in text.
- Private Input Masked Output (PIMO) (*https://oreil.ly/LDA_3*) uses a Go-based engine and has many templates to pseudonymize and mask data.

As you explore the advanced techniques and potential threats in this book, you'll develop a better understanding of what risk level and ease of use fits your team and work. In doing so, it will become clear to you when pseudonymization fits and when it's best to approach the problem with a more advanced and protective technique.

Summary

This chapter outlined what data governance is and how you can and should use it as a data scientist. You learned important avenues that link governance to data science and data privacy, such as finding undocumented data, identifying sensitive data,

---

7 Disclaimer: I cofounded KI Protect and worked on the initial implementations of this library; however, the company now runs without my involvement, and I am no longer a contributor to the library.

managing data documentation, and tracking lineage. You also learned some basic privacy approaches for working with sensitive data, such as pseudonymization.

You should feel like you are getting your foot in the door. You are building your mental map of privacy and what is important and relevant for your work. You may already have some questions about how to practically identify and manage privacy risk or how to ensure you are using privacy techniques effectively. I have some good news: the next chapter helps you think about these questions using scientific methods. Let's move on to differential privacy!

## CHAPTER 2

Anonymization

In this chapter, you'll dive into anonymization: what it is, how to use it, and what factors you need to consider in using it for data science. You may already know about anonymization, and this chapter might challenge or contradict what you think you know! The topic of anonymization is one that has plagued researchers and scientists for decades—and still incites debate between different privacy professionals today. In this chapter, you'll learn rigorous, scientific definitions of anonymization—meaning you will learn about differential privacy. This will help you approach the problem with state-of-the-art technologies and give you tools that empower you to meet strong privacy protections while still performing accurate data science.

What Is Anonymization?

To anonymize is "to remove identifying information from (something, such as computer data) so that the original source cannot be known." [1] When you anonymize personal data, you want to make sure the data cannot be traced back to a particular individual. But how exactly can you do that?

In the past, there have been several approaches, most of which have been debunked and replaced with newer understandings. Some of the initial approaches (categorized under Statistical Disclosure Control (*https://oreil.ly/KfE-z*)) used a variety of no longer recommended methods like suppression, aggregation, and transformations to anonymize the data. These methods were like early cryptographic ciphers. They obfuscated the original source, but a dedicated attacker would be able to infer or extrapolate more information, potentially even revealing the original.

---

1 From Merriam-Webster Dictionary, accessed January 2022

Similar to the developments of cryptanalysis in cryptography, new privacy attacks were developed over decades that highlighted weaknesses in these basic approaches. You might have come across "anonymized" data that had undergone techniques such as the following:

- Removal of particular columns or attributes (i.e., drop the names, addresses, birthdates, etc.)

- Aggregation of certain row attributes (i.e., "5 people in this dataset live in this postal code")

- Scrambling or other transformation methods to obfuscate individual characteristics (i.e., mixing the row attributes from multiple rows so that no single row has its original values, but the overall distribution of values is unchanged)

All of these are interesting obfuscation techniques from a security standpoint, but unfortunately they cannot and do not guarantee privacy.

Cynthia Dwork and several of her peers debunked this type of data anonymization by proving that release of any data has a potential for a re-identification attack or information gain.[2] This is illustrated in the seminal paper via an example. Let's say that you know that a person is 2 cm taller than the average height for people in a particular country. Then, a government agency releases the average height of a large group of people in that country. Now, you know this person's exact height. They don't even need to have been in the dataset!

The essential lesson here is that you cannot know what an attacker already knows about an individual or a group of individuals (often called *auxiliary information*). Auxiliary information contains not only what data is available today but also any data that might become known in the future, making it essentially impossible to estimate. Therefore, you cannot guarantee that a release of information, no matter how obfuscated or benign it seems, will keep a person safe from identification or won't reveal some information about them.

You might be asking, if so, then what even is the point of anonymization? If there is no guarantee that an attacker cannot learn something, then why even try? Even though you cannot guarantee an attacker will learn nothing, you can start to think about how to quantify the amount of information that can be learned. This is what Dwork and several other researchers began to develop after proving these methods for statistical disclosure control were a myth.[3]

---

2 See: Dwork et al., Calibrating Noise to Sensitivity in Private Data Analysis, 2006 (*https://oreil.ly/DDRha*).

3 Aside from the aforementioned paper, you might want to read Dwork, "Differential Privacy" (Microsoft Research, 2006) (*https://oreil.ly/JGyXe*) and Dwork and Roth's publication *The Algorithmic Foundations of Differential Privacy* (2014) (*https://oreil.ly/Bkt4H*), which is freely available online.

Because they were able to prove that anonymized data release as defined in the dictionary, from a mathematical and logical view, actually doesn't exist, the problem at hand shifted from "How can we anonymize data?" to "How can we measure the loss of privacy when data is released"? Their goal was to find ways a researcher could measure things like privacy loss in a data release, rather than guarantee it would never happen. This meant shifting from a binary understanding of privacy—as "on" or "off"—to a gradient of privacy.

This is an important mental shift for you as well. The only guarantee of complete privacy is to delete all data or never collect it in the first place. While I'm a big fan of data minimization, I am also a pragmatic data scientist. You need data to solve problems. Thinking about privacy as a range can help you clarify your needs. How much privacy loss am I willing to create in order to answer this question? How much privacy can I offer and still get reasonable answers to my questions?

To help you reason about these questions and begin thinking in terms of privacy gradients, I've made a small diagram (Figure 2-1) showing the relation between privacy and information. On the far left, there is absolute privacy, which also means zero information—all data is deleted. On the far right, there is absolute information, which means zero privacy (if the data is sensitive to begin with). Along this continuum, you can choose myriad privacy technologies to provide reasonable privacy guarantees and determine an adequate balance for your analysis.

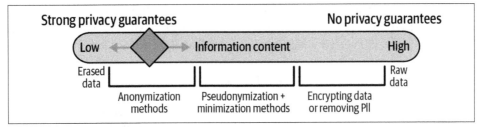

Figure 2-1. Information and privacy continuum

Even though Figure 2-1 is shown as linear with the methods written underneath them, there are anonymization methods in this chapter that can also provide more information, and there are pseudonymization methods that destroy information! The graphic is meant less as an instructive "use this instead of that" and more as an example for thinking about a range of technology choices and a range of information versus privacy. By the end of this book you'll have learned many that can be combined to find the right mix of information and privacy for your work.

Differential privacy can help you measure information content and find a reasonable balance between the problem you are trying to solve while still providing individual privacy guarantees. Let's dive into exactly what differential privacy is so you can begin to imagine your choices along this continuum.

Defining Differential Privacy

Differential privacy is a rigorous and scientific definition of privacy-sensitive information release—that defines a limit or bounds on the amount of privacy loss you can have when you release information. It also gives you a way to measure that privacy loss for any individual in the dataset. It is today's "gold standard" for so-called anonymization. The differential privacy bounds can be tuned by you using particular parameters in the definition—and they are guaranteed by the process that you use to access, query, or release the data. To maintain those bounds, you use algorithms (called *mechanisms*) that release enough information to learn something from your data without revealing too much about any one individual.

One important thing to note about differential privacy versus older methods is that differential privacy focuses on the process rather than the result. In older methods it was often the case that you try to look at the resulting data and figure out if it is "anonymized" enough. This is a fallacy, as you know from Dwork et al.'s work. Differential privacy shifts to thinking about what guarantees a particular algorithm can provide by measuring the information that is being continuously released via the algorithm itself. By focusing on the process and algorithm, you can also build more dynamic systems, change your algorithms, and still analyze privacy loss over time!

 At a high level, differential privacy first defines a particular condition that an algorithm or mechanism needs to meet in order to maintain privacy. Later, you'll learn how algorithms actually meet this strong definition—by establishing certain bounds on each individual's contribution and adding carefully formulated noise. This chapter starts with the original definition and builds up to a toy implementation. It's not essential that you understand all the math described here, but it is worth reviewing to understand why the algorithms work and deliver privacy-preserving results.

The original definition of differential privacy describes two databases D_1 and D_2 with one row difference between them. Either a row representing one person has been added or a row has been removed from the first database to produce the second one. The goal is that a motivated and informed attacker cannot obtain too much information about the person whose data has been added or removed or even *if* the person has been added or removed. You use an algorithm (A) to release the query response, which you want to ensure satisfies the following definition:

$$P[A(D_1) \in S] \le exp(\varepsilon) \times P[A(D_2) \in S]$$

To read this out: the probability P that an attacker can determine based on the response ($A(D_1)$ or $A(D_2)$) if they are interacting with the first or second database is limited by a small value e^ε. Here, e^ε represents the amount of information gained by a dedicated adversary investigating the query response or data release in a worst-case scenario.

In this scenario, the attacker wants to learn information to determine whether or not a person is in the expected dataset ($\in S$) and update their assumptions based on the response. Your job is to limit their ability to do so while still responding to queries. The goal of the algorithm is to keep the amount of information as high as possible but to still provide as much privacy as possible.

The algorithm (A) must hold these bounds no matter what row has been added or removed. When you build differential privacy algorithms, you need to determine what queries are supported. This showcases the difficulty of the problem. What if there is an outlier? What if the query has joins with several different databases? For this reason, tailored algorithms for specific use cases work well for complex problems; formulating your query clearly is an essential step in figuring out which algorithm provides the right balance between privacy and information.

ε defines the bound that gives individuals privacy. Let's define this more practically so you can see how this helps provide the best approximation for anonymization possible.

Understanding Epsilon: What Is Privacy Loss?

When you think about the previous equation, the epsilon is doing a lot of work! For each individual in your dataset, their information leakage is being bound by e^ε. What does this mean in a practical sense?

Let's take a real-world example to make it more concrete. Let's say we both work at the same company, and I want to learn your salary. You are a new joiner, and I thoughtfully took a screenshot of a company-wide dashboard for salary transparency that showed me the average across a variety of roles. After you joined, I compared my screenshot to the updated dashboard and tried to infer what role you have and what salary you have. If the average salary went up by 1,000 monetary units for a particular role and I had an idea of the number of employees for that role, I could use that information to reverse engineer your estimated salary.

My ability to successfully perform this privacy attack is based on my belief that the dashboard is updated, my knowledge about the number of employees for that role, and my assumption that you are the only new joiner. If I am uncertain about the number of employees in that role or about the accuracy of the dashboard result, I insert some estimation of potential error. Instead of being 100% sure that your salary is a certain number, I can now update my suspicion to within a probability range or even begin to think of your salary as a probability distribution (i.e., strongly likely to be between X and Y, but with a small chance of being higher or lower).

This example gives us the tools you need to interpret the bounds you are setting with differential privacy. You would like to quantify how much information an attacker can gain and keep this within some probabilistic range. What is "too much" information gain? Would the ability to update my prior suspicion that a person is in the dataset from an initial suspicion of 25% to 75% after I see a response be too much?

Using Bayes' rule,[4] you can reformulate the differential privacy definition from the point of view of the attacker who is trying to learn the underlying dataset. The posterior or new knowledge of the attacker is based on new information in the response. The attacker is trying to figure out if the database D they are interacting with is D_1 or D_2, based on the response A.

The attacker's prior suspicion is represented by $D = D_1$, the information from the query result is $A(D) = O$ where O is the actual response the attacker sees. $P[A(D_1) = O]$ represents the probability that the result comes from D_1, and the posterior or updated suspicion is $P[D = D_1 \mid A(D) = O]$, which you can read as the probability that the database they are interacting with is D_1 given ($\mid$) the query response. Using Bayes' rule, the differential privacy formula can be rewritten to define the new suspicion (posterior) depending on the prior suspicion (prior):[5].

$$P[D = D_1 \mid A(D) = O] = P[D = D_1] \times \frac{P[A(D_1) = O]}{P[A(D) = O]}$$

In this binary case, $P[D = D_1] = 1 - P[D = D_2]$ because the probabilities must add up to 1 since the attacker is attempting to deduce the shift in the same database. Doing some math allows us to reformulate the equation as such:[6]

$$\frac{P[D = D_1]}{e^\varepsilon + (1 - e^\varepsilon) \times P[D = D_1]} \le P[D = D_1 \mid A(D) = O] \le \frac{e^\varepsilon \times P[D = D_1]}{1 + (e^\varepsilon - 1) \times P[D = D_1]}$$

---

4 Quick reminder: Bayes' rule (*https://oreil.ly/qlsup*) defines conditional probabilities based on observations and known or probable ranges of events. With Bayes' rule, you can calculate posteriors (new suspicion or best guess) and use those to update your priors (old suspicions and best guesses).

5 You don't need to have studied Bayesian theory to understand the following, but it does help to think about priors and posteriors when determining information gain and the resulting privacy loss. If this is new to you, you can familiarize yourself with this theory via many O'Reilly publications and freely available blog, textbooks, and video courses online—choose one that speaks to you!

6 A proof can be found in Damien Desfontaines's blog post (*https://oreil.ly/_4Mhy*).

This equation calculates the potential information gain based on the epsilon and the attacker's initial suspicion (auxiliary information). Your choice of epsilon defines these bounds (lower in best case and upper in worst case) and therefore is a critical choice in operating a differentially private system.

Let's look at this equation in graphical form in Figure 2-2, which is based on Damien Desfontaines's introductory post on differential privacy (*https://oreil.ly/_4Mhy*).

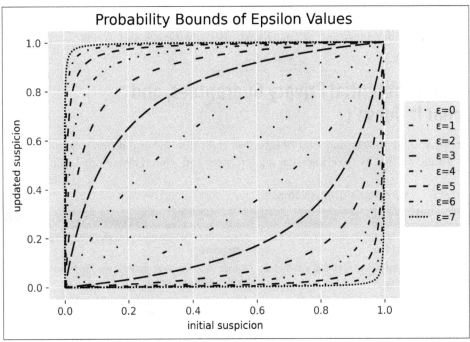

Figure 2-2. Estimating knowledge gain based on epsilon

To read this chart correctly, you want to imagine the x-axis as potential prior information that you cannot predict or prevent. The y-axis tells you how much information an attacker can learn given their prior information. For each epsilon shown in the legend, there are bounds for best and worst-case scenarios showing exactly how much more certain an attacker with a given prior information can get from a query response that uses differential privacy. The graph shows that certain values of epsilon are quite revealing, potentially allowing an attacker to immediately update a suspicion quickly and with higher certainty.

It is often recommended to choose a small epsilon, where epsilon is close to 1 or even below 1. As illustrated in Figure 2-2, this keeps the privacy leakage quite small even in a worst-case scenario. An epsilon of 1 bounds what a Bayesian attacker can learn with an initial suspicion of 0.5 by plus or minus approximately 0.2. You can test different suspicions using the equation derived in the prior paragraph in the book's notebook repository (*https://github.com/kjam/practical-data-privacy*). Remember, this equation calculates the worst-case scenario, which is unlikely to happen but still possible. You'll learn how to reason about this when you build an example mechanism later in this chapter.

How can you actually implement algorithms that satisfy these bounds? In short, specific and calibrated noise is added to the query result that guarantees the information leakage is within these bounds. This noise is not uniformly random but instead is sampled from a particular distribution. This noise distribution allows us to set the privacy loss guarantees and calculate best-case, worst-case, and average-case privacy loss scenarios.

What Differential Privacy Guarantees, and What It Doesn't

I hope you are developing a bit of intuition right now around differential privacy, so let's build on that by covering what it guarantees and what it doesn't in Table 2-1.

Table 2-1. Differential privacy guarantees

Differential privacy is...	Differential privacy is not...
A probabilistic way to bound an attacker's information gain when releasing data	A way to guarantee zero privacy loss where everyone is always "anonymized"
A way to quantify and track privacy loss of an individual in a released dataset	A magic wand that can be applied to every data science use case and its potential privacy risk
The best way experts know to offer individuals in a dataset plausible deniability	A way to block all private information from being learned (especially true for group information)

Differential privacy is the best way experts know to offer data subjects or participants plausible deniability while still conducting data analysis. Results can reveal sensitive information about participants based on their group membership and the conclusions of the research. For example, if I know you participated in a study and the study showed that 80% of women and gender minority participants in the study were paid less than men, then I can infer based on your gender whether you are paid fairly or not. What differential privacy allows you to do is to retain the ability to say, "That may be true for a lot of my peers, but not me in particular." This is your plausible deniability!

One advantage of offering this plausible deniability is opening up research about sensitive topics such as equal pay. Differential privacy can offer participants better privacy guarantees and safer ways to contribute their data for research while still supporting open data and transparency in research.

Another advantage of differential privacy is you can stop talking about auxiliary information and instead reason about probabilities and information gain based on the differential privacy mechanism (A), which means you are not trying to figure out what someone could know (impossible!) but instead using your probabilistic understanding to choose reasonable privacy guarantees. Since you can always calculate the maximum change that a release of data under differential privacy would bring, you don't need to explicitly consider every piece of auxiliary information. Since determining all possible pieces of auxiliary information would be a Sisyphean task, this is a truly liberating revelation!

Working with Legal Professionals

In any environment where you are discussing anonymization or sharing of person-related data, you'll want to be in continuous conversations with legal professionals. You should follow their advice and definitions of anonymization.

In Chapter 8, you'll review several well-known privacy regulations, but enforcement and the legal landscape can change frequently and are often made stricter over time. The good news is that differential privacy is seen by many legal professionals as the "gold standard" because it is state of the art in the technical field. However, this does not mean you get a free pass from the consultation—you must still develop an approach that makes your legal and technical stakeholders confident in data release decisions and reasoning.

Understanding Differential Privacy

To help you better understand how differential privacy actually works with your data, let's walk through a few implementation examples. You'll first analyze a real-world use case and then build your own mechanism and consider its privacy guarantees.

Differential Privacy in Practice: Anonymizing the US Census

The Constitution of the United States of America calls for a full census of all people every 10 years. This count is used for numerous significant decisions, including representation in Congress, federal funding, and monetary support for state initiatives. Getting it right—ensuring that everyone is counted and only once—requires a huge effort. The privacy implications are equally significant.

In the past, the US Census Bureau has used a variety of obfuscation methods to ensure "anonymization" of the results. These included combinations of aggregation and a method called *shuffling* (or sometimes *scrambling*), which took census block data and shuffled the households so that the census blocks were mixed with one another. Because the methods retained information about the individuals, it allowed for private information to leak in ways the original Census workers did not anticipate.

To determine the potential for outsiders to re-identify households in the released data, the Census Bureau ran several attacks on the 2010 Census results. Reconstructing age, gender, and race/ethnicity combinations revealed correctly re-identified data with 38% accuracy by combining the data with an external source that was readily available.

These sources could have been a consumer database, a voting or driving record database (for adults), or even an insurance database. The external sources often had complete identity information (names, addresses, contact information, and other details). For smaller census blocks, they were able to perform this re-identification with much higher success. With ubiquitous data available for free or low prices or when performed by a company with large access to consumer and household data like a large e-commerce provider, this type of attack is not only feasible, it is actively used for direct marketing campaigns and targeted advertising.

How exactly did these reconstruction attacks work? They literally built a system of equations and used a solver to determine potential candidates (more details in this article (*https://oreil.ly/AwIuL*)). From those candidates, they were able to deduce the most probable by linking this information with a few consumer databases or another dataset acquired via a data breach. Although there are plenty of false positives, in less populated regions this proved even more effective (up to 72%).[7] You can find an example notebook from my colleagues Mitchell Lisle and Menghong Li showing how to use solver software to perform a reconstruction attack on a small example dataset in the book's code repository (*https://github.com/kjam/practical-data-privacy*).

As a consequence, the US Census Bureau decided that they would use differential privacy for the 2020 Census. The task at hand—could they create a data workflow that allowed for differentially private census results for 330 million people that was still usable for the critical tasks requiring accurate results?

They refined their privacy parameters using example data and prior census responses, determining exactly what noise measurements and distributions fit their needs. They worked diligently to determine the balance of privacy and utility, preserving accuracy while still guaranteeing basic privacy protections. They built up

---

[7] Even before the US Census released this method, I knew of several data teams using statistical and Bayesian reasoning to perform direct marketing based on census data in combination with consumer databases. Think about what you can already infer from customer databases, particularly with filtering mechanisms that highlight purchase or browsing history to accurately infer income, familial status, and gender, and then combine that with publicly available data—very revealing and quite scary when you think of all the potential implications! More on this in Chapter 4.

infrastructure in Apache Spark to run through, aggregate, and finalize all results, which are available on the US Census home page (*https://oreil.ly/xHWm_*).

A high-level overview of how they implemented differential privacy is outlined in Figure 2-3. They started at the highest population levels (which they call a *top-down* approach), created histograms or sketches of the data, and then added the noise barrier (differential privacy mechanisms on histograms) to create noisy histograms. Then, they did this for each smaller regional set and went back to ensure each level ended up with the same aggregate statistics. One exciting property of differentially private data is that you can do as much post-processing as you want without affecting the privacy guarantees.

For more details, I recommend watching the US Census video from Spark Conference (*https://oreil.ly/kmMxV*) or reading through their blog posts on the NIST home page for differential privacy (*https://oreil.ly/BbSx_*) as well as checking out this comprehensive slide deck on the initial approach (*https://oreil.ly/TVKFW*).

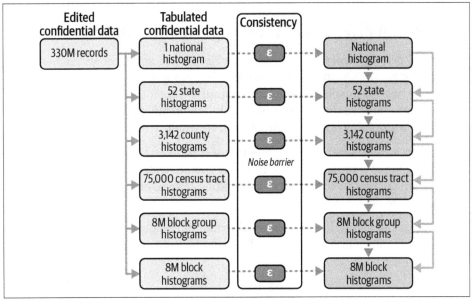

Figure 2-3. US Census with differential privacy

One critique of using differential privacy for public data is the potential of undercounting underrepresented groups. If there is only one person of a given ethnicity in a particular census block, it's unlikely that ethnicity will be represented in the neighborhood histogram. How does this affect federal funding, redistricting, and so forth? Is it better to ensure you are counted and to reveal your private details?

These questions can't be answered by any one person but should be something the industry as a whole and each of us as data scientists considers when deploying differentially private systems. Understanding the implications for underrepresented groups in data will always be a serious point to consider when deploying any privacy protection mechanism. Individuals in underrepresented groups are also at a greater danger with regard to their privacy risk than others and often have less access to privacy in daily life. You must fully explore the trade-off between giving underrepresented groups more privacy as a defense against further targeting and exploitation and ensuring that those groups don't disappear or lose benefit from the outcomes (here: democratic processes). This conversation will be continued in Chapters 4 and 11— and I also recommend following the work of activists and thinkers in this space, like Chris Gilliard (*https://oreil.ly/n4qy1*) and Ruha Benjamin (*https://oreil.ly/FAGuV*).

To better understand how you can approach the technical aspects of the problem and assure you are making thoughtful choices, let's dive into how differential privacy *actually* works!

Differential Privacy with the Laplace Mechanism

Differential privacy theory tells you adding noise to data and/or query results can be effective in guaranteeing individual privacy. What you want to do as a data scientist is add as little noise as possible, finding the appropriate point on the information versus privacy continuum. To do so, you have to fulfill the requirements of differential privacy while determining how to create an accurate result.

One approach to maximize information that was proposed early on and is still commonly used today is to sample noise from the Laplace distribution. This allows us to meet epsilon guarantees for privacy while adding minimal noise. Let's take a look at its properties to analyze why it fits so well.

As you can see in Figure 2-4, the Laplace distribution has qualities similar to an exponential distribution and is sometimes called a *double exponential distribution*.

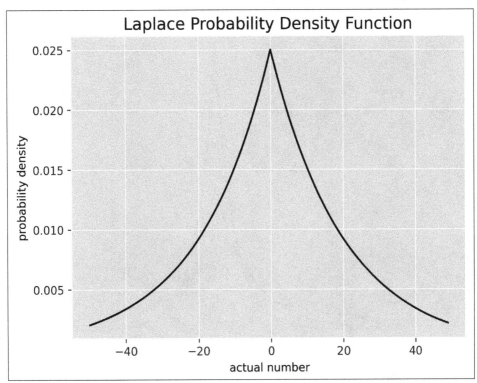

Figure 2-4. Laplace distribution

The probability density function is given as:

$$\frac{1}{2b} exp\left(\frac{- \mid x - \mu \mid}{b}\right)$$

Here, μ is the location where the exponential functions meet (and essentially the peak of the distribution), and b represents the scale of the distribution. You can see how changing the scale shifts the distribution in Figure 2-5.

When you use this distribution as a source of noise with $\mu = 0$, you notice that it has a high probability of ending up with a quite low amount of noise. This is great for retaining information. But there is always a chance of gathering noise from the tails of the distribution (i.e., further from the 0), ensuring plausible deniability. As a consumer of the data, you shouldn't be able to infer whether the noise came from one part of the distribution or another.

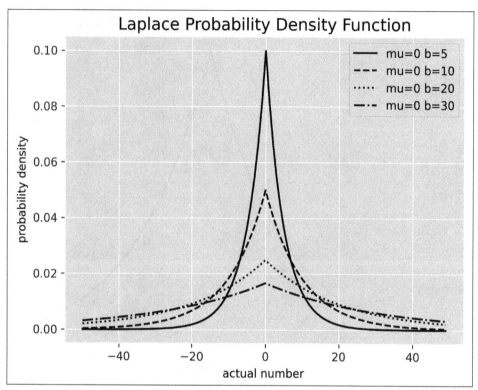

Figure 2-5. *Laplace distribution: comparing scale and location*

Let's take a look at how this might work in a differentially private mechanism. You want to ensure that the noise is added in a way that protects each individual. One such way would be to add Laplace noise to your query result. You're going to do this in a fairly naive way to demonstrate why it doesn't work.

The code examples in this chapter are naive implementations of differential privacy mechanisms and are insecure! Please do not use them for any real use case. By building this mechanism from scratch, you are going to develop understanding about how the mechanism works. In real systems, subtle bugs can occur and negate the privacy guarantees (see Chapter 4 for more). In general, building your own differential privacy is like building your own cryptography—you should do it only if you are an expert, and even then, you should have other experts audit your work!

Differential Privacy with Laplace: A Naive Attempt

In this example, you have a generated dataset of age and salary information. You can follow along and run any of this code yourself, via the book's code repository on GitHub (*https://github.com/kjam/practical-data-privacy*).

You want to allow querying to the data but still protect privacy. Throughout the rest of the chapter, you will be building a differential privacy mechanism from scratch, and you'll learn a few interesting things about these mechanisms and encounter a few gotchas along the way.

In Python, a naive differential privacy implementation using Laplace noise might look like this:

```
epsilon = 1.1

def naive_laplace_dp_mechanism(value, epsilon):
    # Please do not use this function, ever :)
    orig_value = value
    value = np.random.laplace(value, 1/epsilon) # more on this choice later!
    print("Noise: {}".format(value - orig_value))
    return value
```

In this code, you are sampling the Laplace distribution with a particular epsilon. Let's dive into what this calculation means:

```
np.random.laplace(value, 1/epsilon)
```

value here is the μ value or location of the Laplace distribution, telling you where it is centered. In this example, you are setting the location to the value of the input, which means the center of the probability mass is close to the actual input value.

epsilon is your epsilon value for your differential privacy guarantees. In this case, you've defined epsilon=1.1.

From the NumPy documentation, the np.random.laplace method takes the location (μ) and the scale (b) as required arguments. Given the previous definition, the 1/epsilon value directly calculates the scale of the distribution. You'll be evaluating in this section if 1/epsilon is a reasonable choice.

With the random set generated in the notebook, I can run code to try to see the mean of the ages in the dataset, like so:

```
laplace_dp_mechanism(np.mean(ages), epsilon)
```

When I ran this, I got the following result. Your result will be different:

```
Noise: 1.277692233946226
```

```
46.55769223394623
```

So, you can see that the "average age" is around 46.6.

In this toy example, I explicitly added a `print` statement to show how much noise was being added. In a real implementation, you would never see or infer this information directly from any mechanism because it immediately violates the privacy guarantees. To preserve privacy, you need to also conceal how you add noise to your users and yourself; otherwise, you would directly leak the information and probabilistic mechanism that allows differential privacy to function. Because no one knows exactly how much noise was added, you can preserve privacy and give individuals plausible deniability! Since this is a toy example that you will not use in a real system, you can take a look at the internal workings to support your understanding.

But can this be correct? The added noise and the scale 1/epsilon seem to be quite small to account for something like an average age over a large population. When you take a look at Figure 2-6, you can see that the vast majority of the noise values will lie between –2 and 2. But what if my age is significantly low or high compared to the average? This could easily shift the average enough that details about my age are revealed in this result. You can experiment by following along in the example notebook from the book's repository to explore how adding outliers shifts this mean and leaks information!

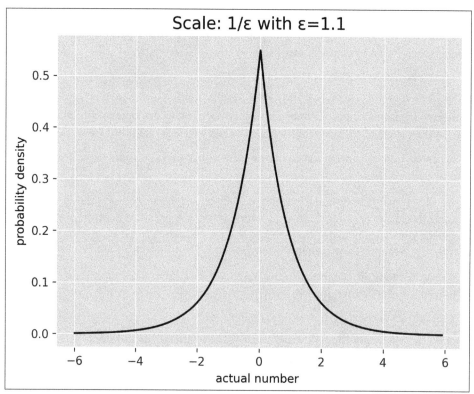

Figure 2-6. Understanding scale 1/epsilon

It seems like I've built something dangerous here, so let's evaluate sensitivity at a deeper level to see what might have gone wrong.

Sensitivity and Error

When I chose 1/epsilon to scale the Laplace distribution, I also set another parameter for differential privacy, namely, the sensitivity of the mechanism. The sensitivity measures the maximum change in the query result based on a change in the underlying dataset. For differential privacy's definition to hold, you need to account for a dataset both before and after a person was added and removed, therefore limiting the change in query results due to their addition or removal.

Sensitivity measures how much a value can change—at most—when one person is added or removed. It is easier to see this sensitivity when you think about something like a count versus a sum (good news for you, as you need both to compute an average!).

Let's say that I am 81 years old. When I am added to the dataset and you query the count of employees over 40, I change the result by 1. But when you calculate the average age, I can presumably change the sum part of that mean result (sum/count) by 81! This means that to properly compute the average age with appropriate privacy controls, you need to figure out a sensitivity for ages in a sum operation.

Some queries (like a sum) will have mathematically unbounded sensitivity where either no upper or no lower limits exist on the individual contribution. A sum of all salaries would leak extensive information if any salary is added—just like the dashboard example. Without a significant amount of noise, I can easily guess the salary of the new employee or the salary of the employee who is leaving! I just take the first sum and see how it changed after the person joined or left.

Another good example of unbounded sensitivity is querying the minimum or maximum value. Although the query response is unlikely to change when you add or remove a random user, when it does, you will again have a very close estimate of the underlying value regardless of the amount of noise added, and this would result in catastrophic privacy loss for that individual.

When a query has unbounded sensitivity, you need to approach it differently than queries that have sensitivity you can measure. One solution is to not answer or allow queries that have unbounded sensitivity. Another way is to introduce bounds and artificially limit possible answers to within a chosen bound. This presumes that no one will show up outside of those bounds, or if so, their existence in the query response will be obfuscated by changing their value to within bounds.

Some queries will have fairly clear and bounded sensitivity. When you want to count the number of users you have, each user should be counted only once. They can affect the output by only 1—therefore, sensitivity is 1 no matter who the person is. If you are building a rating system and each user can rate on a scale of 0–5 only, the sensitivity of a single rating is 5. Similar to artificially bounding the maximum and minimum contribution of any user, there are certain use cases that lend themselves well to measuring sensitivity accurately.

When looking at sensitivity, you are also managing error. When you use a particular noise distribution, you have the ability to estimate error insertion and to look at how that affects relative error, the total error divided by the actual value or measurement. You could create an error estimate based on the distribution and scale you choose and model plausible outcomes by experimenting with similar nonprivate data sources to ensure you understand the impact of this error on later analysis. There are some experiments in the book's code repository that show this approach.

With this in mind, how should you adapt the average query to actually apply differential privacy appropriately? What is the sensitivity of the average operation? You need to bound the ages so that you can appropriately apply sensitivity for the sum operation.

Choosing useful bounds depends on the ages in the dataset, which itself might be sensitive. How can you solve this problem?

In this case, you know that the database is related to employees at a company. A reasonable choice might be that the ages can be bound between 20 and 70. If you had more knowledge you wanted to use to help calculate these values, such as how the recruiting process works and what normal retirement ages are in the industry, you can create smaller or larger bounds. Remember, the bounds themselves also define the sensitivity, which defines the amount of noise. Larger bounding ranges will introduce more noise. Here you are making a key choice in the privacy versus information continuum.

If you are choosing 20 and 70, you can bound the data like so:

```
def filter_bounds(value, lower_bound, upper_bound):
    if value < lower_bound:
        return lower_bound
    elif value > upper_bound:
        return upper_bound
    return value

bounded_ages = [filter_bounds(age, 20, 70) for age in ages]
```

You now know the sensitivity of each query! The count has a sensitivity of 1, and the sum now has a sensitivity of 50. This also means you always need to run this filter_bounds operation when new users join the dataset as part of your differential privacy implementation.

But now you have two calculations rather than one. Because your implementation of differential privacy uses the entire epsilon for one query, you need to change your approach to handle more than one query. This means you need to track privacy loss and epsilon across multiple queries. Let's look at how to do that with privacy budgets.

Privacy Budgets and Composition

Differential privacy was built to answer questions about data and guarantee privacy, but so far you've looked only at how to answer one question via a naive differential privacy mechanism. What happens when you want to answer multiple questions about the data? What happens when you want to open the database for external queries using differential privacy? Differential privacy promises that you can track and measure privacy loss, but *how*?

One amazing property of differential privacy is that the epsilon value (ε) is your privacy loss for one particular response, and it has the property of being individual to each query and yet composable, meaning if you answer two queries, you can add their epsilons to calculate the total privacy loss!

What does this mean in practice?

- There is a way to track this privacy loss; it's called a *privacy budget*. I can budget my total epsilon appropriately over a certain number of queries. This allows me to understand both information gain and any individual's privacy loss when there are multiple queries across the data. As you learned earlier, changing the epsilon changes the information gain and resulting privacy loss.

- Each query can use different amounts of the total epsilon (privacy budget), which allows you to make choices along the information and privacy continuum. You may decide to spend more of whatever epsilon I am using on one particular query than on the others. So if I know the queries in advance—or if I am releasing data all at once—I may want to allocate my budget on a query-by-query basis. For example, the US Census spent more of the budget on the smaller locales (like blocks and tracts) and less on the national level. To choose appropriately, you can keep relative error in mind!

Let's take a look at how this might work by calculating the average age.

To calculate an average, you need a differentially private sum and a differentially private count on the ages. You know that the most a count can change by adding or removing a row is 1, so you can set the sensitivity to 1.

Next you need to run the sum. To calculate this reliably, you already applied a technique called *clamping* with the filter_bounds function. Clamping allows you to create artificial floors and ceilings for values. This bounds the sensitivity in a deterministic way.

You could naively split your epsilon between the two queries, meaning each epsilon would be 0.5. Now you are ready to calculate a differentially private mean. To try out different approaches, please experiment in the notebooks in the book's code repository.

You also need to update your differential privacy mechanism to incorporate sensitivity. The 1/epsilon scale now becomes sensitivity/epsilon, which shows you why 1 was a poor choice for the average before! If you want to refer to Figure 2-5, you can see that queries with higher sensitivity will also have a larger scale, meaning more noise in order to protect privacy. Neat!

```
def laplace_dp_mechanism(value, epsilon, sensitivity):
    # Please do not use this function, ever :)
    orig_value = value
    value = np.random.laplace(value, sensitivity/epsilon)
                            # now you see why 1 was a poor choice!
    print("Noise: {}".format(value - orig_value))
    return value


epsilon_for_sum = 0.5
epsilon_for_count = 0.5
summed_ages = laplace_dp_mechanism(np.sum(bounded_ages),
                                   epsilon_for_sum, sensitivity=50)
count_ages = laplace_dp_mechanism(len(bounded_ages),
                                  epsilon_for_count, sensitivity=1)
summed_ages / count_ages
```

When I run that code, I get the following:

```
Noise: -53.24175804583501
Noise: 1.928454653399541

43.88135047434459
```

The actual mean of the original unbounded age dataset is 45.28, so this result has a relative error (noise added divided by true mean) of about –0.03. Depending on what you were using this for or related queries that this might affect, this error could be reasonable or too much.

 For more examples of using toy examples of differential privacy, please see the book repository (*https://github.com/kjam/practical-data-privacy*)! There are several additional calculations and explanations related to the work in this chapter, and a few notebooks that operate as appendixes for other related concepts (such as local differential privacy and debiasing differential privacy results). There are also notebooks for most chapters there to follow along as you learn!

In the queries here, you split your budget across each query, but instead you could think about budget as you do any limited resource and plan accordingly. This might mean spending more for queries that are more important for your final result or what you are trying to calculate.

You can build up an idea of how these budgets work with example data. I challenge you, at this time, to take some of these toy examples and use them with an actual dataset to which you have access. How does your data operate under these mechanisms? What works well, and what would you need to reconsider?

 You might be now wondering how you're going to actually track budgets when implementing differential privacy. The good news is, you can use a library that automatically does this for you, equipped with ways to minimize mistakes. These could include miscounting the number of contributions a user can make, inadvertently running computations more than once, or even incorrectly calculating sensitivity. Most important—now you know how to allocate your limited budget and make the most of it. In Chapter 3, you'll use a library that does just that!

Exploring Other Mechanisms: Gaussian Noise for Differential Privacy

As you are thinking about creating budgets and tracking and deploying differentially private systems, you might also be wondering if there are other distributions besides Laplace that provide differential privacy guarantees. As a data scientist, you may choose to work with something more familiar than Laplace's distribution—like a normal distribution.

Great news! You can use a Gaussian (normal) distribution to produce differential privacy "noise" with differential privacy guarantees. You then get all the benefits of working with a Gaussian distribution and can better reason about the results and de-bias the answers using familiar tools and mechanisms.

To use Gaussian noise, you first must introduce a more relaxed definition of differential privacy. This definition adds a small delta to the original definition, allowing a relaxation of the probability bounds. This delta accounts for an improbable outcome, which could mean "catastrophic failure" or a so-called distinguishing event.[8]

---

8 The reason why this delta is needed for Gaussian noise is because the probability distribution significantly changes, which means the chance of giving an answer that leaks more information increases when compared to Laplace. For a deep dive into this phenomenon, I recommend reading Desfontaines's post on the topic (*https://oreil.ly/JpmCr*).

$$Pr[A(D_1) \in S] \le exp(\varepsilon) \times Pr[A(D_2) \in S] + \delta$$

How should you properly choose a delta (margin of error)? You could imagine a delta that allows an implementation to, essentially, release *all* information about a small number of rows with no noise added, if that fits within the delta! Take a database of 1 million rows, and release 1 row "in the clear" (i.e., without any changes or modifications); if your delta is $\frac{1}{10^9}$ or greater, then you can call it differential privacy (just kidding, please don't!). For this reason, it's recommended that delta be cryptographically small, or minimally smaller than 1/total number of rows, to disallow this undesired behavior.

Let's take a look at how this relaxation and use of Gaussian noise works in practice. First, you'll need to define the differential privacy guarantees when working with a Gaussian mechanism.

 The following definition for a Gaussian mechanism is only for epsilon < 1 and adds more noise than you actually need or want, as it is based on the original paper. The recommended way to add Gaussian noise at the writing of this book is analytic Gaussian noise, described in Balle and Wang's paper "Improving the Gaussian Mechanism for Differential Privacy: Analytical Calibration and Optimal Denoising" (*International Conference on Machine Learning*, 2018). There is also a blog post you can read showing some of the properties (*https://oreil.ly/g5jhq*). Because that mechanism involves a more advanced formula, you'll use the simpler one here to build initial understanding and then use a library in Chapter 3 to add Gaussian noise efficiently.

A Gaussian mechanism is (ε, δ) differentially private if it follows the criteria and the epsilon is < 1:

$$F(x) = f(x) + N(\sigma^2)$$

where

$$\sigma^2 = \frac{2s^2 log\left(\frac{1.25}{\delta}\right)}{\varepsilon^2}$$

where $N(\sigma^2)$ samples a Gaussian distribution centered at 0 with variance σ^2. Here s represents the sensitivity.

You'll notice that now you must account for delta, which you didn't do with Laplace. This is because Laplace satisfies so-called (ε, 0) differential privacy, where delta is 0, but Gaussian does not.

You know now that delta should theoretically be "cryptographically small" (which is defined as $\leq 2^{-30}$). Since you are going to use a differential privacy mechanism and not some tricky release of a row, you can relax some of this advice. A good choice for delta is somewhere between $\frac{1}{n}$ where n is the number of rows and $2^{-30} \approx 9 \times 10^{-10}$, knowing that a smaller value adds more guarantees.

Let's choose a number to begin with for your age and salary dataset. You'll use $\delta = 10^{-5}$ as an appropriate number between those recommended bounds. With the delta value chosen, you can now calculate and apply a Gaussian-based differential privacy mechanism and compare your results with your Laplace mechanism. But first, let's dive deeper into how these mechanisms will alter your inserted error.

Comparing Laplace and Gaussian Noise

To evaluate and compare Laplace and Gaussian noise, you need to go back to the fundamentals of sensitivity. These two mechanisms have different notions of sensitivity. You know sensitivity so far as how much only one person can affect one value.

But there is actually another variant of sensitivity that you need to address when working with differential privacy. It isn't only how much one person can affect one value. It is actually how often and how much a person can affect values in the data you will release or the queries you will answer.

Let's take a concrete example to make it clear. You are working with human resources to analyze whether particular teams or departments have issues that leadership needs to address. You want to protect the individuals who are contributing these issues. Leadership wants to track problematic areas and properly prioritize, so you need to calculate the average number of complaints per team and/or department and the mean time to resolution for those complaints.

First, you will need to choose clamping bounds, since the number of complaints per month could be 0 to unlimited. You decide on a range of 0–10. You want to also scale mean time to resolution, so each complaint is given a range from 0–5 (for instance, 0 could represent a ticket resolved that day by the employee who filed it and 5 could represent a ticket not resolved after 30 days). This will help highlight chronic issues as opposed to potential false positives, where someone might have miscategorized the complaint.

If you think of your definition of sensitivity so far, this means that for the metrics you are calculating, you likely need a sensitivity of 5×10 to properly protect a person who will add multiple complaints and have them lie unresolved.

Taking a step back, this means that the noise and error will scale linearly with the number of statistics a single individual can influence. To calculate the correlation between several features, if a single person can affect many points, you would need to account for the worst-case scenario or maximum sensitivity every time.

But there are actually methods to help you do this with less error! To find them, you need to think in multidimensional vector space. You have the initial vector representation of the true result of each of the queries without noise. To add a fitting differential privacy mechanism, you must apply the appropriate sensitivity. How can you add enough noise in this multidimensional space to match the sensitivity of each of those queries while still minimizing this noise if possible?

For Laplace mechanisms, you use Manhattan distance (L_1 norm) to optimize and minimize the error and noise. But for Gaussian-based mechanisms, you can use Euclidean distance, because the noise you are adding would be the same noise you would expect from normal error. Gaussian noise will distribute the error normally, and it is best accounted for using Euclidean distance or the L_2 norm.

To find the Manhattan distance or L_1 norm in vector space, you calculate the following:

$$\| x \|_1 = \Sigma_{i=1}^{N} \mid x_i \mid$$

To find the Euclidean distance or L_2 norm in vector space, you calculate the following:

$$\| x \|_2 = \sqrt{\Sigma_{i=1}^{N} \mid x_i \mid^2} = \sqrt{x^T x}$$

To visually inspect what these differences in error and noise mean in two-dimensional space, let's look at a comparison of L_1 versus L_2 distance of two points (Figure 2-7).

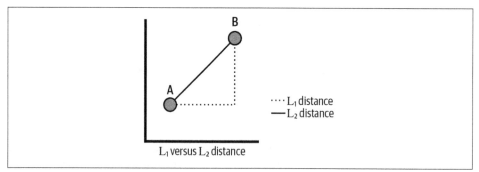

Figure 2-7. L_1 versus L_2 distance

Figure 2-7 makes it clear how the methods get their names. For Manhattan distance, you treat distance like streets in Manhattan, which has a grid-based city design. For Euclidean distance, you are using geometry to find the shortest distance between the two points (which here is the hypotenuse).

To go back to the concrete examples of adding noise to the complaints—if you use Laplace noise and a coworker sends 10 or more complaints that remain unresolved, you need to scale their noise along with Manhattan distance. This means scaling the noise by 5×10. On the other hand, if you use Gaussian noise, the noise will scale by $5 \times \sqrt{10}$. Now you can see the advantage of understanding how one user contributes multiple statistics!

A good rule of thumb is to understand that Laplace noise scales linearly with the number of statistics a person can influence (k), but Gaussian noise scales by the square root of k. So if sensitivity is high and one person can affect quite a few results, Gaussian noise is superior.

What does this mean in practice? Let's add some noise to the salary and age dataset to take a look. You will calculate the mean now with Gaussian instead of Laplace noise. This simple implementation does not account for the optimizations you can leverage with Euclidean distance as it is a toy example and should not be used in any real-world situation. In the Gaussian notebook you will see a comparison that you can play with to build your understanding, and in Chapter 3, you'll use a library that has the latest techniques already implemented:

```
count_epsilon = 0.20
sum_epsilon = 0.79
delta=10**-5


def gaussian_dp_mechanism(value, epsilon, sensitivity=sensitivity):
    # Please do not use this function in real life - it is susceptible
    # to well-known attacks. Instead, use a well-known and audited
    # open-source differential privacy library
    orig_value = value
    gauss_scale = sqrt((2*sensitivity**2*log(1.25/delta))/epsilon**2)
    value = np.random.normal(value, gauss_scale)
    print("Noise: {}".format(value - orig_value))
    return value

summed_ages = gaussian_dp_mechanism(np.sum(bounded_ages),
                                    sum_epsilon, sensitivity=50)
count_ages = gaussian_dp_mechanism(len(bounded_ages),
                                   count_epsilon, sensitivity=1)

mean_age = summed_ages / count_ages
mean_age
```

When I run this code to see how much noise is added, I get this result:

```
Noise: 332.0995166206894
Noise: 25.527328637215277

38.7015287377063
```

The real average age for this newly generated dataset is 45.28, giving a relative error of about 0.15, which is about 5 times the Laplace relative error but using a smaller epsilon (0.99 versus 1.1). It is difficult to make an apples-to-apples comparison as you've implemented the simplest versions of these mechanisms and there are optimizations you haven't yet done. In addition, each time you run the experiment, the noise will change (by design!). That said, you've also had the pleasure of learning from the ground up—working through the choices that a mechanism has to make in order to deliver differential privacy.

You should now have a solid mental model you need for making decisions. There's not enough room in this chapter to cover all the methods you could use, but you now have the basis for evaluating how sensitivity, noise, and error relate.

Real-World Differential Privacy: Debiasing Noisy Results

When you are using differentially private data, you are essentially using data with higher error. You want to start thinking intelligently about how to use the results you get. What can you do to reduce errors inserted by differential privacy?

Noise reduction has been a long-running area of study for statisticians and data scientists alike. Recent innovations like diffusers and Stable Diffusion (*https://oreil.ly/ UYZX3*) have brought these techniques to new problems, allowing noisy images or audio to be "denoised" into realistic content. It would be interesting to apply these methods to differentially private outputs, which would mean learning to predict differential privacy noise and therefore be able to remove it. As you could never reach 100% accuracy unless the mechanism is improperly implemented, you could safely denoise the results while still holding the privacy guarantees, as the certainty of the attacker remains unchanged (i.e., your denoiser cannot guarantee that the output is the original value nor can anyone prove that unless they are inspecting the mechanism at runtime, which is strictly forbidden).

You could also use Bayesian reasoning to develop assumptions about the queries and their real output. To model those assumptions, you could use a Bayesian library like PyMC3 to run a series of experiments. By properly identifying, documenting, and modeling your priors, you can see if your experiments match the behavior of the differentially private data source. If your model looks incorrect, it probably means you need to update your priors!

One reason to prefer Gaussian noise is that scientific inquiry often assumes errors are distributed normally in the first place. Whatever error normalization or correction you have built into your initial design and reasoning likely works well when using Gaussian noise.

 In this chapter, I've used the terms *noise* and *error* at times interchangeably. This is on purpose to highlight that data already has an element of error and noise. There is no such thing as "ground truth" or "pure data," which means when you insert artificial noise via differential privacy, you are modifying one already error-prone version of reality to another.

Another good reason to look at Gaussian noise for data science is the properties of a normal distribution. If your dataset or minimally certain variables in the dataset are also normally distributed, you still end up with a normal distribution. Normal distributions also have nice properties for linear algebra and machine learning—like when you need to apply linear and affine transformations to matrices or vectors.

Of course, approaches to differential privacy are still actively under development and research, and new ones can pop up at any time. Try to look at the bigger picture, developing your understanding of this technology as you determine what works best for your use case. Let's review a more abstract, theoretical view of differential privacy to support these decisions.

Sensitivity and Privacy Units

Up to this point, you defined the sensitivity as relating to one person added and one person removed. This is also called the *privacy unit*. There are times when one person as a privacy unit may be a poor fit for the privacy problem you are trying to solve.

What if a device is used by multiple users (such as a car, home assistant, or wireless router)? You might then want to ensure the privacy of that device for all users is protected, making the difference between D_1 and D_2 device-based.

If you want to investigate user behavior over a long period of time, such as browsing history, location history, or purchasing history, you run into another problem. Running multiple queries on this data over a long period of time would likely use up the privacy budget without any fruitful analysis. You might then choose to make the differential privacy budget bound to a particular interval, which will reset when that interval is over. Or you might choose a smaller set of actions rather than all user actions that a user can perform as the basis for your guarantee (where you will then try to protect the privacy per click or per action).[9] Of course, these guarantees then

---

9 For an example of this method, you can take a look at Facebook's public release of actions (*https://oreil.ly/jHFez*), which was created via an action-level differential privacy mechanism.

become weaker when releasing on a smaller privacy unit, such as guaranteeing privacy on only a per-day or a per-week basis or for a click or other user action rather than for all actions a person can take. If an attacker has auxiliary information, they can use the differentially private queries or data release to increase their suspicion with more information over time. It also shows how so-called superusers end up overexposed even in differentially private results.

 If you are performing anonymization to comply with data protection legislation, like differential privacy to anonymize data under the GDPR, a discussion with your legal team regarding these choices is particularly relevant (more on this in Chapter 8). If you are willing to implement novel approaches, looking at research literature around a particular algorithm or use case you have in mind might uncover an implementation that best meets your privacy and utility requirements.[10]

You'll dive into one of the useful open source differential privacy libraries in Chapter 3, which should make practical approaches more tangible, but you might still be wondering if there are other definitions of anonymization. Maybe you've heard of k-anonymity? Let's explore what it is and why it's no longer recommended for use.

What About k-Anonymity?

K-anonymity is an older approach to anonymization created by computer scientist Latanya Sweeney (*https://latanyasweeney.org*) after she demonstrated that she could de-anonymize medical records released by the State of Massachusetts. The governor, William Weld, had proposed a release of all state medical records for public review, claiming they had been properly anonymized. By joining the public medical records with easily purchased voter registration records, using age, zip code, and gender, she was able to single out his medical records in the release. After she mailed his records to him, he revoked the public release.

K-anonymity was first created as an attempt to mitigate this type of linkage attack. When using k-anonymity, you group people with similar sensitive attributes (like age, zip code, and gender), and you don't release groups that have less than k people in them. For example, if you had a table that looked like Table 2-2:

---

10 When learning about potentially interesting differential privacy papers as well as new developments in the field, take a look at privacy-oriented technical conferences, like PETs Symposium (*https://oreil.ly/iC9v4*), the USENIX Privacy Engineering conference (*https://oreil.ly/DeHye*), or PPML conferences like the ACL's (*https://oreil.ly/m0s1t*) or IACR's (*https://oreil.ly/H8iON*). That said, privacy is now a major topic for all technologists, so there are always new papers across many technical conferences!

Table 2-2. Start dataset

Age	Zip code	Diagnosis
54	11189	Covid-19
44	11188	Normal Flu
22	11187	Covid-19
25	11189	Covid-19
44	34555	Covid-19
72	34555	Covid-19
66	34556	Normal Flu
77	34555	Normal Flu
78	11189	Normal Flu
75	33444	Covid-19

you might update it to look like Table 2-3, setting k=2.

Table 2-3. Dataset with k=2

Age	Zip code	Diagnosis
40-60	1118*	Covid-19
40-60	1118*	Normal Flu
20-40	1118*	Covid-19
20-40	1118*	Covid-19
60+	3455*	Covid-19
60+	3455*	Normal Flu
60+	3455*	Normal Flu

As you can see, you've generalized some of the groupings to preserve more privacy and to ensure that no one person can be singled out. You've also dropped some rows to let k=2, and any singletons are therefore removed. Is privacy protected?

If I'm fairly certain you were in the dataset and you are in your mid-20s with a zip code that begins with 1118, I can immediately deduce that you probably had COVID-19 because 100% of the 20- to 40-year-olds in this dataset and that zip code had a positive diagnosis. This isn't what you wanted or intended. Information like this has been exploited in several k-anonymous datasets, including a public edX dataset that was de-identified via LinkedIn data (*https://oreil.ly/gTcKg*).

When noticing public attacks on these weaknesses, researchers proposed a new method for use in conjunction with k-anonymity called *l-diversity*. L-diversity states that there must also be variance in related sensitive attributes, so the k-anonymity process doesn't create homogeneous groupings where sensitive attributes are unintentionally exposed.

Unfortunately, l-diversity created additional problems for using the data. In the process of creating the groups, data could become skewed, rendering it useless for processes such as machine learning or statistical inference as well as creating imbalanced groups that were nonrepresentative of the actual data. For example, what if you proposed a value of k=2 and a value of l=2? You would end up only with the rows in Table 2-4.

Table 2-4. Dataset with k=2 and l=2

Age	Zip code	Diagnosis
40-60	1118*	Covid-19
40-60	1118*	Normal Flu
60+	3455*	Covid-19
60+	3455*	Normal Flu
60+	3455*	Normal Flu

Not only have you significantly reduced the information you have and the data you can use, but you also now have a skewed dataset that shows a higher incidence of the normal flu than COVID-19, which was not the case in your full dataset.

To try to manage this problem, t-closeness was proposed, which stated that the l-diverse groups needed to have t-closeness to the global distribution of these attributes. Therefore, you now need to create groupings that more closely reflect the global distribution of these related attributes. Let's try that in Table 2-5.

Table 2-5. Dataset with k=2, l=2, and t-closeness

Age	Zip code	Diagnosis
None	None	None

Yes, that's correct. You cannot release any data and match these requirements.

I think you're starting to see the limitations by now. K-anonymity is like taking a hatchet to your dataset when a chisel might work best for what you are actually trying to achieve. K-anonymity provides no way to quantify privacy guarantees, must be customized to each dataset, can take a lot of compute power to properly implement, and adds large amounts of bias to the dataset. Unlike differential privacy, there is never a way to interpret how much information an attacker can learn or to reason about privacy loss of individuals in the dataset. Therefore, it is not generally used or recommended today to anonymize data.

You might be also wondering about synthetic data. I'll address potential uses of synthetic data in Chapter 10, but so far synthetic data with realistic properties has been difficult to produce without using real data as a basis, which can lead to potential leakage. Gretel.ai has ways to generate synthetic data from real data while still applying differential privacy (*https://oreil.ly/bcZun*). In Chapter 4, you'll learn more about the privacy risks associated with generating realistic data from real data without differential privacy.

Summary

In this chapter, you learned to define privacy in a rigorous and scientific way via differential privacy—the leading solution for anonymization. You implemented naive mechanisms and compared different types of noise, started your own privacy budget, and developed an initial understanding of how differential privacy works in a practical environment. You now understand how difficult it is to comprehensively build mechanisms that address complex topics such as sensitivity and find balance in the privacy versus information continuum. And you evaluated older approaches that are not often recommended.

In doing so, you've begun to appreciate the complexity of the privacy problem at hand. In the next chapter, you'll apply your new understanding of governance, data protection, and differential privacy to real systems today by leveraging available libraries.

## CHAPTER 3

Building Privacy into Data Pipelines

Now that you've evaluated different approaches to pseudonymization and anonymization, let's explore how you integrate these approaches directly into normal data workflows. Pipelines and other large-scale data infrastructure are a sustainable and extensible approach to designing privacy into your data architecture. When you scale privacy methods, defined by a multidisciplinary team of experts and implemented by a group that understands not only the privacy technologies but also the infrastructure of the company, you move from piecemeal, one-off operation to maintainable Privacy by Design.

In this chapter, you'll learn about how to incorporate privacy technologies into the data engineering infrastructure and software.[1] You'll also learn tips for working with data engineering teams (in case you aren't in one already!). Finally, you'll learn how to engineer privacy into your data collection methods and how differential privacy looks as part of your data collection pipeline.

How to Build Privacy into Data Pipelines

In Chapter 1, you looked at data governance basics and how to apply basic privacy protections. In Chapter 2, you learned anonymization and differential privacy methods. Now that you understand the basic building blocks of privacy, it's time to experiment with them and then automate and scale them into real data infrastructure.

---

1 If you don't normally work in data engineering or infrastructure, I recommend learning some of the basics by reviewing data pipeline and data architecture books, videos, or blog posts.

Before you begin building privacy into these workflows, you need to have properly outlined the risks, documented the data (as best you can), understood the use case and data sensitivity, and outlined your processing and privacy plan for others. You've used the process from Chapter 1 to determine governance and sensitivity, so you now know the required method to collect, use, or transform your data. Whether you are using masking, pseudonymization, or differential privacy, you can follow these steps to engineer your privacy efforts into pipelines.

Design Appropriate Privacy Measures

You might have hundreds or thousands of data engineering jobs running daily to process data. Regardless of the scope of an extensive data processing setup, clearly outline to everyone involved what privacy-preserving measures you will take for the variety of data types you are consuming. Not sure what the appropriate privacy technology measure should be? Start small, with something like masking or redacting sensitive fields, and experiment. You are looking for the sweet spot between information and privacy—enabling enough data utility for the purpose it was collected while preserving privacy for the individuals. Collecting personal or sensitive data that just sits around because no one uses it is always a bad idea!

Let's walk through a few critical questions and recommendations that will help you assess whether your measures match the use case:

Define your purpose and use case
> What is the purpose of collecting this data? Who will use it and for what? Define your use cases clearly with the internal users or end users. If you aren't sure why the data is being collected or used, you need to talk with others about whether it is worth the risk of collecting data you might never use. Follow and learn more about data minimization (*https://oreil.ly/SK8Xq*), which is the best privacy-preserving mechanism available. Out of the use cases, prioritize one that has higher privacy risk for your first implementation.

Maximize privacy
> Based on your initial use case, what is the maximum privacy you can offer while still getting your job done? Sometimes this means experimenting with different privacy technologies and seeing the results. To do so without losing data, create a temporary, secure, internal storage or sample that has no privacy protections. Test different methods and have the team or data consumer take a look and see if they can answer their questions. If you can, begin with higher privacy (i.e., removal of fields, masking, and/or differential privacy). Like when you are defining a new product, find out what they need; don't just give them what they ask for.

First, you as a privacy specialist might see ways to meet their needs in a more privacy-friendly way. Second, they might be focused on their own analysis and not balancing their needs with data subjects' rights. As always, have the conversation! After a few rounds, you'll be building experience and knowledge for yourself and the team on what measures are appropriate for what types of tasks. You will also learn new libraries and approaches as they become available via your experiments.

Expand use cases

When the appropriate privacy-utility equilibrium is reached for the initial project, what other tasks, use cases, or data consumers would fit the same or similar requirements? If your organization has strong data classification bounded by consent or usage, start with use cases that have those same classifications and usage requirements. Try an agile approach where you are rolling out these small changes and learning and adapting one more use case or task at a time. Your data consumers or end users are also learning as they go, and they might have different needs that will require fine-tuning. When an approach works across multiple teams and similar use cases, it can become a standard method or approach. This can be documented and taught to new data engineering or data privacy joiners. If, for some reason, the approach fails after a certain time, ensure there are ways for the data consumers to communicate what has changed!

Experiment, learn, and adjust

When new privacy technologies become available or when you grow the privacy skills on the team, identify where can you optimize and adjust. The space is constantly growing and changing; always have a few team members looking at what is next. Is there a new version of a library you are using? If so, what new features does it have? Is there a new team member who brings a particular expertise or was a new privacy engineer hired? How can you integrate their advice into your workflows? Evaluate planned changes to privacy policy and other data governance measures at the organization and collaborate on new policies, standards, and implementations. Being forward looking will ensure your privacy measures are fitting and appropriate now and in the future.

 As you learned in Chapter 2, differential privacy is a rigorous definition of privacy that provides provable guarantees. All other methods are therefore less safe and less recommended. In terms of practical data privacy, you will likely need to use methods that are not as secure and rigorous as differential privacy. My goal is for you to use the knowledge in this book to push for the most secure method that gets the job done. If that means field removal instead of differential privacy, then it is also your job to ensure your team and others who use the data understand the risk.

Once you've found the measures that work for your use cases, it's time to solidify them into each workflow. But before you do that, let's discuss building data flows that work for everyone involved.

Meet Users Where They Are

Who is receiving the data at the end of your pipeline? What requirements do they have from a data privacy and data quality perspective? Figuring out who is your "data customer" is an important part of building better and more useful pipelines.

By getting to know their needs and use cases, you will better understand the best approach for privacy and how to institute checks that ensure everything is operating as planned.

As you learned in Chapter 2, building in differential privacy requires a good understanding of the data, the use case, and the sensitivity involved. Each of these factors will change over time. Performing regular check-ins with the data consumer will confirm that the differentially private data is still meeting expectations and fulfilling the needs of the team. If that changes or if the underlying distribution fundamentally changes (e.g., from a change in the software or application that produces the data or a shift in the population), then the differential privacy mechanism should be re-architected to fit. This might be as simple as adjusting the clamping bounds, sensitivity, privacy unit, or epsilon or as complex as developing a new algorithm.

It is equally important to communicate shifts the data consumers will see due to the privacy protections in place. Ideally, this is an ongoing conversation as the team implementing privacy controls adjusts them to match the needs of the business as well as compliance, legal, and other stakeholders. Teaching people how to use data that has undergone privacy measures will now be a new required skill in privacy and data teams. Ensuring this conversation goes smoothly and that everyone feels empowered to ask questions and experiment will be a key factor in the success or failure of your privacy initiatives.

I am personally a big fan of meeting people where they are in terms of user experience. If you run into an analyst or engineer who has spent 20 years doing their work in a particular way and you're about to change it, figure out how to minimize the disruption. They might have been using the same methods for many years, and it's important to ensure you don't disrupt their work and that you are enabling them to embrace privacy technologies. Make small changes almost imperceptible, walk them through changes step-by-step, listen to their concerns, and incorporate them into your architecture and planning. Keep interviewing during the process to determine if it is working for them. A little bit of psychological safety can go a long way!

By making this effort, you will also figure out ways to take small slices of work and incorporate them into your pipelines.

Engineer Privacy In

As you build out data privacy automation, try to embed it directly into your systems instead of creating one-off, user-defined functions. Even if that is where you start, take a step back to determine if there are holistic ways to engineer privacy into the system once your experiments have shown positive results.

One way to do so is to create small software packages in whatever language or platform you are using that perform these steps. If you are already using software that supports some of the functionality (like Apache Beam with built-in support for differential privacy (*https://oreil.ly/24cOE*)), leverage those tools whenever possible! If you are using Spark, you can also use the Tumult Analytics library (*https://oreil.ly/fNrKw*) (coming later in this chapter) or the PipelineDP project (*https://oreil.ly/jA1Xs*). Do the heavy lifting only if a specific use case requires it, for example, a very particular type of format-preserving encryption to fulfill a particular team's requirements.

In addition to leveraging privacy technologies directly in the pipeline, you'll also want to test and validate that things are working as you expect.

Test and Verify

You are already testing your pipelines, aren't you? This has been a best practice for many years now, allowing you to better understand and validate they are working. In addition to unit testing or running integration tests, testing the actual data being transported is essential to determining the health of your system.

I've been a long-time fan and user of Great Expectations (*https://greatexpectations.io*) for this work, which has a fairly intuitive interface that allows you to both use built-in expectations and build new ones. You can think of this as static analysis for your data. Does the data pass the smell test?[2] If not, you can have the data flagged or halt the entire process. This saves you compute expenses and speeds up identification and rectification of system and pipeline errors.

When you think about using a tool like Great Expectations for privacy, what should you test? Well, you might test that particular fields are present or missing if you have added fields post privacy processing or if you expect particular sensitive fields to be removed or not included. You can also test if differentially private clamping bounds are working as expected. You can even come up with fairly clever tests to assure that particular fields are hashed or encrypted (by testing string entropy) or that certain masking tokens are present in fields where you expect them to be.

---

2 A smell test (*https://oreil.ly/rnO2I*) in computer science means assessing if the code quality is high. You want to assess if the privacy standards are being properly enforced and keep the privacy standards properly distributed across the organization and many data flows.

To take these guiding principles and standards and make them more practical, you'll explore how to actually engineer these with an example.

Engineering Privacy and Data Governance into Pipelines

Now you're ready to actually engineer the initial use case or several use cases. To get your tested and approved privacy transformations into a production environment, you'll want to ensure they match your current data workflows and are properly implemented and well-tested.

Let's see how this can work with a concrete example of sharing data between different departments at a company.

An Example Data Sharing Workflow

Sharing data across an organization or even between organizations is common. How can you do this in a secure and privacy-aware manner? You have two goals: the privacy of the users or employees and the needs of the data consumer. You have consulted with internal experts to analyze the privacy and security risk to determine the appropriate level of protection required.

For this example, you are working at a sustainable chocolate company. You hold purchase data from users via the website. The marketing department wants to use this data to measure the effectiveness of their campaigns on a user-by-user basis.[3]

Based on your initial analysis, you have a plan for how the data should be transformed to apply the fitting privacy and utility for the use case. That plan:

- Remove personal identifiers with the exception of the user ID, which is hashed so that if the marketing team comes back with specific questions, you can answer them by finding the matching user ID.

- If the user session came in with a tagged campaign, retain campaign information; otherwise, leave blank.

- Retain billing city and state, as this was specifically asked for by the marketing department to effectively answer questions for their campaigns.

- Join order data and aggregate order quantity (number of orders) and order value (sum of quantities) per user.

---

3 User-level data is never a great idea for privacy but is common practice for marketing departments. When presented with these cases in your work, you'll need to determine your best advice for the task at hand. In my opinion, marketing questions can often be answered in aggregate data (which might even benefit from adding differential privacy, depending on the audience and how widely it will be shared).

- Bound outliers that have exceptionally large or small amounts of customer value (if needed, you can create a written summary of these for marketing review).

Let's outline how this might look in a workflow. In pseudo-Python it might look something like this:

```
order_dataframe.drop(['street_address', 'first_name',
                      'last_name',...])
browser_dataframe.drop(['ip_address', 'browser_user_agent',...])

order_campaign_df = order_dataframe.merge(browser_dataframe,
    how='inner', on=['order_id'])

# here you would use a key that was securely generated and stored
# for this particular job the key is maintained only for the duration
# of the data investigation and then destroyed
order_campaign_df.user_id.map(lambda x: encrypt(x, key))

order_campaign_df = order_campaign_df.groupby('order_id').agg(
    {'campaign_uri': 'first',
     'user_id': 'first',
     'city': 'first',
     'state': 'first'
     'total': 'sum',
     'num_items': 'count',
    })

order_campaign_df = order_campaign_df.total.map(remove_outliers)

# then export and share with details on processing!
```

There is a working example of this process in the Jupyter notebook in the book's repository (*https://github.com/kjam/practical-data-privacy*). Adapt these examples to fit the framework and languages you use at your organization.

How do you know if the pipeline is properly working? You test it, of course!

To do so, let's use a few expectations from the Great Expectations library. First, you can import Great Expectations directly into your notebook and set it up so that you can sample data directly from the Pandas dataframe:

```
import great_expectations as ge
context = ge.get_context()
```

Next, you can explore what expectations are available by creating an augmented dataframe that has the expectations built in. Do this by using the Tab auto-complete function in Jupyter by typing **expect** and then pressing Tab. You'll see a long list that you can navigate through:

```
ge_df = ge.from_pandas(summary_by_order)
ge_df.expect #  Now press Tab!
```

The following example tests that you have removed outliers from the `total_price` column. You could also define it to, instead, look at percentiles, max, and min as well as standard deviations.

```
ge_df.expect_column_values_to_be_between('total_price', 1500, 27000)
```

Normally you'd then continue to add expectations by hand, but there are ways to run a Great Expectations profiler and build a set of expectations automatically from the data. At the end of your exploration, you need to save the expectations and set up the pipeline to run them as a step in the processing. There are more details to get it working in your setup, with many guides available via the Great Expectations documentation (*https://docs.greatexpectations.io*):

```
ge_df.get_expectation_suite(discard_failed_expectations=False)

# Here you can check that the expectations meet your needs!
# After you do so, write them to a JSON file and set up your system
# to use this file plus GE to test data as it processes!

import json
with open("order_summary_for_sharing_expecation_file.json", "w") as my_file:
    my_file.write(
        json.dumps(ge_df.get_expectation_suite().to_json_dict())
    )
```

Now you can be certain that, should anything malfunction, you will be alerted. During the first few runs, check with your data consumers and ask if their analysis is going well. Have they noticed changes in their analysis or processing? Have they talked with their data consumers or people who use their analysis? I recommend daily check-ins the first week and then once-a-week check-ins for a month. Have someone on the team look at the overall statistics for Great Expectations as part of a weekly health report for all pipelines and note any massive deviations that would require further investigation. Set up alerting for errors that should not happen and ensure team members receive alerts and understand how to troubleshoot.

Let's investigate another type of use case to explore data governance in pipelines. How do you get the order and session information in the first place?

Adding Provenance and Consent Information to Collection

After reading Chapter 1, you learned how important it is to collect and attach consent while you collect data. Automating this type of collection and structuring it for easy use is essential for building privacy into data collection.

Ideally, consent would be given not only for data collection but also data usage. This is not how most systems and interfaces are designed today. Generally, the user encounters a list of data that will be collected and then a long terms-of-service or privacy policy. This is meant to be all-encompassing rather than outlining use cases that the user can then opt in and out of.

If you're at a company that wants to approach privacy differently, you could design your policy and data collection differently. It might look something like Figure 3-1. When a user first opens the application or site, the initial settings are loaded, and the interface is shown. Defaults should be privacy-first, ensuring only absolutely required data collection is on and all other settings are turned off. When new features or processing are added, the user is prompted with a notification to adjust their settings. In addition, there are options for local-only data storage where data is stored only on-device and not shared with a central server or application unless absolutely required for functionality (more on this in Chapter 6).

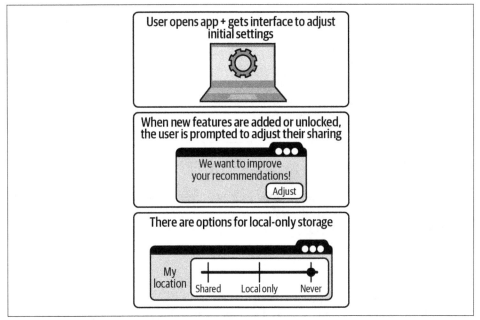

Figure 3-1. Privacy-aware consent and data collection

If you want to change the use cases or had a new way to use the data, like a new machine learning model, you would push that to users and explicitly ask for consent for the new use case.

Another user-friendly option is to give users an interface to review all of their consent options with each use case and allow them to toggle them individually. That could look something like Figure 3-2. This interface states what data is needed for each different data use case, and the vocabulary used is easy to understand. The user is given a variety of choices, including the ability to anonymize data or to keep data on the device.

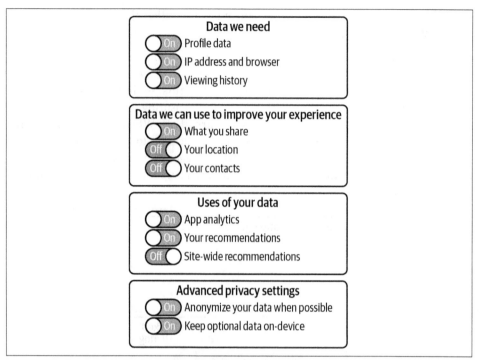

Figure 3-2. Fine-grained consent management interface

There's been a lot of user design and user experience research into better privacy interfaces—like ind.ie's Ethical Design Framework (*https://oreil.ly/Oqzox*) and Privacy UX (*https://oreil.ly/o0cO5*), as well as what not to do, like the University of Ulm's work on bad privacy design patterns (*https://oreil.ly/qrmP1*).

 If you have customer experience designers at your organization, it's worth starting a conversation with them to determine how to align workflows and enable better consent collection and clearer messaging.[4] As a user of consent interfaces, you know it is a lot easier to opt in when it's clear what your data is being used for and why—as well as when there's a place to review these settings. This is also a core requirement of the GDPR (more in Chapter 8).

Even if you cannot redesign consent collection in a meaningful way, you should note what consent data you have at the time of collection. As you know, the regulatory landscape is dynamic; knowing which privacy policy terms were used during

---

4 I recommend reading Vitaly Friedman's Privacy UX Experience on Smashing Magazine (*https://oreil.ly/ HE4NK*) and consulting with your UX team to determine potential changes for your organization.

collection can help you make better decisions later with regard to data usage, retention, and minimization.

How would privacy-aware consent and data collection work in practice? Let's outline collection requirements and design a schema that is useful for later privacy needs. Here's an example of what to collect:

- Privacy policy version
- Retention period
- Date the user accepted the policy
- Compatible purpose of processing (i.e., for what reason is this data being collected?)
- Terms and conditions version
- Data subject localities
- Usage preferences (i.e., please use my data for this service but not related partner services, or please use my data for machine learning but do not share it with other companies)
- Provenance details

Remember, it's not really developed until it has been tested and validated. How can you ensure that consent data is properly tracked?

Here's an example schema validation to ensure this data is properly collected and stored. This example uses Apache Avro syntax (*https://avro.apache.org*) as another way to test data schema and validate data structures in pipelines:

```
{"namespace": "example.avro",
 "type": "record",
 "name": "User Consent Data",
 "fields": [
     {"name": "username", "type": "string"},
     {"name": "policy_version", "type": "float"},
     {"name": "retention_months", "type": "int"},
     {"name": "agreement_date", "type": "datetime"},
     {"name": "processing_purposes", "type": "array",
                                      "items" : "string",
                                      "default": []},
     {"name": "terms_version", "type": "float"},
     {"name": "data_localities", "type": "array", "items" : "string",
                                 "default": ["us-aws-east"]},
     {"name": "usage_detail__location_on", "type": "bool"},
     {"name": "usage_detail__location_ml", "type": "bool"},
     {"name": "usage_detail__location_analytics", "type": "bool"},
     {"name": "usage_detail__location_sharing", "type": "bool"},
     {"name": "usage_detail__actions_on", "type": "bool"},
     {"name": "usage_detail__actions_ml", "type": "bool"},
```

```
                {"name": "usage_detail__actions_analytics", "type": "bool"},
                {"name": "usage_detail__actions_sharing", "type": "bool"},
                {"name": "provenance_location", "type": "string"},
                            /* application or website, etc */
        ]
    }
```

In this example, the usage detail fields are flattened, making it easy to filter data based on the type of fine-grained consent. This allows continuous integration pipelines for machine learning to easily select the users who have given consent automatically and route that data immediately for inferences or training.

You also now have data on when the policy says to retain data and when the agreement date was made, which makes it quite easy to batch anonymize or delete records that are expiring soon because they have reached the full retention period. Building pipelines for these tasks is a smart thing to do before those expiration dates get too close. If you want to retain the data and have cleared differential privacy as an anonymization mechanism with legal (more in Chapter 8), this means integrating differential privacy as a normal part of your data workflows. Let's take a closer look!

Using Differential Privacy Libraries in Pipelines

When adding differential privacy for current or new pipelines, it's best to use a well-supported library that integrates into the technology that you currently use. If you are already using Apache Beam on the Google Cloud Platform, I recommend using its Codelab notebooks (*https://oreil.ly/IKHm4*) to explore ways to implement differential privacy.

If you are using Spark, I recommend the Tumult Analytics library (*https://oreil.ly/idW3D*), with built-in privacy accounting and a variety of other features.

 The Tumult Analytics library was fairly new as this book was being written, so you will want to check out the documentation (*https://oreil.ly/gl2ia*) in case anything has changed. The notebooks from the book repository will also be regularly updated, so please refer to them to try the library.

Let's take the Tumult Analytics differential privacy library for a spin to see how it would work as part of your normal workflow. You can use a new dataset that is referenced in the Tumult documentation (*https://oreil.ly/gl2ia*) or just use it directly from the book's code repository.

To begin, start a Spark session and initiate a differential privacy budget. Here, you will use an epsilon value of 1.1:

```
session = Session.from_dataframe(
    privacy_budget=PureDPBudget(epsilon=1.1),
    source_id="members",
    dataframe=members_df,
    protected_change=AddOneRow(),
)
```

In this dataset, you have a list of library members and their activity. Let's first check the columns:

```
members_df.columns
```

This outputs the following:

```
['id',
 'name',
 'age',
 'gender',
 'education_level',
 'zip_code',
 'books_borrowed',
 'favorite_genres',
 'date_joined']
```

Let's say you're curious as to whether there is a correlation between the amount of books borrowed and education level. To take a look at categorical columns using Tumult, you need to create a KeySet (*https://oreil.ly/4vHVJ*), allowing you to define the categorical variable values you expect to see and would like to group by:

```
edu_levels = KeySet.from_dict({
    "education_level": [
        "up-to-high-school",
        "high-school-diploma",
        "bachelors-associate",
        "masters-degree",
        "doctorate-professional",
    ]
})

edu_average_books_query = (
    QueryBuilder("members")
    .groupby(edu_levels)
    .average("books_borrowed", low=0, high=100)
)
edu_average_books = session.evaluate(
    edu_average_books_query,
    privacy_budget=PureDPBudget(0.6),
    # I am saving some budget for later, so
    # I'm only spending 0.6 of my epsilon (1.1 total) now.
)
edu_average_books.sort("books_borrowed_average").show(truncate=False)
```

Here, the Tumult KeySet and QueryBuilder (*https://oreil.ly/-DcfZ*) classes create a differentially private query. The example code clamps the number of books borrowed to between 0 and 100, as you learned in Chapter 2. To evaluate the query, you need to tell the library how much of the privacy budget you want to spend. When I ran this, I got the following output. Note: yours will be different due to the use of differential privacy:

```
+----------------------+----------------------+
|education_level       |books_borrowed_average|
+----------------------+----------------------+
|doctorate-professional|18.929587482219063    |
|masters-degree        |19.1402224030377      |
|bachelors-associate   |19.173858890761228    |
|up-to-high-school     |19.361286812215194    |
|high-school-diploma   |19.57674149725407     |
+----------------------+----------------------+
```

You can see that there is no discernible difference in this particular dataset between education level and number of books borrowed. The library members don't change their borrowing behavior significantly based on this feature. The clamping range might also be high, so you could take a look at updating that in future queries.

Let's see if folks borrow differently based on an intersection of education and age. First, you need to create age bins (*https://oreil.ly/ihlxx*) so you can group by them:

```
age_binspec = BinningSpec([10*i for i in range(0, 11)])

age_bin_keys = KeySet.from_dict({
    "age_binned": age_binspec.bins()
})

binned_age_with_filter_query = QueryBuilder("members")\
    .filter("education_level='masters-degree' or"\+
            "education_level='doctorate-professional'")\
    .bin_column("age", age_binspec)\
    .groupby(age_bin_keys)\
    .average("books_borrowed", low=0, high=22)

session.evaluate(binned_age_with_filter_query,
                 privacy_budget=PureDPBudget(0.4)).show(truncate=False)
```

When I run this code, it outputs the following:

```
+----------+----------------------+
|binned_age|books_borrowed_average|
+----------+----------------------+
|100-109   |-2.0                  |
|80-89     |11.476923076923077    |
|40-49     |11.034418604651163    |
|30-39     |11.501822600243013    |
|70-79     |11.256830601092895    |
|20-29     |11.08816705336427     |
```

```
|50-59    |11.599250936329588  |
|10-19    |14.0                |
|90-99    |-24.0               |
|60-69    |10.970472440944881  |
|0-9      |19.0                |
+---------+--------------------+
```

Wow! You can see that there is a lot of differential privacy noise added to some of these columns because some of the values are even negative. What went wrong? In this case, the code filtered on age and did not take into account that some of the age groups represented would likely be underrepresented in the filter. The likelihood that a 8-year-old has a master's degree is quite small.

This example is a great reminder: thinking about your data and clarifying your queries and hypotheses to plan your analysis before you run any code are necessary when working with differential privacy. In this case, you could have run a query to get an idea of the age ranges or run a map to show what age ranges are present (with or without counts), giving you a better understanding before writing the queries that will focus on what you are trying to learn. If using Tumult Analytics, you can start with an unlimited privacy budget to get an idea of how small changes in epsilon will change your results. You'll also learn more about how to approach differential privacy and other mechanisms in the entire data science process in Chapter 5.

Data Access and Privacy

In a scenario of using differential privacy at scale, you might end up building different access paths with different privacy guarantees. Here are a few scenarios to think through:

Differentially private access restrictions
Company-wide access to data is only via differentially private queries but allows a small number of data team members to have access with a very large epsilon or no differential privacy at all.

Third-party data sharing with differential privacy
Use a differential privacy mechanism for all data shared with third parties.

Differential privacy for data science workflows
Tie differential privacy to a particular part of the data science workflow—after you perform some initial exploratory data analysis (EDA) and better understand the data. Remember, your goal here is to learn how to better protect the data while still allowing users to analyze it and answer important questions!

Experiment and learn what works for your organization, ensuring that you are evaluating the privacy versus information continuum and figuring out how to protect data and provide access at the same time.

You can see more example queries with this dataset and library in the book's repository, and you can experiment with the library on your own dataset. If you are just experimenting, you can set your privacy budget to infinity! But, in reality, you will need to set an epsilon and determine how to split your budget. If you see an error similar to this one:

```
RuntimeError: Cannot answer query without exceeding privacy budget:
it needs approximately 0.100, but the remaining budget
is approximately 0.000 (difference: 1.000e-01)
```

you know that you've allocated too little budget to answer the query.

I highly recommend using an example dataset and getting to know the capabilities of the Tumult library, or any well-reviewed open sourced differential privacy library! Tumult isn't the only library that works with Spark; you can also use PipelineDP, which is maintained by some Google team members alongside the OpenMined community (*https://www.openmined.org*). They also have several examples in their GitHub repository (*https://oreil.ly/Xjk4z*).

 Not every library has what are called end-to-end differential privacy guarantees, meaning that budget tracking and allocation become a difficult and error-prone task. If you are getting started with differential privacy, I recommend sticking with libraries that will manage the budget for you.

As you learned in Chapter 2, building your own differential privacy mechanism and tracking the privacy budget can be a lot of work and fraught with complex edge cases and errors. It's wonderful that data science is entering an era when open source libraries can support this work. Now that you've seen the internals of building your own simple mechanism, you can also understand how to spend your budget accordingly and ensure that the privacy guarantees are well understood for the data participants. You can also inform downstream recipients of the processing so they can better understand and address the inserted error.

You might be wondering if you can use differential privacy at collection, and there are actually quite a few different ways to approach this. Let's dive into anonymization in data collection!

Collecting Data Anonymously

Now that you are able to use open source and audited differential privacy libraries in your pipelines, you can think about collecting data in an anonymized way. This brings several new considerations such as how do you know sensitivity of data if you don't have access to it? And what privacy guarantees can you offer if anonymization is moved to collection?

To investigate what is possible, let's examine how Apple implemented its initial privacy-aware emoji sampler to see how local differential privacy works (as compared to central differential privacy, which you learned about in Chapter 2).

Apple's Differentially Private Data Collection

Apple was one of the first companies to deploy internet scale local differential privacy (adding a differential privacy mechanism before data is collected and centralized). They have a team of scientists and engineers who work on privacy systems and have decided, as a brand and company, that privacy is a product differentiator.

Apple wanted to improve its emoji suggestions but didn't want to send private text data to its servers to learn what emojis occurred near what text. They determined that emoji frequency and neighboring tokens would solve the problem and went about implementing it for iOS devices with differential privacy included.

In the initial paper released about its differential privacy mechanisms (*https://oreil.ly/AtH_I*), Apple included several useful graphics that show device-level differential privacy before data collection. The data is sent to Apple servers after the differential privacy mechanism is applied.

As shown in Figure 3-3, the specified noise is added to the emoji on the actual device. If you have an iOS device, you can look at the epsilon values on your phone by going to Settings > Privacy > Analytics and looking at Analytics Data in entries that begin with "DifferentialPrivacy." After noise is added, the differentially private emoji representation is sent to Apple servers where the IP address and origin information is dropped. The results are aggregated in a statistical distribution, which can then be denoised due to the scale and knowledge of the differential privacy parameters used. Figures 3-3 and 3-4 show the entire pipeline.

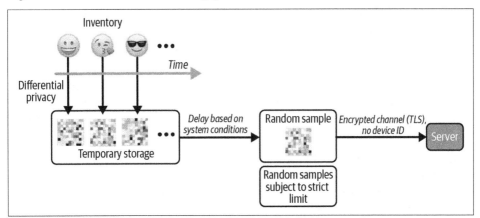

Figure 3-3. Apple's emoji use data collection with local differential privacy

In Figure 3-4, you see that the initial differential privacy mechanism is applied on the device (also shown in Figure 3-3). When the anonymized data is then sent to the server, the IP address is dropped so that no one can trace the data directly to a user, as this would immediately counter all privacy guarantees gained from differential privacy. Internally, Apple uses an ingestor and an aggregator, which transform the incoming data and aggregate it for analytics use. Finally, there are internal dashboards and insights used by the data team and application developers. Each of the dotted lines represents a trust boundary; if the processing violates this boundary or if an internal employee can trace the data, it nullifies the privacy guarantees.

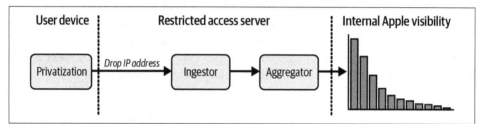

Figure 3-4. Apple's emoji data collection pipeline

What Is a Trust Boundary?

A trust boundary is like a border where security changes in a fundamental way. Usually these boundaries mean that users and operators of one area should not have the same access in the other area. Here are a few examples, to make the definition clearer:

External to internal
> When a user enters data into a web application form and sends it to the application server, it crosses a trust boundary. Ensuring the request is properly formulated, validated, and contains no malicious commands (such as a SQL injection attack) is required before the server can properly respond—and this needs to happen under the purview of the server and application administrators.

Secure environment to less secure
> When moving data from a secure architecture controlled by specific standards to a less secure one, you also cross a trust boundary. This can mean crossing from an on-premise system to the cloud or from a highly restricted area of the architecture to a more lenient one.

Downstream data flows
> When producing data workflows, you might have multiple data consumers. These will often have different access rights and audiences, meaning these flows also operate across trust boundaries. Thinking through trust boundaries for your data workflows is an important step in determining where to apply privacy controls and technologies.

Once the pipeline is done, the resulting analytics are interpretable. This means each user has culpable deniability of which emojis they use, but the keyboard team now has information on how to better deliver emojis for different keyboard languages. The analytics shared in the paper are in Figure 3-5, showing a difference in emoji popularity between French and English keyboard users.

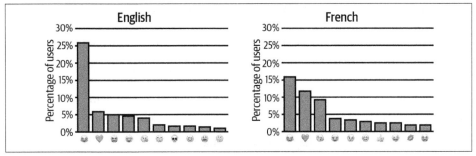

Figure 3-5. Differentially private keyboard emoji use analytics

This approach might be useful if you have some simple sketches or distributions that you want to learn and you have device-based data collection. One thing to note, which you will learn in the next section, is that this is really only feasible at large scale, due to the amount of noise inserted on the individual level.

Apple's differential privacy team regularly publishes their latest research (*https:// oreil.ly/20UxD*), which might be of interest to you if you are thinking of implementing differential privacy at the device level.[5]

What about other ways to collect data with respect to privacy? Google developed an approach that they later sunsetted, which is a use case you can learn from.

Why Chrome's Original Differential Privacy Collection Died

RAPPOR was one of the first successful deployments of differential privacy at scale. It was released by Google in 2014, and you can still see the implementation details (*https://oreil.ly/sqy3M*) and code (*https://oreil.ly/bqz1o*) via the open source repository and documentation.

RAPPOR was built to report sensitive data from Chrome browsers in a privacy-preserving way. To do so, the teams implemented randomized response in a library

---

5 Although Apple is a market leader in embracing privacy technology, it does not mean that there aren't examples where they follow the footsteps of many technology companies when collecting data. An ongoing lawsuit at the writing of this book challenges Apple's privacy-first marketing (*https://oreil.ly/gysAJ*), arguing that there is no real way to turn off all data sharing. In this book, you'll learn more consensual ways to communicate collection to users, employing privacy-first design with a user focus and better empowering users to control their own data.

that was used to collect basic statistics in the form of bitstrings. On the machine, there might be a series of events or metrics that interested the Chrome developers, such as whether a particular add-on was used, if a particular error had occurred, or some information on the user's Chrome history.

Let's stop here and define randomized response (*https://oreil.ly/EPUBT*). It was a technique first proposed in 1965 by survey researchers because they needed to interview people about sensitive topics and they wanted real answers. They came up with this method, which is also differentially private, to give people plausible deniability.

In an example coin-based randomized response, the method would be:

1. A sensitive question is posed, and the person answering has a coin that they flip.
2. If the coin shows tails, they answer "yes" regardless of the truth.
3. If the coin shows heads, they answer truthfully.[6]

You can see how this offers a differential privacy mechanism with quite a low epsilon and a lot of noise! To debias the results, you would assume about half of the yes answers are false and remove them. Should you know more about the population, you could also do this more intelligently. If you would like to learn more and experiment, there is a notebook in the book's code repository (*https://github.com/kjam/practical-data-privacy*) with a longer walk-through and some links.

RAPPOR used a three-part workflow to report metrics from a local machine over a longer period of time while still offering differential privacy guarantees. The guarantees are similar to the randomized response methodology. At a high level, the workflow encoded responses into a bitwise sequence. Each of these responses was related to a small data point. Then, this bitwise sequence was hashed into a Bloom filter. This filter is put through a randomized response process and is saved as a permanent data storage on the device. Then, a bit array is prepared with some additional noise insertion. This is to prevent the possibility of someone learning the permanent responses stored on the filter array over time.

The graphic (Figure 3-6) based on the one in the original paper is quite instructive. The permanent RAPPOR response (B') is stored, and the instantaneous randomized response has additional noise to provide local privacy guarantees. Use the vertical lines to follow the bits from the message down to the report to see this combination of information (original message) and noise (permanent Bloom filter and randomized response) in action. What bits got sent, and which did not?

---

6 There are many variants of randomized response, some which involve dice, or cards, or flipping a coin a second time. This is the simplest version for brevity, but if you are curious to learn more, I recommend diving into research on the topic of randomized response in surveys.

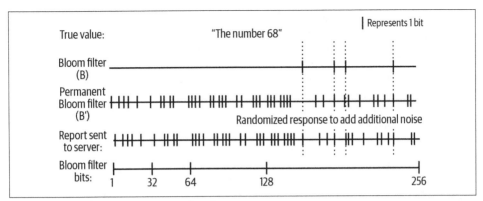

Figure 3-6. RAPPOR report visualized

Google open sourced the project in 2014 and then stopped updating it in 2016. Why?

The relative error of randomized response compared to other methods in centralized differential privacy (like in Chapter 2) is quite high. To get semi-accurate results for randomized response, you not only must collect large quantities of data but also account for a large error in the data.

To get differential privacy guarantees in a centralized model with Laplace, the distribution and resulting noise are scaled to sensitivity/ε for the total data points (k). To get the same guarantees for a local differential privacy mechanism you need to add error of sensitivity/ε for *each* user. This means the relative error for local differential privacy scales with the users at approximately $\frac{1}{\sqrt{k} \times \epsilon}$, much steeper than the relative error of a centralized model, which would be approximately $\frac{1}{k \times \epsilon}$.

If you want to provide local differential privacy (as RAPPOR did, and as Apple does in their collection), you need to reason about a truly large amount of error over time. It's likely that the data analysis that the Chrome team needed was not possible with this much error, which is why it eventually stopped being maintained and is no longer currently used or supported.

The takeaway? Ensure you understand what you want to do with the data and how you want to analyze it over time before investing engineering time and resources in architecting a differential privacy solution that doesn't actually fit your analysis. As of the writing of this book, local differential privacy and the accompanying large noise is often too much for successful exploratory analysis unless you clearly understand exactly what you are trying to learn (as in the case of Apple's emoji analysis).

Google later developed the Prochlo method (*https://oreil.ly/-z4dX*), which uses its processing infrastructure, trust boundaries, some noise, and encryption to provide differential privacy guarantees for data at collection. The paper is worth a read to see how differential privacy guarantees at scale can combine ideas from local and central differential privacy to implement a solution. This type of solution works only if your architecture can support hard trust boundaries!

As this history points out, working with stakeholders to properly explain the error introduced, explaining the questions that can or cannot be answered, and figuring out what fits for the long-term strategy are all parts of designing an appropriate privacy engineering system.

In this chapter, you've explored how to add governance and differential privacy to your workflows. But you're not operating alone. How can you create a team-based approach and win support across the organization?

Working with Data Engineering Team and Leadership

If your organization is large enough, it likely means you have separate data science and engineering teams. In my opinion, this is an unfortunate development because the two teams are irrevocably intertwined. If the communication between data engineers, data scientists, and data managers or data stewards breaks, then the ability to use the data appropriately breaks, too. This affects data and privacy decisions. Data privacy methods work for all parts of the organization when leadership and the entire data team understand the standards and the methods, how they affect the data and data work, and why they are essential.

In case your organization has hard walls between departments that need to work together on these topics, see if you can be the friendly hand over the wall. A little bit of effort here goes a long way toward improving communication.

Share Responsibility

Automating data workflows is not only the job of data engineers or data management teams. It is also the job of data scientists to properly define the types of problems that are important and what data is required.

The data science team must outline business needs and goals, understanding them well enough to anticipate product decisions or features that need data science. Data science expertise should anticipate potential gaps in the current data collection and guide other teams that manage collection and software to fill those gaps. If you are on a data science team, this is also a great time to suggest potential privacy requirements as that data is collected.

Data quality, interoperability, and standardization are part of data governance and should be coordinated across teams regardless of organization size. To do this properly, organizations should have a governance committee, council, or guild and regularly update the standards and guidelines based on community feedback. With your new data governance and privacy knowledge, you can assist these conversations and act as a bridge between parts of the organization.

Check that the standards and guidelines are in place and that the data is meeting the needs of all parties by regularly testing and reviewing the data as a multidisciplinary data team. The last thing you want to learn is that an additional field you requested has not actually been collected for the past 6 months or that the format of another field is indecipherable and not what you needed. Ensure pipelines and other processing have working tests—like what you implemented earlier in this chapter—and are regularly updated with input from all data users.

Finally, to keep larger organizations aligned and communicating, document your work. Let's cover how to do this for privacy workflows.

Create Workflows with Documentation and Privacy

Well-documented systems are easier to use, operate, and manage. This means if you are already working in a shared repository and jobs are clearly documented as a part of this repository, adding a section to this documentation that outlines privacy requirements and recommendations should be easy!

You learned plenty of documentation tips in Chapter 1, but here are some extra ideas to inspire you to integrate documentation into your normal work process:

- Add privacy documentation to your code repositories and notebooks.
- Outline how privacy techniques can be used in an internal knowledge base.
- Give a series of internal talks on the topics you learn in this book.
- Encourage contributions and pull requests to internal repositories for managing privacy.
- Add a "Privacy Measures Enabled" step to your team's Definition of Done (*https://oreil.ly/KJ1dw*).
- Plan a study group and work through this book, the book repository, and the related research. Document as you go!

If you have a few good examples of workflows that have added proper privacy measures, ensure they are properly documented. Then, link to them or give a short internal talk on how you did it. Often folks just need a few good examples to get started and a point person for questions that arise. All of this work supports the data governance documentation as well as creating a culture of privacy at your organization.

Privacy as a Core Value Proposition

Your life will be a lot easier if privacy is seen by numerous team members—or the whole company—as a core value proposition. If this is new, try thinking about what parts of your product or offering touch upon privacy topics and what the value of integrating privacy would be to your organization overall.

If you directly handle consumer data, it's quite obvious. Offering your customers more privacy guarantees goes a long way toward establishing trust and creating a brand that people see positively. Talking about your efforts publicly not only creates this trust but also might attract new talent looking to work in an environment where privacy is taken seriously.

If you work in business-to-business (B2B) or only with internal data, there are also benefits. Working with internal data in a privacy-respecting manner means that there is less invasion of privacy for your coworkers and yourself. For B2B customers whose data you manage, they certainly appreciate the extra effort to make Privacy by Design possible and might be able to pass that message onto their customers. Finally, it could be that the company or organization itself values these topics as a normal part of everyday business.

Building a culture of privacy, where the questions raised in this book become a natural part of conversations about data, is a multiyear journey. Similar to building a champion culture for security, there will be some folks who immediately take to the topic (like yourself, perhaps?) and who bring it to others' attention.

 The security community has done a great job of building cultures inside organizations. Developing bridges with the security experts at your organization and learning how they build security into the culture and foster champions across the organization will be very helpful in determining how to do the same for data privacy. Often, you'll find they are willing to include privacy advocacy into their normal educational work.[7]

The end goal is to ensure that enough folks look at these topics from many perspectives. It doesn't have to be everyone, but it should be enough that things don't slip through the cracks and end up deployed or near deployment without someone considering the privacy questions.

---

7 For additional tips on building a culture around privacy by learning more about security techniques, I recommend reading Chapter 15 of *Agile Application Security* by Laura Bell, et al. (O'Reilly, 2017) (*https://oreil.ly/YNS4v*).

Summary

In this chapter, you learned how to automate privacy in pipelines by first analyzing the privacy needs of the system and finding places to build in privacy. Congratulations! This is a major part of engineering privacy into your data workflows and products.

In doing so, you learned how to design workflows with privacy in mind. You implemented new privacy and data governance technologies at several different parts in the pipeline. You had a chance to experiment with a differential privacy library that you can integrate with Spark-based systems. You learned about local differential privacy and differentially private collection mechanisms. You also evaluated how to collaborate across teams and the organization to bring privacy awareness to all the teams responsible for managing data workflows.

In the next chapter, you'll learn about privacy attacks—getting to know exactly what things you are trying to protect against and solidifying your understanding of privacy risk.

## CHAPTER 4

Privacy Attacks

In this chapter, you'll think like a security analyst and an attacker. Proactive privacy and security creates a cyclical approach, where you spend time envisioning potential threats and attacks and then experiment with how you can protect against them. Because security is never done, you continue this cycle as threats evolve and as your system changes.

When you complete the first round of interventions and mitigations, there is usually another round waiting for you. Since security is always evolving and so are new attacks, this chapter acts as a foundation for your understanding, but you'll want to keep up-to-date by following research, trends, and threats.

Privacy Attacks: Analyzing Common Attack Vectors

Thinking like a security analyst requires knowing what is possible, what is probable, and how to best plan for potential attacks in a proactive, rather than reactive, way. In this section, you'll analyze well-known attack vectors, where both researchers and curious data folks were able to reveal sensitive details meant to remain secret. By analyzing these attacks, you will build an understanding of the more common approaches to reveal sensitive data and be better able to protect data against them.

Netflix Prize Attack

You may think that your online behaviors are fairly general and nonidentifiable. Although some of your behaviors might be more common, such having a Gmail address, liking a popular post, or watching a popular video, there are likely some combinations that make you you.[1] Your collection of interests, your location, your demographic details, and how you interact with the world and others make you stick out, especially over a longer period of time. Let's investigate how this happens by looking at an attack on the Netflix Prize Dataset.

In 2007 Netflix ran a competition, called the Netflix Prize, for the best recommendation algorithm to predict user ratings. As part of the contest, Netflix shared a "random" sample of users' viewing history and ratings that were "anonymized."[2] It contained 100,480,507 records of 480,189 users; the data was protected by removing "identifiers" but replacing them with pseudonymous IDs so that participants could use these individual identifiers to see content the user had rated.

Arvind Narayanan and Vitaly Shmatikov were two researchers with interest in data security at the University of Texas, Austin. They wondered if the individuals in this dataset could be de-anonymized (or re-identified) by looking at potential patterns and outliers. They began evaluating the users in the dataset and identifying those who were overrepresented as part of the sample.[3]

They were able to then compare the most active users in the dataset with a dataset they acquired by scraping IMDB, the popular movie website. By constraining the search space to a small date range from the date in the Netflix set, they were able to match similar reviews for the same content. This allowed them to successfully link individuals in the Netflix dataset with IMBD profiles.

Figure 4-1 shows the probability of linkage (or re-identification) based on this technique. The time span ranges for the bar legend show the number of days used to define the window of time between the review in the dataset and the online reviews. For each of the buckets on the x-axis, you can see the chance of finding the individual based on the number of reviews found online, such as when three out of four reviews in the dataset were found online.

---

1 Of course, your actual account details are definitely unique! What I am referring to here is that the act of using Gmail is not unique.

2 Reminder: if you release data publicly, you'll want to first spend significant time determining how to protect it and how to describe the process used to protect it. Saying something is anonymized means that security and privacy researchers will feel invited to prove otherwise.

3 Indeed, this calls into question how random the sample was to begin with, and if Netflix preprocessed the data to segment a group of more active users. As you know from Chapter 2, outliers would be present and at greater risk for exposure.

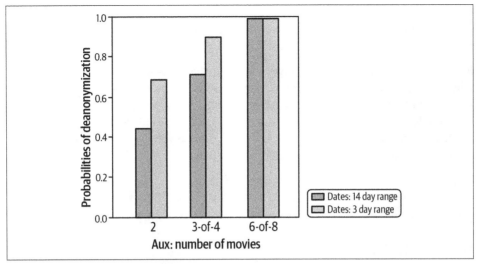

Figure 4-1. Netflix Prize reconstruction attack success

Although some users change usernames on each website or use pseudonyms that are difficult to link to real identities, some people use familiar patterns, including their actual names. If their IMDB profile or username revealed more information about them (such as a first name, a location, or a set of profiles that had more information), the ability for an attacker to then further identify the individual becomes trivial.

You might be thinking, "So what? They reviewed the movies publicly, why should I worry about their privacy?" There are a few reasons. First, most users and people do not have an accurate way to gauge their own privacy risk. This means they can greatly underestimate their risk of posting things in a public forum or other service. It could also be that they did *not* post some of the videos they privately watched on Netflix, which would now be public if Netflix released those reviews. As you recall from the Preface via Nissenbaum and boyd's work—technology obfuscates the context and user choices—meaning users are often confused or unclear what level of risk they are taking on and how to control their own privacy. An absolutist view would be to never post anything publicly, but insisting people sacrifice the utility and enjoyment of technology as the only secure or private option is setting them up to fail.

Second, users cannot anticipate future data releases or breaches and their effects on prior decisions. Unless people live in a jurisdiction like the EU that gives them the right to be forgotten or to request removal of information, many things they did online will remain there indefinitely. Sometimes a user is not aware of the availability of their information—like when the website does not implement Privacy by Design so posts are public by default. Sometimes the data is collected illegally via a breach or when walled garden data is collected without consent for resale or reuse (*https:// oreil.ly/NRHq-*). Sometimes providing data is obligatory, such as to medical providers, to a government, or within a workplace. No one can know the conditions of every data acquisition or release if no consent information is released alongside the data.

Finally, your responsibility—as those who hold the data—is similar to the responsibility of those who build public infrastructure. Protections exist for everyone, not just the most cautious. The governance obligation when you take ownership of data from individuals is to make responsible decisions. Protecting all users, even those who actively participate in public spaces, is part of the job. This work supports the communal nature of the internet and other public spaces.

Thinking more generally about these types of attacks can help you determine how to avoid them when you release data. The Netflix dataset shows the power of linkage and singling out attacks, which are common vectors you should learn and avoid.

Linkage Attacks

Linkage attacks use more than one data source and link them together to re-identify individuals or to gain more information to identify individuals. In general, linkage attacks are successful when attackers have an auxiliary data source that connects easily with another dataset as was the case with the Netflix Prize and IMDB dataset. When you imagine the possible datasets available, you have to think of both privately held and publicly held ones. This can and should include databases you know might have been breached recently or in the past.

One approach to evaluating potential linkage attacks is to actively seek out potential data that others could use in connection with any data you plan to release publicly. Are there public websites that can be viewed or scraped that allow a person to easily gather information they could use in a linkage attack? Are there known public data sources that would easily link to the data you are providing? Or have there been recent large data breaches where data could be used to link individuals in a compromising way?

 As you know from Chapter 2 and your exploration of differential privacy, imagining all possible auxiliary information is an exhausting task that is prone to error. Unfortunately, you cannot know what every attacker will know or have available to them. You can, however, control the data you release and to whom!

Another approach is to ensure all data that is publicly released undergoes state-of-the-art privacy protections, like differential privacy. You might determine this is required for all data shared with third parties, with partners, or even across parts of your organization. As you learned in Chapter 2, this also helps protect against auxiliary information that will get released in the future.

One possible way to determine if your data is easily linkable is to look at the uniqueness of your dataset and the data points themselves. You can determine whether your data is easily linkable by using cardinality analysis, like Google's KHyperLogLog paper (*https://oreil.ly/MSc1L*).

Expansive datasets are part of the problem. When vast amounts of data are collected and are not properly tagged as person-related or where governance and documentation were not properly implemented, a grave danger is introduced to privacy. How do you determine what data is re-identifiable?

Cardinality analysis can help you determine this. When you have a large dataset, it is the many unique combinations of those data points that can reveal or leak information about an individual, such as their device identifier, their location, their website, or their favorite music service. These small points in aggregate get hidden, making it difficult to see each one as unique.

Let's say you have a bunch of different variables in your logging or datasets that are person-related but not necessarily identifiable. You'd like to explore if this data has hidden privacy risks by determining if the variables themselves or combinations of them are actually identifiable. These identifiers can be any piece of data collected from users, but the ones used by the researchers were things like browser agents, logged application settings, and other application or browser details.

What you'd like to find is the uniqueness of any one of these potential identifiers and combinations of them that are potentially or certainly unique. To do this, the researchers developed a two-part data structure that combines the power of two different hashing mechanisms. The first is a K Min Values hashing mechanism, which calculates the density of the dataset, and, therefore, its uniqueness, by looking at the distance between the K smallest hashes. At the same time, the variables and matched unique user IDs are passed to HyperLogLog (*https://oreil.ly/mcvxp*) or HyperLogLog++, which are highly efficient at cardinality estimations. By combining these two powerful mechanisms, the authors were able to create a fast and efficient method to quickly eject variables that were not very unique and variables that had a lot of users.[4]

Not only that, KHyperLogLog data structures can be joined to discover how combinations expose users to privacy risk. With this two-level structure, they can also be used to compare actual PII data with this "pseudonymous" data to determine if some variable combinations function as unique identifiers. In Google's own use of the

---

4 If you have the inclination and time, read "KHyperLogLog: Estimating Reidentifiability and Joinability of Large Data at Scale" (*https://oreil.ly/MSc1L*) or take a look at a more visual walkthrough of KHyperLogLog (*https://oreil.ly/tVuzZ*) to learn more about how these work in detail.

algorithm, they were able to find and rectify privacy bugs, such as storing the exact phone volume location with too high precision.

With these results, you can either recommend that the disparate sources with those unique combinations of variables are never combined or provide appropriate privacy and security precautions to reduce the risk of re-identification attacks or erroneous linkage. This is especially relevant for automated data processing or training large deep learning models, where the linkage could be identified without human oversight and exploited by algorithms or other automations.

This type of cardinality analysis also helps you determine how likely it is that a user can be singled out. Let's explore what attacks are possible if a person is indeed easily identifiable in the group.

Singling Out Attacks

Singling out attacks work by singling out an individual in a public release and attempting to gather more information about them via the same dataset or via other sources. These attacks can also be performed in reverse, by bringing information about an individual to a released dataset and attempting to deduce whether this person is included and can be identified.

Let's walk through an example of each.

Say you are a data scientist querying a naively anonymized database. You want to find out the salary of a particular individual, and you know that she is the only woman over 60 at the company. If the database allows you to get "aggregated" responses without additional security of differential privacy, I can perform a series of queries that targets this woman and exposes her salary to me. For example, if it is truly naive, I can ask for the salary of all women over 60, immediately returning her salary. If it is better protected but still doesn't account for singling out attacks, I can perform a series of queries (one for all salaries of people over 60, one for all salaries of men over 60) and use their difference to reveal her salary.

Another real-world example is the re-identification of celebrities in the New York City taxi dataset. The dataset was released to the public as part of a Freedom of Information Act (FOIA) (*https://www.foia.gov*) request in 2014. A data scientist with the dataset noticed an odd pattern, where the pseudonymous identifiers of several taxi medallions were repeated, sometimes showing the same taxi in multiple locations at the same time. This is impossible, of course, but it left an important clue. The scientist correctly inferred that this value actually represented a null value, where the medallion information was missing.

Via this discovery, the scientist was able to reverse engineer the hashing mechanism used (this was easy, as no salt[5] was added!). The rest of the data was easily reversible by creating a rainbow table (*https://oreil.ly/tzFh9*).

Once that dataset was revealed, it was soon linked to paparazzi photos of celebrities getting out of taxis because the medallion identifier must be visible on many parts of the taxi—the doors, the rear, the license plate, etc. There is a Gawker article (*https://oreil.ly/yCp2u*) that exposes how different celebrities tipped, since the data was now easily linkable. This is an example of bringing auxiliary information to a poorly anonymized data source, making it a linkage attack as well as a singling out attack. Although one might not care about the privacy of celebrities, this also means any other person getting out of a cab in a photo is identifiable. Privacy depends on proper protections, and allowing cracks in the privacy for some (here: celebrities) erodes privacy protection for all.

But singling out and linking data aren't the only types of privacy attacks. Sensitive details exist everywhere, and even when you release aggregate data with some protections, you can inadvertently release sensitive details. Let's investigate how aggregated data leaks information.

Strava Heat Map Attack

In 2018, the exercise tracking application Strava released a global activity map. It allowed users and onlookers to view activities (jogging, biking, hiking) from all over the world. It also boasted that data was anonymized. It took less than a day before interesting less populated areas of the map were highlighted on social media. While Strava had a large user base in North America and Western/Central Europe, it did not have many users in Africa and the Middle East. But there were still active routes there. Zooming in on those routes revealed outlines of previously undocumented US and NATO military bases, which were intended to remain secret.

Figure 4-2 shows a Strava screengrab of a US military base in Afghanistan. This base and similar ones were exposed on the days and weeks following the global heat map release, highlighted in a Twitter thread by a security-minded Twitter user (@Nrg8000) (*https://oreil.ly/ZFX8h*) and several replies. On the day the map was released, many reports made clear that the outliers—data coming from Strava users in Africa and the Middle East—exposed military secrets of more than one nation-state.

---

5 Salt is random data that is used by one-way hashes to protect against rainbow table—or precomputed attacks. To ensure one-way hashes are secure, you need cryptographically secure pseudorandom generation, which salt achieves when used with well-maintained cryptographic libraries.

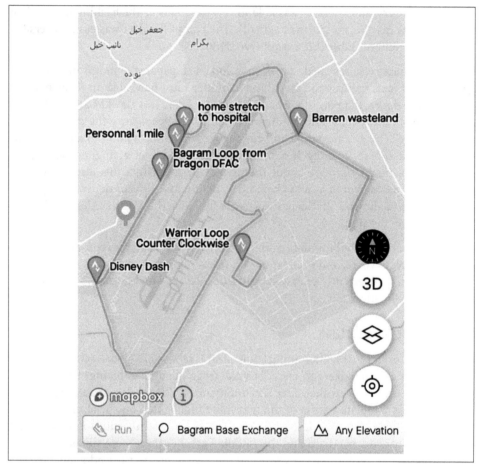

Figure 4-2. Bagram Military Base on the Strava application

This is a great example of how sensitive data can inadvertently link to other sensitive data. Here, personal data for US and NATO service members leaked confidential information about the military bases and operations. This demonstrates how individual privacy and group privacy relate. In this case, individual privacy exposure linked with group membership exposes extra information (here: confidential information).

Individual privacy, as discussed in Chapter 2, allows you to guarantee privacy for a particular individual. Differential privacy measures those guarantees and keeps them within a particular range that you can designate and validate.

Group privacy refers to the ability to guarantee privacy for a larger group. This could be similar to expanding the privacy unit under differential privacy conditions so that it covers a larger number of people (like a household unit for a census). But, as you might imagine, zooming out to say all members of a particular profession, gender, or race/ethnicity would be incredibly difficult if they represented a large portion of the population.

Even when you can guarantee privacy for individuals, you often end up "leaking" information about groups. In a way, this is great, because this is the power of data science and statistics! It is very helpful to use data to investigate, compare across groups, and develop conclusions while still maintaining strict privacy guarantees for individuals.

The Strava example shows how a concentration of users at a particular sensitive location revealed confidential information. But there are other examples where data collected in a voluntary and privacy-friendly way revealed group information. In a lawsuit against Google for underpaying women and gender-diverse individuals as compared to their male counterparts, data was collected internally using a Google form (*https://oreil.ly/VpIxZ*). The sheet asked for voluntary input of the person's engineering grade, their gender, and their salary and additional bonuses paid in the prior year.[6]

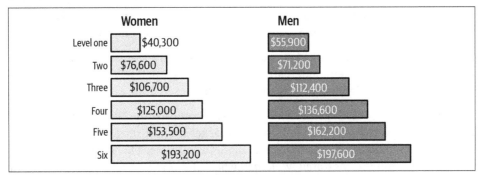

Figure 4-3. Aggregated consensual data collection at Google reveals salary disparity

This data in aggregate revealed a stark salary disparity between male employees and their women and gender minority counterparts at a variety of engineering grades. Figure 4-3 shows the details of this disparity and was used as evidence in court. At

---

6 This type of data collection does not provide the strict guarantees like with differential privacy. It was voluntary disclosure, and the organizers did toggle what options were available to them and built the questionnaire to allow for more privacy. Creating anonymous and differentially private survey infrastructure would be a wonderful contribution for these types of use cases—keeping privacy guarantees high and providing ways that sensitive data can be used for equality and justice.

every level, except level 2, women and gender minorities were paid less than their men counterparts.[7]

As you can see, group privacy may at times be undesirable, because you want to make decisions based on private attributes. However, in the case of the secrecy breach for Strava users, it would have been useful to let users opt in rather than deploying a default opt-in. Strava later fixed this option via an opt-out option, but only after secret information was leaked. This is a good example of how Privacy by Design principles can help you choose safe defaults and consent options!

Another interesting attack on privacy and group identity is called the *membership inference attack.*

Membership Inference Attack

What if I told you that I could determine if your data was used to train a model. This might not matter if billions of people were used to train the model, but it certainly would matter if the training set was much smaller and if your membership in it revealed something particular about you, such as your sexual orientation, illnesses or other health-related information, your financial status, and so on.

In a membership inference attack, the attacker tries to learn if a person was a member of the training data. When models are trained on smaller datasets or if a person is an outlier, this person might be particularly vulnerable.

Reza Shokri discovered membership inference attacks in 2016 (*https://oreil.ly/DKAvU*). The process works as follows: the attacker trains a shadow model, which is a model that should be as close to the real model as possible. This mirrors the process of transfer learning (*https://oreil.ly/pR9qc*), where the goal is to adapt information in one model to quickly train another—usually in a related field, such as when sharing base weights and layers between large computer vision models helps speed up training. Then, there is a Generative Adversarial Network (GAN)–like architecture (*https://oreil.ly/TznAI*) that trains a discriminator, which is used to determine if a person (in vector form) was in the training dataset or not. This discriminator infers, from the output of the model itself, whether the data point was included in the

---

7 This data was collected prior to 2017 and released in 2017. Several other studies and actions in large US technology companies have revealed similar pay gaps or other mechanisms that oppress women and gender minorities—including an overrepresentation in junior roles. Several recent studies show this trend is changing, with now women and gender minorities earning more than male counterparts when they reach high levels, but with the same overrepresentation in junior roles. Analyzing data like this in a consensual and privacy-aware manner can help expose unfair and unequal treatment and track if diversity and equity initiatives are working.

training data.[8] You can see the full architecture in Figure 4-4, which shows the many shadow models being trained, with their output feeding into the "Attack training set," which operates as data to train the discriminator.

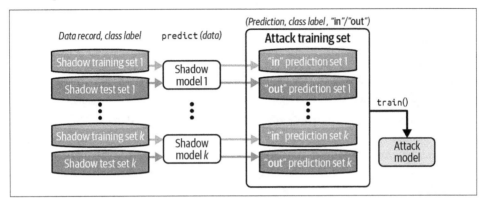

Figure 4-4. Membership inference attack architecture

You can probably guess what this process reveals! If a model overfits or if an outlier leaks particular information about itself into the model, it will have fairly different probability ranges for the training versus testing data. This is also why it's particularly dangerous for outliers, models trained on a small dataset, or models with poor generalization.

 A membership inference attack points out the importance of models generalizing well and the impact of outliers on the resulting model(s). Privacy techniques and technologies can help reduce the influence of outliers and promote generalization. Your goal as a data scientist is to ensure that your models are performant, which means to avoid this type of private information leakage. In Chapter 5, you'll review ways to train models on personal data using differential privacy.

Let's walk through the required steps to perform a membership inference attack:

1. Adequate training data must be collected from the model itself via sequential queries of possible inputs or gathered from available public or private datasets to which the attacker has access.

---

8 If GANs are new to you, the high-level idea is that they have two machine learning models. One tries to make a decision based on the output of another, which then helps correct the error of the first. GANs are often used to produce different types of content and media, ranging from machine learning art to generated text photos or videos, including content like deep fakes.

2. The attacker builds several shadow models, which should mimic the model (i.e., take similar inputs and produce similar outputs as the target model). These shadow models should be tuned for high precision and recall on samples of the training data that was collected. Note that the attack aims to have different training and testing splits for each shadow model, and there must be enough data to perform this step.

3. Once the shadow models are trained, the predictions for examples from the other datasets that were not part of their training as well as data from their own training dataset are recorded. This is now the training dataset for the discriminator.

4. The attacker trains a discriminator with this new training dataset. This discriminator is used to evaluate the target API and determine whether a datapoint is in the target model by evaluating the API model output with the discriminator. These attacks can, therefore, be run without full access to the model or in what is called a *closed-box* environment.

Shokri and his fellow researchers tested these attacks against Amazon and Google Cloud machine learning systems and a local model. In their experiments, they achieved 74% accuracy against Amazon's machine learning as a service and 94% accuracy against Google's machine learning as a service, making it clear that machine learning tasks expose private information. In a more recent paper (*https://oreil.ly/Ijzl7*), researchers were able to run this attack within private and decentralized systems such as federated learning (see Chapter 6), a type of machine learning architecture supported by Google and other large companies to promote private data use in a secure and privacy-friendly machine learning system. Since then, Shokri's research group has released an open source library (*https://oreil.ly/1Ftx5*) to measure membership inference attack privacy leakage.

 Recommender systems are becoming increasingly more personalized—employing demographic information, net worth, and other sensitive fields. For models trained on a small population, an attacker who knows a few pieces of information about someone can then determine if they were included in the training dataset so long as they can mock the probable input features. This applies to other information used for selection of the training data population, such as gender, age, race, location, immigration status, sexual orientation, political affiliation, and buying preferences.

In later research, Shokri and several other researchers found that model explanations leak private information (*https://oreil.ly/WFJlc*), particularly for outliers. When using standard ways to explain why a model reached a particular prediction or output, these explanations leaked information about outliers in particular. This type of behavior is likely more prevalent the more that sensitive data is used to make decisions in the model.

This increased model granularity and sensitivity has other risks, including exposing these sensitive attributes for people who are curious what types of people were included in the training data.

Inferring Sensitive Attributes

Membership inference attacks can be generalized to describe group attributes of the training data population, called an *attribute privacy attack* (*https://oreil.ly/OENQ1*). In this case, the attacker wants to learn things about the underlying population and uses the same technique to test theories about types of people who might be represented in the training dataset.

This attack reveals sensitive group details. If you are training a model with your user base and they are predominantly from certain regions, have certain personal characteristics, or are in a small targeted group with a particular shared attribute, such as their browsing or spending habits, this information could then be available to anyone with access to the model endpoint, so long as these attributes can be exposed via feature input or model behavior. At this point, it would not only be a privacy attack but also likely a proprietary information leak!

This isn't the only way sensitive attributes are leaked, however. A research paper from 2013 (*https://oreil.ly/wtdqw*) demonstrated that Facebook likes were a strong determinant of private attributes, such as sexual orientation, gender, political leaning, or drug use. This research was performed at Cambridge University; one of the researchers went on to work with Cambridge Analytica, where these types of patterns were exploited to manipulate voting behavior.[9]

This underscores the guidance from differential privacy research. It is extremely difficult to determine what attributes an external source might be able to find, use, or link. It serves as an example of how revealing seemingly innocuous data points—such as Facebook likes or web search behavior—can be. Whenever you are collecting data from humans, you need to be aware of the possibility that this data will leak other sensitive attributes.

For these reasons, it's important to treat all data collected about humans as potentially sensitive and to use the techniques in this book, along with your further research and experimentation, to protect this data and the related persons.

---

9 Cambridge Analytica ran political advertisements on platforms like Facebook (*https://oreil.ly/ANM31*), which aimed to influence voters in the UK Brexit referendum and 2016 US Presidential election. It is difficult to determine how successful these targeted advertisements were, but the profiling used private attributes—such as voting behavior and political affiliation—inferred from Facebook likes and profile information.

Learning sensitive or private attributes from seemingly nonsensitive data points is a significant contributor to model unfairness and discriminatory models. If the resulting model learns sensitive attributes leaked via training data correlations, these models reproduce societal biases and accelerate systemic oppression. This problem goes beyond the scope of privacy as well as this book; I recommend reading *Algorithms of Oppression* by Safiya Umoja Noble (NYU Press, 2018) and following the work of Timnit Gebru and team at DAIR (*https://www.dair-institute.org*) and the Algorithmic Justice League (*https://www.ajl.org*) to learn more.

Other Model Leakage Attacks: Memorization

Part of the problem with how models learn is they can end up memorizing or inadvertently storing information. This occurs easily if the examples are outliers. It also can occur if a particular sensitive example is shown many times. This phenomenon is correlated with parameter and model size (more parameters, more memorization). Findings from the Secret Sharer (*https://oreil.ly/AAhWH*) demonstrate this, but several other research circles confirmed this at the time of that publication.

What Carlini et al. showed, in the Secret Sharer, was that large models have a tendency to overfit and memorize parts of the dataset. In this case, it was a large language model that memorized secret tokens in the dataset (such as credit card numbers, Social Security numbers, etc.). I presume that Google was able to identify this behavior in other nonpublic and non-research-facing datasets, which led to the publication of this particular piece of research that was specifically trained on the Enron emails.

Therefore, the larger models grow—which at this point seems to have no upper limit—the greater the chance of some semblance of memorization and overfitting, particularly for outliers, both via their characteristics and/or their frequency.

You can also see this behavior in synthetic GANs, as explained in This Person (Probably) Exists (*https://oreil.ly/F0J8G*). This research pointed out that GANs based on person-related data, such as the faces on This Person Does Not Exist (*https://thispersondoesnotexist.com*), are often actually traceable to the source dataset. This was reported in several other cases where professional models were paid to sit and have photos taken. Later those photos were used to create fake influencers. In the faces and bodies of those synthetic influencers, the original human models could find parts of their faces and bodies. This obviously means those people do exist, and so do the parts of them that ended up in an influencer without their explicit consent. I like to call these types of GANs *data washing*, because—via the machine learning training—personhood, authorship, and attribution are removed. The result is, supposedly, a completely new creation, but you now know this is not really true.

These types of models are growing every week, and it's hard to keep up with all of them. If you have used any of the large GPT-based models such as ChatGPT, I challenge you to find a person who you think might be part of the scraped training data but not someone too popular where they would appear in many sources. Ask the model who this person is and compare it with text from the person's website, Wikipedia, or social media sites. You might be surprised to see these outliers' own words parroted back from the "AI."

By now, you might be realizing how valuable and sensitive trained models can be. Let's review ways that attackers have stolen models from production systems.

Model-Stealing Attacks

Models are increasingly valuable assets, and the more you integrate them into production systems, the more they are shipped to the edge of the infrastructure. There, they are either on the public-facing internet or deployed directly on user devices—laptops, smartphones, and appliances. The result is an increasing threat of model-stealing attacks, where an attacker is able to get either the model itself or a close enough approximation that they could use it for their own machine learning or to extract other details.

Why is this a problem? Well, if the model contains sensitive or proprietary information or is seen as a company asset, then this type of attack is as bad as someone stealing money or data from your organization! If the model is already open source or a fine-tuned model built on a large open source model, the risk or threat is much lower.

How do these attacks work? One of the first papers articulating this type of attack was released by Florian Tramèr et al. in 2016 (*https://oreil.ly/C9DE0*). The group was able to train several models using the Amazon and Google Cloud APIs that were available at that time. They generated and gathered a dataset that reflected the data that this model used. They set up a series of API requests and were able to optimize their requests to span the search space of the input data. By saving those data points, they now had a training set and could build a variety of models. Then, a cyclical approach to fine-tune the model was used to ensure the model closely matched the production system.

I taught an O'Reilly live course on several of these attacks in the past, with example notebooks (*https://oreil.ly/4I_46*) (and a few more (*https://oreil.ly/irvSK*)) if you'd like to walk through some attacks. There are also many implementations available on GitHub, likely with updates for a particular architecture or language if you have a specific use case you'd like to test.

When you ship models to a device, users have an even easier way to inspect the behavior of the model and to run queries in a low-latency environment. Several (*https://oreil.ly/50xHz*) researchers (*https://oreil.ly/Xhv1w*) and enthusiasts (*https://oreil.ly/NdMH-*) have explored models shipped to Android and iOS devices and how to reverse engineer the model weights and architecture. Protecting models that are shipped to end devices is still very much an open problem. One piece of advice is to use differential privacy as part of your training steps (see Chapter 5), obfuscate the model architecture using transfer learning and distillation, or keep multiple models as part of a process, shipping only those that are required to run offline to a phone. You might also find that using federated learning—where the model is owned by all devices—fits the scenario best (see Chapter 6). As this is an active area of research, I recommend searching for recent research and discussing these concerns openly with the security and privacy experts at your organization in order to find a fitting mitigation.

Similarly, model inversion attacks exploit models to target an individual user. In 2015, researchers were able to extract noisy images from facial recognition models (*https://oreil.ly/72pkx*) that revealed semi-accurate photos. The only data needed to perform this attack was the target class they were trying to reveal and access to the model prediction API. They used a search method that aimed to maximize activation, allowing them to get closer to the optimal input: in this case, a person's face (see Figure 4-5 to view the extracted image versus the real image; this was generated using an open source repository modeled after the initial research (*https://oreil.ly/PLZ5y*)).

Figure 4-5. Extracted noisy face from a model inversion attack (left) and a training set image of the victim (right); the attacker is given only the person's name and access to a facial recognition system that returns a class confidence score

If a model is particularly sensitive, you should treat it as a high-value asset, wrapping it in several layers of protection. That said, you'll need to balance the usability of the system with the model value. Privacy technologies are handy for this. In Chapter 6, you will learn more about shipping parts of models closer to devices while keeping them updated and safe.

So if privacy technologies can help create models that leak less information, is there any way to attack these privacy technologies? Let's explore ways researchers have proven that privacy technology itself can be attacked.

Attacks Against Privacy Protocols

When I discussed differential privacy in Chapter 2, I referenced attacks against differential privacy mechanisms. Let's dive a bit deeper into the types of attacks that have been performed and what libraries do to prevent those attacks.

In 2012, Ilya Mironov was able to perform an initial attack on a differentially private mechanism that used a Laplace distribution (*https://oreil.ly/fgZDr*) due to how floating-point systems function. When you sample from a Laplace distribution, you attempt to model a continuous space, but this isn't how computers actually work. What researchers have been able to show is that there is a tendency for floating-point machines to sample randomness in predictable ways. This makes sense, if you think about the need for someone to write code that creates entropy—generally, computers are not very good sources of true entropy.

In this attack, the attacker will observe several query responses for this differential privacy mechanism and try to determine whether or not it came from a random distribution sample. If the attacker knows the type of distribution (e.g., Laplace or Gaussian) and the mechanism uses no special source of randomness—but instead calls built-in functions for random sampling methods—this attack can succeed.

To prevent this attack, some post-processing needs to be performed on the addition of random noise to the distribution. This post-processing should be built directly into the library, be peer reviewed and audited, and use methods that will work across all machines.[10]

 Successful attacks on k-anonymity and weaker mechanisms for anonymization are commonplace enough that they often don't get much attention. That said, a simple search in ArXiv for "re-identification" can turn up the latest research. I also recommend reading Aloni Cohen's successful attack on k-anonymous EdX data (*https://oreil.ly/t3I3v*).

---

10 If you'd like to learn more about these approaches, I recommend taking a look at Tumult Analytics' approach (*https://oreil.ly/6SG26*) or the Google paper on secure noise generation (*https://oreil.ly/Sdwqy*).

Timing attacks have also been proven to work against differential privacy mechanisms. The attacker observes the amount of time the response takes and then builds a statistical model to discern what part of the noise distribution was selected. Timing attacks are common against computationally complex operations—like cryptography—and notoriously difficult to prevent when rapid responses are the goal.

To be clear, these attack vectors are not all the possible privacy attacks on data or machine learning systems, but they should help you be alert and thoughtful. I hope this overview gave you an idea of what to look out for and how to reason about the more common types of attacks.

 You haven't even begun to scratch the surface of other types of attacks on machine learning models, such as adversarial attacks that attempt to "trick" the model into a particular result or poisoning or Byzantine attacks, which make models drift in a particular fashion. For a good overview of that space, I recommend starting with Battista Biggio's Wild Patterns paper (*https://oreil.ly/cHZxg*) and then checking out the latest on ArXiv! There are also some interesting conferences, such as the ACM's AI and Security conference (*https://aisec.cc*) and the NeurIPS's Safety Workshop (*https://oreil.ly/Ajcg0*).

In the next section, you'll learn data security basics as an overview in case you are new to security. You'll see how working with data security professionals helps manage attacks and related risk and supports privacy and security concerns in your data science work.

Data Security

Data security overlaps with data privacy and data governance in fairly significant ways. Security is a required step in data governance—restricting access, preventing insecure or questionable usage of data, setting up security controls for safer data, and assisting when something goes wrong (i.e., data is breached or stolen). Obviously, if data is breached, so is privacy. These fields complement one another, but they are definitely not the same.

Although these systems and processes are not often the responsibility of the data science team, you should be familiar with these measures and the conversations around them. They will come up when you are managing and maintaining sensitive data. This knowledge will also help you consider potential attacks and protect the data you are using.

Data security is almost always concerned with the CIA triad, which stands for:

Confidentiality

Data that is sensitive or confidential is made accessible only to those who should access the data. The data is not available—in any way—to others inside or outside of the organization.

Integrity

The data can be trusted. It is valid and has not been tampered with by internal negligence or external tampering.

Availability

The data and related services are properly available for their intended purpose. This usually has to do with agreements like service level agreements (SLAs) or service level objectives (SLOs) that outline availability metrics.

Clearly, these are also the goals of most data teams, but there is a focus on potential malicious activity or actors—external or internal (referred to as *internal threats*).

Figure 4-6 imagines some of the intersections between these topics in data security via a data science lens. It is not exhaustive but should provide guidance and inspire ideas on how these fields overlap.

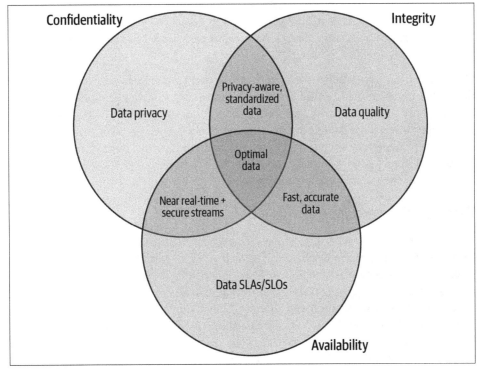

Figure 4-6. Data security principles in data science

Data security professionals have several major concerns when it comes to managing data, implementing data governance, and supporting privacy initiatives. In the following sections, you'll learn key building blocks and technologies you will encounter when working on these systems with security professionals and get a few tips for collaboration.

Access Control

Access control systems, often connected with authentication and identity providers such as Microsoft Active Directory, Google Single-Sign-On (SSO), and AWS Identity and Access Management (IAM), allow administrators to manage who has access to what data and in what form. These systems allow you to form groups of individuals and/or services that have the proper authentication credentials to access, read, change, or add to data. There are several reasons why access control in this manner is useful. For example, you might want to shut down write access to the data in case the service is ever compromised by a malicious actor who might use the service to manipulate the data (perhaps by encrypting it in a ransomware attack). And, of course, it is possible that even a read of that particular data by a malicious actor can create a significant security risk.

For example, you might have an API service for a machine learning model that pulls data for training and testing. This service requires read-only access, as it will not—and should not—modify the data.

Or, suppose you have a person-related database that you'd like to secure more heavily than other databases. You could set access controls for a smaller group of individuals as well as use built-in security features to ensure that every access is logged and that each query returns masked content for some of the fields. Pseudonymization techniques (see Chapter 1), such as masking, or ideally the use of differential privacy (see Chapter 2) would provide extra protection for access and also allow for a stronger audit trail in case there is a suspected breach.

Data Loss Prevention

Data loss prevention technologies measure ingress and egress interfaces for systems or networks to determine if sensitive data is leaving a trusted region. They are often used by data security professionals to provide an extra layer of protection for sensitive data and to guard against data exfiltration attacks—when someone is exporting or moving data in an unapproved manner. A malicious actor might break into the network to take files and data, or this can happen via an internal threat, such as an employee exporting data to another party or device for unapproved usage. It could also be nonmalicious and insider, for instance, where "shadow IT" operations have made the transfer of sensitive data internally commonplace (although still not approved!).

Data loss prevention technology can often detect these data flows by looking at network activity and network packet headers or metadata. Many of the top solutions available use statistical modeling and/or machine learning as part of the offering. Your skills in data science will help you understand that anomalous network behavior (like gigabytes of data flowing to a new IP address) or data flowing at odd hours is a good indication something might be amiss. Depending on how the network is architected and managed, there may also be deep packet inspection, allowing the network administrators and the data loss prevention technology a closer look at what *exactly* is being sent over the network.

If your organization uses data loss prevention technology, it's important for the data team to understand where and how it is being used so new data services you build don't get flagged as potentially malicious. It might also be interesting to learn more about the technology in use, in case you would like to support those efforts. For more detail regarding data prevention technology, I recommend reading through the documentation provided by Google Cloud's service (*https://cloud.google.com/dlp*).

Extra Security Controls

Additional security measures, beyond basic access control mechanisms, are commonplace at most organizations today, ranging from encrypting all data at rest and ensuring encryption keys are rotated to changing server access points via networking restrictions or cloud identity services like Amazon's Identity and Access Management (IAM). The purpose of extra security controls is to reduce the risk of an internal or external attack by adding protections and defenses.

Development teams—including data scientists—often complain about these protections that make data *harder* to access should an intruder infiltrate the servers, network, or systems. It can mean a few extra steps for well-intentioned actors, like a data analyst trying to get their job done.

That said, these protections help ensure data accessibility is appropriate. The more valuable the data, the more controls and protections it should have. Lead by example and help champion these measures, which also provide better data privacy. Most technologists have learned and used these basic data security measures, such as using authentication systems, managing keys, and checking proper access, and data folks need to learn them as well. If you end up specializing in data privacy and security, you might even suggest and implement these systems one day.

Threat Modeling and Incident Response

Security professionals often use threat modeling and incident response to assess security risks. These are commonly performed by the information security (infosec) teams, in conjunction with relevant compliance, audit, or legal experts.

Threat modeling involves mapping current processes, data flows, and procedures and then considering what malicious actors might do to attack the infrastructure or how they might trick employees to provide access or use the services for unintended purposes. When performed effectively, threat modeling is a continuous and agile exercise that keeps the data, applications, and humans as secure as possible.

 In my experience, I've worked alongside amazing infosec professionals, who were open to learning about the data and machine learning topics I know and sharing their knowledge on topics like threat modeling. Your security team will know a lot more about the types of attacks that affect the systems in your organization and may be willing to teach you more. This knowledge will help you better assess risk and threats internally and externally. For a quick overview of agile threat modeling, I recommend reading Jim Gumbley's Agile Threat Modeling post (*https://oreil.ly/ygpiU*).

Incident response refers to the actions you need to take and the plan to use should you discover a security incident, such as a network intrusion, data breach, or other information leakage. An incident can be as small as someone posting a username or email on an internal log. But it can be huge—posting full credentials to a public repository or leaving a database open to the public with a poor password or none at all! Unfortunately, these incidents happen regularly, in part because many developers and data scientists are not taught about security hygiene—a term used by security communities to describe risk awareness and best practices.

Incidents will happen. When they happen, your team already should have worked through several incident response plans and know how to proceed. Security professionals create these plans, often with input from other teams that develop and maintain the affected platforms and/or services. Privacy professionals also often have a data breach response plan, which is particularly helpful for your work and often integrated into the incident response plans.

If you discover an incident, the first step is to take a deep breath, refrain from touching or doing anything, and contact security. They may need to collect forensic evidence and determine what services and storage were accessed or impacted along with attempting to identify the entry point, privilege escalations, as well as other evidence left behind. Think of it like a crime scene, where every fingerprint and smudge matters! Only once you have the all clear to turn off services or remediate the problem should you proceed with ways to help mitigate the incident. You may need to update a password, rotate a key, or change the networking rules if something was exposed. No one wants to be part of an incident, but having a plan in advance can make these events less chaotic and error prone. I recommend working on incident response plans with your security team as they relate to your privacy concerns about the data you use.

Probabilistic Reasoning About Attacks

What is reasonable to expect when preparing to defend your query mechanisms, APIs, and models against attack? How can you determine when you have built in *enough* privacy and security?

Security practitioners ask these questions daily. Generally, the advice is to ensure that enough mitigations are in place for the likelihood and potential impact of any threats. Let's analyze how to think about these problems using probability.

An Average Attacker

Is there a such thing as an average attacker? Well, I ask you this: do you have an "average user" in your population? Probably not!

You might be able to cluster your users and find an average per "type" of user (for example, superusers, or beta testers/early adopters), but humans aren't often average. Therefore, the idea of an average attack is flawed.

But can you use data to reason about expectations for a "typical" attacker and use probability to assist in how your organization thinks about attacks? Absolutely!

When you participate in a threat modeling exercise, you identify and then sort potential attack vectors by value (i.e., financial or reputational risk/reward) as well as likelihood. This is where your understanding of probability can help. Depending on the data at your organization, you might actually have hard information to support your reasoning around likelihood.

Humans are not very good at reasoning about likelihood without actual data. Research shows, in fact, that even security experts asked to rate risk and likelihood in a given scenario will rate it differently when they see the same scenario another time. Figure 4-7 shows data from a study in which Douglas Hubbard and his research team asked experts to rate the same scenarios over a period of time. His group was trying to determine if experts would rate these similarly every time—as expert assessments are often used as the sole data point to assess risk. If this was the case, you would see a perfect line where the x-axis equals the y-axis. Instead, you can see that there is often no consistent rating over time—even for the same rater and the very same scenario.[11] This means that much of the way organizations currently classify risk is inherently malleable.

---

11 Douglas Hubbard and Richard Seiersen's book, *How to Measure Anything in Cybersecurity Risk* (Wiley, 2016), is a great read for understanding the security community's approach to data. Although the recommended methods are dated compared with today's data analysis and probability, the foundational approaches can help you understand the lack of data and large problem space in which cybersecurity professionals operate.

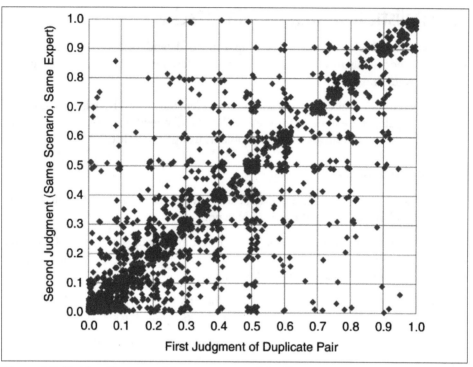

Figure 4-7. Hubbard's expert risk assessment and its divergence

This is similar to the issue of "averaging" risk. When you reason about average risk in quantifiable privacy, you end up actually overexposing vulnerable populations in an unequal way. As described well in an article by DifferentialPrivacy.org (*https://oreil.ly/HU3YO*), when you make average-case assumptions about the privacy risk, you risk overexposing outliers due to their already more precarious place in the data distribution.

So why, exactly, should you use probability to reason about privacy and security risk? Let's take a look at current ways of measuring risk (not averaging it!) and determine if there are some places where data science can be useful.

Measuring Risk, Assessing Threats

You might be familiar with the tried and true risk matrix, which attempts to map and then block risk into different regions to determine what should be addressed. This system would be great if inputs were actually consistent, quantifiable, and realistic measurements, but inputs are often riddled with personal biases and high uncertainty.

As a data scientist, you are tasked with reducing uncertainty via observation, experimentation, and scientific inquiry. Sometimes it works and you build a probabilistic model of reality; other times it doesn't and you can measure only how much uncertainty to expect (or keep experimenting!).

Your data science toolkit can assist in assessing threats and measuring risks, but only when there is historical data. If there is not a quorum of experts to help model, if uncertainly is high and information low, you are unlikely to provide significant assistance.

However, there is a growing push in the security communities to create more quantifiable risk scenarios; here you can help model the question to make it answerable. One way might be to think through dependent and independent variables of a complex problem or threat, identifying those that change often versus those that are fairly static. There might also be open data or internal data to support an assessment of the distribution of these variables over time.

 Modeling experiments have proven quite fruitful in security research. One great example of this is the initial research that uncovered Rowhammer (*https://oreil.ly/oQv9n*), a way to exploit dynamic memory and read from your neighbors in large data centers. This research showed that this threat vector—previously believed to be quite uncommon—was occurring at much higher rates. Building data-driven security experiments to validate threats can help ensure that these models are based in reality.

For data science purposes, the main risks that need to be managed are access to the data, data infrastructure, and models. Let's review a few mitigations that can help ensure that you have appropriate protections in place.

Data Security Mitigations

With your improved understanding of data security, you can now select the areas of data security that you want to incorporate into your work. In this section, particularly relevant protections for data science and machine learning work are highlighted, but, of course, the field is large. This can be your starting point, but it is not a comprehensive list.

Applying Web Security Basics

Since data work often involves offering data via endpoints and APIs, explore how those are accessed to borrow ideas from already well-defined approaches and apply them as you see fit.

For many decades, the Open Web Application Security Project (OWASP) (*https://owasp.org*) has outlined what the top threats are for web applications and websites. OWASP also outlines protective controls (*https://oreil.ly/FMgtB*), including protecting API endpoints by using access control and validating inputs. These controls are also useful for anyone creating a model API that will be available to users directly or indirectly.

Ensuring all model or data query endpoints are thoroughly tested is another useful measure. Work with the software engineers to outline potential attacks on models—adversarial attacks, poisoning attacks, and the privacy attacks outlined in this chapter.

If you are exposing a model directly for use, implement rate limiting and determine who your users are by requiring a clear sign-up process with human verification. If rate limiting is not an option, ensure you are validating input and that you have a response—for invalid queries or requests—that does not leak extra information.

Finally, if at all possible, do not connect your models or query interfaces directly to the public internet. Require an access control process that involves identity verification or wrap your model in several input processes, making the public internet data one of many data sources or one that never directly touches your model input.

Protecting Training Data and Models

As you have learned in this chapter, protecting your machine learning is about more than just protecting the model itself; it's also about protecting the infrastructure that helps build and train your models.

Think about the technological supply chain verification (i.e., technological bill of materials)—you must ensure the data entering your model is properly protected. Therefore, you must automate your machine learning systems and your data workflows whenever possible. Ensure they are properly designed and tested for privacy and security concerns.

Goals for data usage are different from organization to organization. Here are some questions to explore and address as you design:

- Does this data flow have person-related data? What have you implemented to mitigate privacy concerns?

- Do you understand your organization's interpretation of regulation enough to provide guidance regarding proper mitigations? If not, whom can you ask to assist in translating the legal concerns into technical concepts?

- Does this data flow cross trust boundaries? If so, how are you addressing security concerns?

- Have you implemented testing as part of this workflow to ensure that the mitigations are actually working?

- Have you spoken with data consumers on data quality and analysis requirements so they can keep using this data?

- Have you documented assumptions and governance requirements so others can easily understand this workflow?

- Can you run integration tests to regularly sample data and ensure the system is working as expected?

- Have you automated all that you can, but left human-readable documentation so others can validate or update the privacy and security controls should something shift?

- Do you know what happens when something breaks?

In addition to addressing issues like these, you can also implement proper version control on your workflows and determine if version control for their resulting datasets or models is appropriate (see Chapter 1). As you learned in Chapter 1, ensuring that your workflows support self-documenting lineage and governance will already go a long way toward implementing data governance. This also helps accelerate and expand security and privacy work, as systems are well understood.

Now you've done what you can, given what you know about the threat landscape and regulatory environment. But, you know that keeps changing! This requires you to stay informed on new attacks and threats on the horizon. How can you learn about new attacks?

Staying Informed: Learning About New Attacks

You already know that new developments in machine learning and data science happen quickly. It's unlikely that you have time to read every paper on the topic or to keep up with every conference talk, especially as interest in this topic continues to grow. How can you stay current enough to ensure you have things covered?

From a security aspect, I would recommend taking a look at some of the leading conferences, which are now beginning to have dedicated tracks for data privacy and security. For example, the long-running DEFCON conference now has a dedicated track for AI attacks called the AI Village (*https://aivillage.org*).

There is also a great community around privacy technologies called OpenMined (*https://www.openmined.org*). Their Slack community—as well as their courses and conferences—focus exclusively on privacy in data science and machine learning.

Some additional newsletters and blogs might be of interest, including mine! Here is a short list:

Probably Private (https://probablyprivate.com)
> My newsletter on data privacy and its intersection with data science, with updates for this book and related topics

Upturn (http://www.upturn.org)
> Newsletter on justice and privacy in technology

Bruce Schneier on security (https://www.schneier.com)
> Security expertise blog covering a wide variety of security topics

Lukasz Olejnik on cyber, privacy, and tech policy critique (https://blog.lukaszolej nik.com)
> Security, privacy, web technology, and tech policy

IAPP's Daily Dashboard (https://iapp.org/news/daily-dashboard)
> Daily updates from the International Association of Privacy Professionals (IAPP)

 What I would recommend—more than anything—is finding your passion and niche within the community and following researchers and organizations that are doing interesting work in that area. This way, staying up-to-date feels more like following the work of good friends.

If you miss things and it's important, it will likely come up in the context of your work. If you've built your connection with infosec coworkers, they will usually also keep you in the loop should anything of particular interest arise.

Summary

In this chapter, you learned about a wide variety of attacks on privacy—attacks to reveal extra information in the data, attacks against machine learning models, and attacks against privacy protections themselves. You also learned about collaboration with security peers and how working with them on privacy risk and mitigation is essential.

Security is a constantly evolving field—by the time this book is published, new attacks will have been created and used. Use this chapter as a start for your understanding of privacy and security risk that you will grow alongside your work on protecting privacy.

In the next chapter, you'll dive deeper into your normal workflow to start exploring how to protect privacy in machine learning and data science.

## CHAPTER 5

Privacy-Aware Machine Learning and Data Science

In Chapter 4, you learned several different attacks, including attacks on the machine learning models themselves. You might have never thought about how to protect machine learning models from exposing private information; you presumed or heard that regularization and generalization would remove the privacy risk. Unfortunately, that is not the case, especially as models grow in size and parameters.

In this chapter, you'll explore ways to add anonymization to machine learning workflows and dive into research on privacy-preserving machine learning and data science. As this field is fast-moving and actively being researched, you'll want to understand the core concepts and compare today's leading methods. You'll review an open source library that is readily available and examine how to integrate the methods learned in previous chapters into your normal data science experimentation and workflow. This will allow you to develop skills in evaluating mitigations and determining the best approach for your use case.

Using Privacy-Preserving Techniques in Machine Learning

Machine learning offers a workflow where privacy techniques can easily be incorporated. For most machine learning applications, you are already investigating the data, cleaning or wrangling the variables you would like to use, preparing the features, and applying training and testing. Because of the heavy involvement of data science professionals at each stage in this process, experimenting with privacy-preserving techniques is an easy addition.

Privacy-preserving machine learning (PPML) is an area of machine learning that investigates privacy-enhancing technologies and how to incorporate them into machine learning workflows. This could mean incorporating differential privacy into machine learning, or finding other ways to balance the privacy versus utility trade-off when approaching machine learning problems.

Research has shown that privacy-preserving techniques can improve generalization (*https://oreil.ly/rywNM*). This makes sense when you think of the problem of overfitting. You don't want the model to memorize private attributes of any one individual or even a small cluster of outliers. It would be better to have a useful generalization of the available feature space and how that maps to your decision space. In an ideal world, all models would be privacy-preserving because they have actually learned a general approach that maps to reality.

Since the world is not always ideal, let's investigate how to apply your newly acquired knowledge within a machine learning setting.

Privacy-Preserving Techniques in a Typical Data Science or ML Workflow

When approaching a problem in machine learning, you should evaluate the information and privacy continuum and determine exactly what information is required to appropriately train a model and ensure some level of privacy.

In this section, you'll review two common steps of the machine learning or data science workflow: the exploratory data analysis (EDA) process, where you explore the data via several methods to discover if and how it will fit your use case, and feature preparation, which is a data preparation step before machine learning. After these steps are done, you normally move onto model training and evaluation, which is covered later in the chapter.

Exploratory data analysis

Let's begin with the part of the EDA process when you are evaluating the data to determine what might be useful for training a model. This involves deepening your understanding of the data, determining what might be useful for your analysis or machine learning task, and finding relationships in your dataset. One common practice is to test the correlation of input variables (or combinations thereof) with target variables or test information gain or mutual information equations to determine what information could help train a performant model.

As you might recall from Chapter 3, adding differential privacy at the EDA or even feature engineering stage would require local differential privacy because it is likely that each data point represents a person. In fact, a person might contribute many data points, which complicates sensitivity further. Adding sufficient noise to each individual tensor and/or data point would be too noisy for optimal outcomes in EDA.

This is one of the catch-22s of privacy-preserving data analysis. You need to understand the data to decide the best privacy protections, but you need to see the data before you can understand it! Therefore, the practical recommendation is to determine a smaller set of data scientists and analysts who can see some representative samples of the data at hand. Their job is to perform enough analysis to understand the data and prepare the appropriate privacy mechanisms. Their recommendations will then create ways for others to access the data—via either a differential privacy mechanism, a set of tools, or protections applied before the data is released or used by a wider audience.

For a data source where you believe anonymization via differential privacy is best suited, you would first use unprotected data analysis to determine appropriate bounds, epsilon, noise distribution, and library choice. You can then experiment with different approaches and add differential privacy at the analysis or machine learning step—before the data is seen or used by a wider audience.

To perform privacy-preserving data analysis and open the data to a wider audience, you'll need to fit your privacy-preserving mechanism to the type of input data you have. Table 5-1 shows some examples to give you an idea of what techniques might be available to you.

Table 5-1. Privacy-preserving mechanisms for EDA

Data type	Available mechanisms	EDA example
Integer	Perturbation, bounding, differential privacy	Using a differential privacy mechanism to access the data
Float	Rounding, perturbation, bounding, differential privacy	Rounding and bounding all floats to a particular floor or ceiling
String	Redaction, format-preserving encryption, cipher or hashing, masking	Using a library to cipher all strings or find potential PII and mask or redact
Vector	Differential privacy, perturbation	Using Gaussian differential privacy

When managing data and releasing it for EDA or other analysis to a larger group, it is safest to start with differential privacy mechanisms or full redaction of sensitive fields and then test to see if the wider audience can still properly analyze the data. In your best-case scenario, this means you do not need to use sensitive information to learn what you need to learn!

If it becomes clear that differential privacy will not work, you can use a crude measure—such as perturbation, rounding, or bounding within the nearest range—to see if these help. Again, these techniques will not have the guarantees or security of differential privacy.

When you find that a highly sensitive attribute has a strong correlation with the target variables, stop for a minute to think about why that might be. It is often the case that unjust and unfair models exist when target variables and historical data show a correlation between race, gender, nationality, neighborhood, or other sensitive details about personhood and a particular outcome. Think critically and holistically when you find these connections. Some models should never be built.

For text-based or natural language processing work, you'll need to think through differential privacy as part of the training mechanism. You will not, however, be able to use that as part of your EDA process unless you are already working with machine learning models or with tensor representations. For example, if you are using a pretrained language model, you could fine-tune the model with differential privacy.

Another method that might work with text data involves using a library to scan and remove potential PII. As mentioned in Chapter 1, this process can be error-prone and should not be trusted to remove 100% of the sensitive information or PII—but it can provide a starting point when working with structured and semistructured data. When managing large data systems, this is a privacy protection required for normal access criteria. There are several libraries and database systems that implement simple protections like tokenization, masking, and format-preserving encryption, such as Microsoft's Presidio (*https://oreil.ly/Tao7Z*) or Google's Data Loss Prevention library (*https://oreil.ly/8zM-v*). For a further review, please refer to the pseudonymization methods covered in Chapter 1.

You can also decide to eliminate words or tokens that appear in very few—or only one—text. Removing these outliers can help remove sensitive information that might identify one speaker or writer versus others[1] but is unlikely to affect the output or performance of your model should you have a representative dataset. If you would like to keep the tokens, you can always use masking or format-preserving encryption (see Chapter 1) to ensure that the tokens retain some of the information but not all of it.

In general, removing outliers is a good everyday practice to incorporate privacy into your regular data analysis and exploratory work. As discussed in Chapter 4, outliers leak an exceptional amount of information and, therefore, always pose a greater privacy risk than their counterparts. If those outliers are critical to your analysis, such as in anomaly detection, then consider your work highly sensitive in nature. Make certain those workflows are properly protected from curious people inside and outside the organization.

---

1 Google used federated learning with secure aggregation (*https://oreil.ly/FrRjc*), which you'll learn in Chapters 6 and 7, to ensure this type of text did not enter potential models used for text selection prediction.

Feature Engineering

As you move into the feature engineering part of the process, it's a good time to experiment with a more robust privacy mechanism, particularly if the features are going into a centralized feature store or might be used by related teams or projects. At this point, your process must ensure features that are sensitive are easily distinguishable from less sensitive features via proper cataloging and data governance tools.

For weaker privacy mechanisms, such as pseudonymization or simple rounding, think about documenting a data expiry period. This is where having the original data around how it was collected, how consent was generated, and when the data should be removed would be extremely helpful. Under the GDPR requirements, users have the right to be forgotten, so if you are using user data without proper anonymization mechanisms, you will need to figure out ways to delete that data, including copies or artifacts of that data (i.e., models, feature tensors, reports, or dashboards) held in other locations.

> Under the GDPR, a user should be able to remove all data they have produced. This has often been interpreted by legal departments as data they have directly entered (like into a form) rather than data they might have created when using an application and platform. While that practice is safe at the writing of this book, it is not considered to be the intention of the law, and that means enforcement advice can change at any point in time. Therefore, thinking about proper anonymization methods (like differential privacy) and data minimization is a good way to future-proof your models and data work. More on this in Chapter 8.

In the next section, you'll learn how to train models with differential privacy without having to add noise to each feature individually. "Engineering Differentially Private Features" on page 124 and "Applying Simpler Methods" on page 126 explore several other methods for privacy-preserving feature generation that can be explored further should differentially private training be a poor choice.

Let's first look at privacy-preserving machine learning to see if it fits your use case.

Privacy-Preserving Machine Learning in the Wild

There has been increased motivation to implement privacy mechanisms, like differential privacy, in machine learning over the past 10 years, with increased success. The field continues to grow and change, but, in this section, you'll see how PPML was first used at scale. Choosing the best approach for your use case—and what you should try—requires knowing your current architecture and workflows. You'll also need to determine how you will set up privacy technologies in your machine learning operations.

One of the first papers to implement differentially private machine learning at scale is Nicolas Papernot's PATE architecture (*https://oreil.ly/GkiSN*), which he developed in a research role at Google Brain in 2016. The concept: you have sensitive or private data to use in your training. You split it into N groups (the highest performance in the paper was 5,000), as shown in Figure 5-1. The data is now completely separated, so no dataset overlaps with any other dataset. You use those separate datasets to train N teachers. These can be whatever algorithm, architecture, or estimator you want—in the paper they used a deep neural network. Now you have 5,000 models, and you want to aggregate or distill this information into one model you can query.

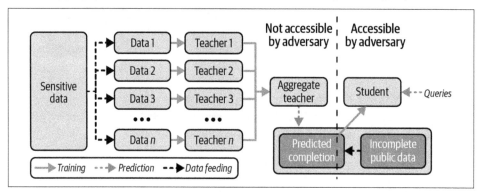

Figure 5-1. PATE: privacy-preserving machine learning

The PATE architecture, outlined in Figure 5-1, takes these many teachers and trains a single student. This student is trained on public data where the labels are collected via aggregated teacher votes. How does this account for differential privacy? Well, a teacher can vote at most once, and each teacher influences the vote by at most one. Sound familiar? As you learned in Chapter 2, this means if you employ Laplace noise with sensitivity equal to one at the aggregation point, you can guarantee differential privacy so long as you trust that no one is watching the process or has access to the aggregator. This guarantee presumes that the N groups have properly divided up persons so they are seen by only one teacher.

At the end, you can guarantee not only the differential privacy budget that was used but also that the student has seen only public data. Of course, all of the labels are actually coming from the private or sensitive data that the teachers learned via their training process. The differential privacy mechanism at the voting aggregation step ensures that no one single teacher leaks too much information from their individual training set.

In the paper, the researchers showed a drop in accuracy of about 10–15% compared with normal training without any privacy on the raw data; however, that drop in accuracy is generally for near-misses—the student model ends up being more uncertain about data near decision boundaries and data that may be incorrectly labeled. You might have trained models with adversarial training or SVM-kernels, which use similar strategies for uncertainty at boundaries to improve model performance.

Differentially Private Stochastic Gradient Descent

There have been significant advances since the PATE paper in adding differential privacy noise during training. As you learned in Chapter 2, you can measure sensitivity in L_2 distance and apply noise via a Gaussian-based mechanism. Because of this you can directly add noise during training to tensors—or, more accurately, calculations thereof—regardless of the particular algorithm and architecture you are using.

The difficulty in applying differential privacy in machine learning is actually determining what the sensitivity of a given training tensor is. Let's presume that one person equals one sample for your algorithm or machine learning process. You then need to ensure you have bounds for each tensor's contribution to the machine learning process.

To properly address sensitivity of tensors, several deep learning libraries use differentially private stochastic gradient descent. Figure 5-2 walks through the steps to clarify the process.

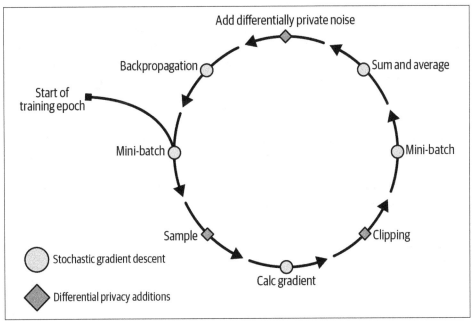

Figure 5-2. Differential privacy stochastic gradient descent

First, you need to understand vanilla stochastic gradient descent (SGD), so let's walk through that process briefly. You have an optimization function (or loss function) you would like to minimize. To do so, you need it to be convex and differentiable. To find the lowest point in this function, you take random points on the function (samples), and you calculate the gradient (vectorized representation of the function slope given those points). Here, the gradient is actually showing the way to reach the maximum of the function, but if you go in the opposite direction (descend the gradient), you should get to the bottom eventually, where you have minimized the error. The size of your "step" down the gradient is determined by your learning rate. So you can take big steps, but you might not find the global minimum because you actually *overstep*. Alternatively, you can take tiny steps, but that might end up taking a long time. This is why adaptive learning rates are also favorable (big steps first, smaller steps later) or more exploratory methods that allow a wider search space at the start.

I hope this high-level overview of SGD helped if it was a new concept for you. Now, how can you use it to implement differential privacy? First, you want to create a measurement that shows the contribution of a single individual in the training set. The idea supported by differentially private SGD (DP-SGD) is to use the gradient itself as the measurement of a single person's contribution; it will calculate the "learning" you get from one sample. Note, however, that this presumes that each person is seen only once—more on this later!

In SGD, you can have unbounded gradients, which means your first problem is the amount of privacy leakage you have in these unbounded gradients (especially with outliers). As you learned in Chapter 2, you need to choose sensible clamping bounds for each gradient, which introduces the idea of gradient clipping. You might have already heard about gradient clipping as a technique for regularization, but here you use it to clamp the amount that any one sample (read: person) can contribute to the learning process.

You might be familiar with gradient clipping from handling exploding gradients—which can create instability or unreliability during training. Normally, this involves creating a unit vector by dividing the gradient by its norm if the gradient is above a certain size and then multiplying this by a particular constant. When you apply this method for differential privacy, you then control the constant because it defines your sensitivity bounds.

Once the per-sample gradient is clipped and scaled, you need to combine these per-sample gradients back into a batch update. You can then sample noise via a differential privacy mechanism—and since you have bounded each contribution, you can appropriately scale noise. In your machine learning processes, you typically expect a Gaussian error, so Gaussian noise fits quite nicely with the loss functions, algorithms, and architectures you design.

At this point, the learning process starts with a new stochastic sample (i.e., randomly chosen data points from your training set), and you continue the learning process until the loss method is at a stopping point.

To properly calculate sensitivity, you must ensure you know how many samples a given person can contribute to the overall training data and make certain your sampling mechanism obeys these constraints. For example, a truly stochastic sampling could easily choose the same training sample multiple times in multiple batches or epochs—essentially breaking your sensitivity guarantees.[2] This is another good reason to never roll your own library and use open source, well-reviewed, and maintained solutions.

The following section provides examples of how to use open source implementations of DP-SGD in a model training. If you are not using an algorithm or architecture that can work with stochastic gradient descent, search for a well-reviewed and, ideally, already open sourced implementation for your algorithm or architecture. There have been many recent contributions such as sarus.tech's DP-XGBoost (*https://oreil.ly/4lf3D*). Extensive research on differential privacy exists for a variety of other machine learning algorithms like SVMs, clustering, and Bayesian models.

DP-SGD has also been used in mitigating data poisoning attacks (*https://oreil.ly/Zgj5x*), as it limits the impact of any one particular participant in the training process.

Let's dive into using an open source library for DP-SGD.

Open Source Libraries for PPML

After reviewing the available libraries, I strongly recommend Opacus, from the PyTorch team, which makes it fairly easy to add differential privacy mechanisms to your training optimizer.

Unlike adding a differential privacy mechanism to a single directed acyclic graph (*https://oreil.ly/O6FdB*)—like a data pipeline—in privacy-preserving machine learning you must consider the repetitive and parallel actions of a machine learning training process. For example, when you optimize a model by iterating over batches, it requires that you split your epsilon over quite a lot of iterations.

---

2 This also applies to multiple iterations of training and parameter optimization as the epsilon must be shared across all training epochs and other parameter tuning rounds.

If you are already using PyTorch, the team has built-in methods for tracking this privacy loss over time directly into the optimizer step. Therefore, as your model is training, you will get a running update of privacy loss in terms of epsilon and delta values.

There is a notebook that walks through training a model with Opacus in the book's repository and also several tutorials in the Opacus documentation (*https://oreil.ly/ XYA-h*). In the notebook, you set up a BERT-based natural language classification model that uses Steam game reviews to predict positive versus negative reviews. Because it is only fine-tuning, using a Transformer model, you only have to update a smaller set of weights and parameters, spending less of your epsilon budget than if you were training a large language model from scratch.

The notebook walks through preparing the data, setting up training and testing datasets, and setting up the model to fine-tune the top layers. Finally, the optimizer is set up to use Opacus, making the training differentially private using DP-SGD and setting up a privacy budget to track privacy loss during training.

To use the optimizer, you need to set a few parameters:

```
privacy_engine = PrivacyEngine()

model, optimizer, train_dataloader = privacy_engine.make_private_with_epsilon(
    module=model,
    optimizer=optimizer,
    data_loader=train_dataloader,
    target_delta=DELTA,
    target_epsilon=EPSILON,
    epochs=EPOCHS,
    max_grad_norm=MAX_GRAD_NORM,
)
```

Here, you can set the target epsilon, delta, and maximum gradient norm (or the gradient clipping setting). You can also fine-tune your batch size and epochs as you normally would based on your data and architecture. Ideally, you use smaller batches, or a smaller learning rate, because the added noise could mean that you need to spend more time to hit an optimal model.

After you set this optimizer and begin training, you will get updates on the current values according to the privacy accountant, which is pretty neat:

```
Epoch: 1 | Step: 1500 | Train loss: 1.928 | ... | Eval accuracy: 0.698 | ε: 3.68
Epoch: 1 | Step: 2000 | Train loss: 1.834 | ... | Eval accuracy: 0.720 | ε: 3.94
Epoch: 1 | Step: 2500 | Train loss: 1.711 | ... | Eval accuracy: 0.785 | ε: 4.14
```

Behind the scenes, Opacus tracks per-sample gradients and feeds these into the backpropagation and layer update steps. User privacy is guaranteed at the sample level, which means you are making assumptions about the individuals in the dataset. Appropriately scaled noise can be reasoned about at the layer level as the Opacus team optimized the process so each pass has only one backpropagation where all sample-level gradient updates are combined and applied with noise at the layer level. This is also why models that use BatchNorm need to be converted into GroupNorm, which allows Opacus to split updates across layers or parts of layers (*https://oreil.ly/ MZZqs*).

Opacus actually uses Rényi differential privacy (*https://oreil.ly/2_eRs*) with Gaussian noise to add the noise when updating the layer weights. This tracks epsilon and delta but uses a relaxation based on "average" privacy loss. Reading through the second blog post from the Opacus team (*https://oreil.ly/lBFHJ*) details interesting optimizations built to appropriately parallelize and vectorize layer updates.[3]

Monitoring Your Training

Using an interface like TensorBoard (*https://oreil.ly/3ZFuq*) during your training will help you determine how your noise addition is affecting the training overall. Since the noise scales with the gradient size, your training may, at times, behave erratically.

For many algorithms and architectures, the overall resiliency of the iterative process means your training will stabilize. Keep an eye, however, on the size of your norms during the training process to help spot potential problems early and address them by adjusting your training data, features, or even thinking through how to remove outliers before training.

You can also optimize your machine learning usage of differential privacy by using base models that have been trained on publicly available data and then fine-tune these models using the private data. Freeze the base layers and add noise to the higher layers, achieving less noise addition overall. This is standard practice, especially for computer vision or language models, and it allows you to use publicly available models as a starting point and improve them for your particular use case using your training data, with privacy-preserving training.

If you aren't using PyTorch, take a look at other libraries, such as TensorFlow Privacy (*https://oreil.ly/9Y1R7*). If you aren't using deep learning, keep reading for tips on other PPML methods.

You might have noticed that the epsilon values when using Opacus are higher than you expected when compared with your learnings from Chapter 2. This is an open critique and danger of using DP-SGD and many differential privacy mechanisms for training, where accepted epsilon values are much higher than you would expect from a query-based mechanism. Research from privacy and security experts in 2023

---

3 Recent research shows new optimizations, including research from Google on improved privacy accounting (*https://oreil.ly/R4Yni*) and DeepMind DP-SGD optimizations at scale (*https://oreil.ly/099eC*).

(*https://oreil.ly/OaqcI*) demonstrated that these levels are dangerous and can lead to privacy assumptions that are simply inaccurate. They recommended standard over-fitting mechanisms instead of DP-noise during training to provide more robust privacy guarantees.

Practically, you need to assess a range of possibilities, including differentially private training, overfitting mechanisms or other methods that surface as a result of research, and differentially private feature engineering, which you'll learn about next. As with other privacy technology that you have learned in this book so far, there is no one magic bullet to address these concerns—and staying up-to-date and thoughtful on emerging privacy risks and mitigations will assist you in choosing the best approach for your use case.

Engineering Differentially Private Features

If you aren't using TensorFlow or PyTorch to do your training or if you are using an unsupported architecture, you need to find other ways to anonymize the data during training. Adding differential privacy during training is optimal; consider writing your own implementation based on the latest research. This will scale only if it's maintained by a larger team that is willing to document it, keep it up-to-date, and invest in having it audited by experts.

Otherwise, think about building differentially private features. If these are aggregate features, you can potentially categorize the population, build a differentially private histogram or distribution for the population, and then use that as an encoder.

You could also investigate other ways to minimize the amount of personal data used in training. Possibly, that personal feature based on individual input is not as meaningful as you imagine, and exploring other data reveals other trends or patterns with more relevant information.

If you need to use personal data or input to have your model succeed and you cannot add noise during training, you should apply differential privacy as you create features by adding noise to the representative data and features of each individual. This means you are looking at local differential privacy if each person can contribute one tensor to the feature—which puts you squarely in the space that it might not work at all because your noise will scale with the size of your dataset. You must also figure out how to track budget across many features that you might use in a model. Basically, it gets complicated!

This section covers local differential privacy for machine learning—which has all the same problems of local differential privacy covered in Chapter 3 in systems like RAPPOR. The amount of error you add will scale with the size of your dataset, which might make the features completely useless for your task. Whenever possible, avoid local differential privacy in favor of a centralized model, which means either training using differential privacy or thinking through other methods, such as federated learning (see Chapter 6).

To do so properly, you'll need to meet the following criteria:

1. Determine what sensitivity you have for each feature and how you want to implement clamping. This might mean you experiment until you find a useful mix. Remember, when you are experimenting, you are not providing differential privacy guarantees, so keep in mind that the results of your experiments and intermediary data artifacts are just as sensitive as the data itself!

2. Figure out how many contributions a user can make to a particular model (i.e., how many features based on a particular user you will use in a given model) and use this to help determine how you want to track epsilon over time. Think about what type of noise you would like to use and how this will insert larger error into the model.

3. Build or use a library to produce a differentially private tensor (or sets thereof). If you build your own, please take time to get it audited if you are going to use this in a production system or regularly for your research and work.

4. Try training a few different types of models with your differentially private features and see how your results work on a nonanonymized test dataset. Do you have enough accuracy to make it worthwhile to invest more time in this approach?

5. Make sure you are not building it alone. Long-term buy-in and support from a larger team are essential to ensure the implementation lives on and produces value for the team during your tenure and beyond.

As you consider building your own features, you might want to investigate queries that are more difficult to answer. For example, you might want to evaluate if a particular feature is worthwhile to include given its sensitivity. This likely means performing covariate and correlation analysis on these features and your targets. Again, if you find a high correlation between a sensitive attribute (like postal code) and your target (like credit availability), then stop to think about if this has unjust and unfair implications in the world. I repeat: some features should never be used, and some models should never be built.

You must also bear in mind the appropriate expiration or deletion of features. For example, can a user interaction from three years ago really predict current behavior or provide guidance on the current behavior of people like that user? Several large corporations were able to meet stringent GDPR requirements for data retention because they determined that older data was too stale to predict current trends, interactions, and desires. For example, Google moved to 18-month data retention (*https://oreil.ly/xZHkp*) for advertising purposes.

You could regularly test and review models and remove older contributions to determine if they add value. Allow these models to shadow working models in production systems and switch to them based on a performance threshold determined by your team. Doing so regularly will not only support compliance efforts for data retention, especially if you can simply delete older data that is no longer useful or needed, but also increase awareness within the team that more data does not always mean better performance.

Develop the strategy; then write tests and build automation where possible. Although a smaller group might maintain this software, there needs to be a larger group that can use this software without having to fully understand how it works. Provide useful documentation, easy-to-use libraries and APIs, well-tested and automated code, and a process for filing tickets and asking for support as needed.

There will be times when creating a differential privacy mechanism is just too much. In such situations, you will need to apply simpler methods and figure out how to build a privacy-aware workflow.

Applying Simpler Methods

If incorporating differential privacy doesn't work for the particular model or feature, then you will need to look at other methods, such as redaction, pseudonymization, format-preserving encryption, or potentially engineering new features that are more privacy-aware.

Let's explore these solutions. Suppose you are building a personalization engine, where you want to recommend products based on personal details or combinations of user activity. Your first question is, what are the business goals, and is there a privacy-aware way to reach these goals? If there is no privacy-aware way to reach the goals, you should question the goals themselves.

Assuming you can align both business goals and privacy needs, use your privacy knowledge to minimize personal or sensitive data while still meeting business objectives. Perhaps you remove clearly personal and sensitive attributes from the data. This at least removes them from the model directly learning them as part of feature input. However, this mitigation alone will not prevent all possible avenues. As you know from the attacks described in Chapter 4, the ability to statistically learn these details still remains as these attributes often correlate with website activity, shopping behavior, and other data used in training.

Once you have maximized data redaction, you can move onto other techniques such as pseudonymization or format-preserving encryption. Masking, generalization, and bounding pseudonymize particular aspects of personhood. For a birthday, you could generalize to the birth year or even decade of birth if this was necessary information.

In addition, there may be new ways to find the information you think you are learning via other variables. For example, US postal codes are often a correlated variable for class, race, socioeconomic status, and ethnicity. If postal codes hold a lot of information about what you are trying to learn, it's possible that you are building a model that is making a decision based on income, socioeconomic status, race, and/or ethnicity. First, stop and ask if this model is going to harm people. Determine how to raise your concerns within your team and organization.

Next, consider encoding this information explicitly. If your recommender does well deciding via postal codes and you find that these decisions are made on socioeconomic lines, you can better protect people's privacy and be more explicit about what your model is doing by creating a categorical variable that uses geographical income data to map postal codes to income groups.

You can then create a new variable "Neighborhood income bracket" and map postal codes to these ranges or generalize them even further into categories, such as lower income, middle income, and higher income. Now you are being very clear about what the model is doing, which can help later in evaluating whether it meets internal standards for equitable machine learning.

Finally, you may be able to provide more privacy and reduce the risk of exposing outliers by "zooming out" from a particular granularity level. For example, if you use shopping or viewing history to improve your recommendations, you could generalize particular clicks or purchases into broader product categories and avoid using the specific item purchased or link viewed. Depending on the size of your categories, this can act as an aggregation mechanism and add better privacy protections to your data workflow.

It is absolutely essential that you document your decisions continually. This helps not only others who will touch these workflows but the entire data governance process at the organization. Let's dive into documenting machine learning, specifically for data privacy.

Documenting Your Machine Learning

As you learned in Chapter 1, data governance requires that you document your efforts and that this documentation is readable and editable by others. If you build data automation, you should also automate documentation for those systems when possible.

For machine learning, this could mean developing self-documenting machine learning pipelines, which document models produced by them as part of the pipeline. Research and attention in recent years has focused on developing model documentation that can be understood by a multitude of users. For example, model cards were proposed by a group of researchers who formerly worked at Google (*https://oreil.ly/lYUXA*) showing how models can be documented with regard to fairness and justice concerns and criteria.[4] This evaluation and card generation was supported via software in a semi-automated fashion—making it easier to integrate into normal workflows and improving documentation. Releasing model cards with open source models is now more common, even if the card itself sometimes lacks thorough documentation (see the model card for GPT-3 from OpenAI (*https://oreil.ly/PfxVM*)).

What could a model card look like if it was reimagined for privacy (see Figure 5-3 for my proposal)? Let's take a look at a few aspects you could document and share:

Data lineage
> Where did this data come from and under what conditions was it collected or transformed? What were the consent information and privacy policies for this data? Showing the original source and data processing using a lineage tracking tool or other visualization will help people understand the data sources and related sensitivity.

Data retention and protection policies
> What are the internal or external policies that apply to this data? How long can it be used without anonymization mechanisms applied? Should this model be deleted at a particular point in time? Provide a policy perspective and your professional opinion, based on the sensitivity of the data in the model.

Privacy risks
> What risks were in the data before preparation and training? How did you evaluate them? What risk does continued use of the model pose? Were outliers analyzed for impact on marginalized populations in the model? If your organization has a risk evaluation framework, you could integrate it for this analysis.

---

4 Most of the original researchers for this paper, including Timnit Gebru and Margaret Mitchell, were subsequently fired by Google (*https://oreil.ly/T63w4*) for related research about Google's own unjust and environmentally unsound machine learning practices when training and distributing large language models (*https://oreil.ly/0nQsM*).

Privacy techniques applied

Enumerate the techniques applied to the data preparation and training. If you experimented with several options before choosing a particular technique or technology, a short summary of prior methods provides background and insight to others.

Approved usage

You want to explicitly outline recommended conditions for model use. For example, you could recommend deploying the model only to internal systems, not to devices. You might even suggest appropriate use cases or propose restrictions on sharing the model internally, as you would any other sensitive data source.

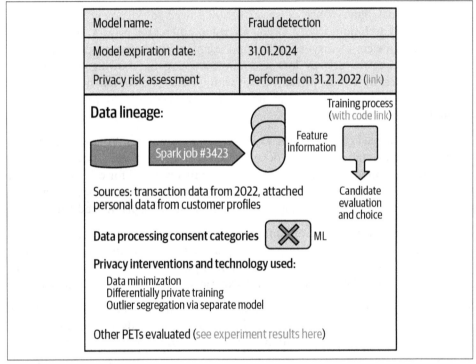

Figure 5-3. Privacy card for machine learning models

Showing privacy to users and practitioners visually has a long history. In fact, the CMU CyLab Usable Privacy and Security Laboratory released a design with privacy label (*https://oreil.ly/Dg1d_*) with pretty neat visuals (*https://oreil.ly/CTdcQ*) in 2010 to show users how their data was going to be used. And there are several visual elements of the GDPR and other compliance documentation, such as the Data Protection Impact Assessment (DPIA) (see Chapter 8).

Ideally you would be showing visuals and clear explanations of your data use internally and externally at your organization. My proposal for model privacy cards aims to communicate privacy concerns in models to software engineers and machine learning scientists. A document like a DPIA communicates privacy risks and mitigations to internal legal and technical stakeholders as well as external regulators and auditors. A privacy label clearly and visually explains to users how their data will be used. If you can create and extend governance systems to display this information with different views for different users, you would presumably have only one central knowledge system to manage. From this centralized data governance and documentation platform, you could serve multiple users with varying needs. This collective understanding and knowledge would also greatly support privacy champions and likely inspire new privacy initiatives across the organization.

From a basic data governance perspective, you'll need to document model lineage and how PPML techniques work. If you are using differential privacy, document the choice of parameters in easy-to-understand language. Perhaps you develop a brief interactive to explain privacy loss and information gain, showing how different parameters affect individual privacy. Or sit with the risk and compliance department to co-develop language that communicates the organizational approach to privacy risk and risk mitigation.

Models will also need creation dates, expiration or retraining, and/or evaluation dates and usage documentation. Provide details on the overall population used to train and when you'd recommend retraining or evaluation; this is useful for others who might use this model for a related use case. Include performance and accuracy metrics and documentation on how those changed after privacy mechanisms were added.

If there is no established guild or community for machine learning at your organization, consider launching that group. Develop some basic standards on documenting machine learning—beginning the conversation inspires knowledge sharing and facilitates communication between curious and experienced engineers and scientists.

This shift can initiate a community of practice around privacy and privacy-enhancing technologies in machine learning. As the community builds understanding and expertise, it creates new opportunities to investigate nonobvious approaches to protecting privacy or approaches based on different understandings or meanings of privacy.

Other Ways of Protecting Privacy in Machine Learning

As explained in Chapter 4, privacy is not only about individual privacy and differential privacy; you may have other privacy concerns regarding your machine learning engineering and setup. These could include leaking information from your training data, accidentally uncovering more than you expected about individuals, or dealing with data security and secrecy concerns around the training data itself.

Let's say you are concerned particularly with membership inference attacks or leaking information about your training population. Some mitigations to these attacks have been proposed to help defend against them. The researchers who uncovered this attack followed up with a paper to show how one can use adversarial regularization (*https://oreil.ly/74LEw*) to defend against membership inference attacks. This approach confuses the discriminator and increases its uncertainty regarding inclusion of a given person in the training data.

In general, if you are worried about leaking details about your populations, you should consider normalization and regularization as options to eliminate some encoded information. You could additionally protect the model by implementing API rate limiting and account-based API access. As another option, use a wider and more diverse data sample so your risk is mitigated as individuals in the training set are less prone to information leakage.

You might be concerned about model fairness and the effect of using individuals' data for model training. What if, based on the data, the model learns to discern between different types or groups of people and negatively affects one group more than another? This is a real and growing concern in the machine learning community and world, and as you have seen in Chapter 4, private information leakage occurs even when you don't directly include private attributes into the training data.

If this is a problem, methods like differential privacy can inspire new ways of imagining machine learning. Cynthia Dwork et al. released a paper on this relationship in 2011 called "Fairness through Awareness" (*https://oreil.ly/6SMbw*). In the paper, they posited that—if there are two individuals similar in many aspects but different in one private attribute like gender or race—it is possible to create a transformation that allows these persons to be represented close to each other when they are encoded.

This is illustrated in Figure 5-4, where the vectors in the input space are mapped to a new vector space. You can see that the distance between the vectors in initial input and decision space (X) can be compared to that in the transformed representation space (Z). In this case, the persons in the dataset change their relationship to one another, moving closer as their private attributes have been removed. The decision boundaries of the function you are trying to learn (f) have also shifted; this shows that the encoded representations now enforce statistical parity. Ensuring that the private attribute was actually private in the transformed representation means that people who are similar in other aspects are also represented quite similarly.

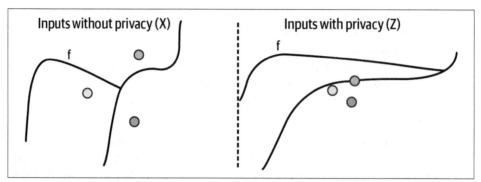

Figure 5-4. Fairness through awareness

Their initial paper presented this in theory. Later, a group of researchers implemented it and demonstrated its viability in machine learning systems. Using several datasets linked to discriminatory treatment of individuals, including the UCI Adult dataset, which classifies income based on other personal attributes, they showed that creation of these fair representations enhanced the privacy of the individual and fair treatment of the group.

Figure 5-5 displays their results, compared with several other methods for enhancing fairness in a dataset. Their resulting model is both more performant and fairer. On the left are the results from minimizing discrimination; you can see the dark blue here is the learned fair representations (their model). In comparison with the baseline—a logistic regression trained to the far left—you see far less discrimination and about the same accuracy. The chart on the right shows optimizing for the maximum delta between accuracy and discrimination, and you see similar performance. The other bars represent a fair naive Bayes model and a regularized logistic regression approach for fairness.

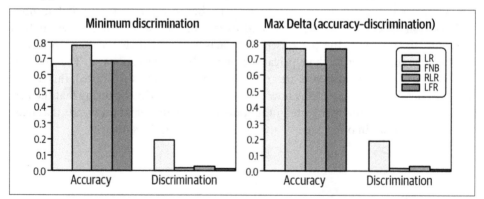

Figure 5-5. Fairness through awareness performance

Here is the process the researchers used to create privacy-aware and fairer representations, in case you want to implement this approach. Here, X is the initial dataset, Z is the transformed representations, y is your target, and f is what you are attempting to learn:

1. The mapping from X to Z satisfies statistical parity between groups.

2. The mapping to Z-space retains information in X (except for membership in the protected set).

3. The induced mapping from X to y (by first mapping each x probabilistically to Z-space, and then using Z to learn y) is close to f.

This shows that there can be some interesting intersections between fairness and ethics in machine learning and data privacy. Indeed, if you use sensitive and private data, you are often giving information about personhood to a probabilistic algorithm and asking it to reproduce potential societal harms seen in the dataset. If you can remove some of these private attributes in a holistic manner—rather than just removing a few fields and hoping it works—you are one step closer to building fairer models.

 Some problems don't lend themselves to fairness transformations because they are inherently unfair. You must think not only about your data and the data's view of the world but also what your model is attempting to do. Don't work in a vacuum, where you search for technical solutions to societal problems. Only a multidisciplinary team with an opinion on societal change can adequately approach these problems in a comprehensive manner. Initiating the conversation and pointing out injustice you see in your work is a wonderful starting point. I highly encourage you to do so, as algorithmic solutions will never be the sole or primary way to address these issues.

Finally, there are times when you are primarily concerned with the confidentiality or secrecy of a particular input or several inputs. For example, you might want to make a service that takes photos and evaluates them for a particular health condition. In doing so, you need to provide the users with a strong guarantee their data is properly protected and no one else can see their photos.

This is the problem that was posited in Cryptonets by the Microsoft researchers (*https://oreil.ly/pM9Dl*). Could they provide a service to make predictions on encrypted data? The machine learning model took encrypted tensors as input and output an encrypted prediction that the user could then decrypt. This is enabled by a technology you will learn about in Chapter 7 called *encrypted computation*.

What privacy does this offer? Presuming there are no additional listeners on the infrastructure or cached tensors and predictions, this approach can support high confidentiality guarantees. It does not provide privacy for the training data itself, although there are ways to combine approaches—using differentially private mechanisms and encrypted computation together. As you learn more in this book, you will see a wider array of options, approaches, and tools for your toolkit!

Solving the privacy part of the machine learning problem means looking more holistically at what problem you are specifically wanting to solve. This usually means figuring out how the use case will be architected, deployed, and maintained.

Architecting Privacy in Data and Machine Learning Projects

Training is clearly not the only part of the machine learning process. As larger data science, analytics, and machine learning systems are built, they require a broad expanse of software and data as well as architecture, DevOps, platform, and infrastructure support to deliver and integrate software and machine learning workflows.

Understanding Your Data Privacy Needs

As Chapters 1 and 3 note, it is important to have comprehensive data governance initiatives and implement them into your platforms and workflows. Because you have proper lineage, consent, and provenance details, you can use this information to investigate what data is available and useful for your use case.

You can even use data catalogs or other documentation to make this information easily accessible. For example, you might want to build a new machine learning service that helps suggest payment options based on your understanding of the customer. Suppose customers with fairly regular purchasing get a different set of options than those who are new. From a privacy aspect, this would have quite sensitive data. If you had a catalog to query which data sources have customer purchase and payment information, you could examine those datasets to determine which are useful for your model. Governance details, such as the collection process, consent details, and anonymization and/or deletion requirements, would help you find data that fits your use case and deployment requirements. This information can also tell you the sensitivity of the resulting model and help you plan should the model need retraining often to meet expiration requirements.

At the beginning of a project, it's often useful to evaluate approved libraries and tools for building privacy into workflows. If you are a data or technical team leader, create an evaluation and approval mechanism for technical governance as well as a place to learn about approved libraries. This sends the message that privacy is a normal part of developing software and tooling. A list of tools and examples of their use can really accelerate adoption!

As with most fun problems in computing and data, there is no silver bullet when it comes to privacy. You will continually need to consider the privacy versus information continuum and make decisions for your use case. As you learned in Chapter 2, applying anonymization works best when you can directly calculate data sensitivity and decide on clamping bounds. If differential privacy doesn't work for your problem space (*https://oreil.ly/15HLr*), you need to make some hard choices and document them so others can make sense of your model or analysis. Develop sensible defaults and decisions for your organization in support of data governance. These can help people understand the overarching guidance and empower them to make decisions in your absence.

To automate privacy in your workflows, build consent and governance into your data management platforms, ensuring the necessary consent, lineage, and collection details remain close to the data. If your organization has a data management team or data platform team, they can build this in; the data science team can automate querying and retraining models without concerns that data is miscategorized or misused.

Above all, I recommend bringing in privacy libraries and frequent experimentation. Building privacy directly into multiple use cases provides the blueprints needed so others can get started too. Rather than waiting for the perfect moment to introduce privacy, I recommend testing it directly and building in automations when possible. If you have machine learning engineering or MLOps infrastructure already in use, build privacy practices into these that are available to all. Implement early and iterate; this supports the team by ensuring some privacy tooling is immediately available.

Privacy tooling and technology can be a normal part of workflows if effort is made to build the tools in, test them, experiment, and learn. It is also helpful to have a culture that is thoughtful about privacy and a process to encourage newcomers to get started. Some privacy is better than no privacy, so start small if there are no current practices. Evaluating privacy technologies and creating ways to tie them to business goals helps leadership understand the importance of privacy and contributes to team alignment.

Monitoring Privacy

As you build privacy into your data science and machine learning infrastructure, it is possible to add privacy monitoring to your normal infrastructure systems. This might also mean building privacy into your current monitoring systems—particularly if there have problems in the past with logging sensitive information or ensuring that the infrastructure is respecting the data privacy and security policies.

One good starting point is to monitor outliers and to determine how they will be handled. Doing so can also improve your data quality and data understanding, so you might already have tooling that works for this task. As you have learned in Chapters 2 and 4, outliers present special risks around privacy because they leak extra information. Some outliers are easy to identify as the data comes in because their inherent values are outliers. These are the obvious outliers to address—sort them for later analysis if there is suspected error or directly apply regularization or normalization to keep them within clamping bounds or an acceptable range. If you sort them into a separate data storage or tag them so you can follow up, make certain that they are protected the way you would other sensitive data. You must treat them with a higher level of privacy or determine how to integrate them into normal analytics and operations.

But other outliers are more difficult to identify, like a user who contributes to a new application as an early adopter or a superuser who is overrepresented in the population. The privacy risk from these users can be more difficult to identify or automate and requires regular analysis of sampling and population choices.

You may wonder about how to monitor and sample appropriately if the data you are using is extremely sensitive. First, you'll need to ensure your monitoring and logging is not leaking information. If so, use differential privacy on a particular statistic or redact and/or encrypt sensitive information in logging systems. There are also some interesting ways to provide differentially private sampling (*https://oreil.ly/0f6iZ*) (or to begin thinking about synthetic data approaches, which you will learn in Chapter 10).

When monitoring privacy, you want to confirm the privacy automation you are enabling is working appropriately. Test the automation regularly and continuously and log any anomalous or error-prone behavior in these workflows. If you are using a library, it should provide ways to hook in logging and monitoring software to track errors. You may also need to alert the infrastructure, DevOps, platform, and software teams about this software and its usage.

If you find that your privacy engineering, especially differential privacy mechanisms, is contributing to low data quality due to significant shifts in the data itself, you'll need to begin again at the EDA part of the process and determine what is acceptable. This might mean finding new bounds for individual contributions or changing some of the privacy-preserving transformations you've automated thus far. Ensure you are talking with downstream data owners to address potential data quality problems early and often.

For predictable errors, incorporate error handling to avoid monitoring overload. Again, start small—using the errors you collect from the first hour, day, and week of use. As you roll out new privacy technology, try to plan an extra two or three weeks (or a full sprint if you are using sprint-based or agile project planning) just to monitor the system, build in more integration testing, and handle unanticipated errors as they emerge.

As you learned in Chapter 4, machine learning explanations and predictions can leak sensitive information, particularly about outliers, and should be handled as sensitive data themselves. Some machine learning systems, as part of their processing, produce explanations or log predictions, which need to be treated as sensitive data. The same is true for logging user behavior or even user-generated errors in software systems. Embed processes for managing sensitive data in logging or monitoring systems themselves; managing potentially sensitive logs in the same way you would manage sensitive data is absolutely required.

As the expanse of your privacy infrastructure grows, it is essential that your monitoring and logging are set up appropriately and scale with your needs. Develop monitoring as you go and plan time to review it and how to address it when alert fatigue hits. Keeping your monitoring healthy and functioning is as important as the rest of your software and applications and can help you quickly spot errors and manage privacy risks.

Summary

In this chapter, you've learned how to apply core privacy principles and techniques you learned to the data science and machine learning workflow. By evaluating these technologies in the context of exploratory analysis, feature engineering, and machine learning, you can identify areas you need to address to apply theory to practical situations. You've evaluated the pros and cons of applying privacy protections at the various stages and experimented with an open source library for PPML. It should be clear now why starting with governance basics, like documentation, lineage, and data understanding, can have a massive impact on your ability to leverage more advanced technologies and utilize them in your data work.

You now understand how to add differential privacy in machine learning use cases. In the next chapter, you'll build on that by exploring how federated learning and distributed computation scenarios can enhance privacy guarantees and provide interesting opportunities for data sharing.

## CHAPTER 6

Federated Learning and Data Science

At this point, you've built an understanding of and appreciation for the scope of the data privacy problem and, if you are anything like me, you wonder why organizations collect so much data in the first place. Isn't there a better way?

Actually, there is! Federated learning and distributed data science provide new ways to think about how you do data analysis by keeping data at the edge: on phones, laptops, edge services—or even on-premise architecture or separate cloud architecture when working with partners.[1] The data is not collected or copied to your own cloud or storage before you do analysis or machine learning.

In this chapter, you'll learn how this works in practice and determine when this approach is appropriate for a given use case. You'll also evaluate how to offer privacy during federated machine learning, along with what types of data or engineering problems federated approaches can solve and which are a poor fit.

Distributed Data

In data science, you are almost always using distributed data. Every time you start up a Kubernetes or Hadoop cluster or use a multicloud setup for data analysis, your data is de facto distributed. Because this is becoming "the norm," it means that distributed data analysis is increasingly built into the tools and systems you use as a data professional.

---

1 In this chapter, I'll use the term *edge* to refer to the "edge" of your graphs or networks, where the nodes are as far as you can access or "see." This is part of edge computing (*https://oreil.ly/vcNsn*), where processing is pushed to devices that are not specifically in large-scale centralized data storage and compute.

But what I am referring to in this chapter is taking distributed data and moving it farther away from your core processing. What if, instead of distributing data in your own data centers or clouds or clusters, you actually kept data where it originated and ran your analysis across hundreds, thousands, or even millions of smaller, distributed datasets? What if you never pulled data from an application, phone, browser, or database or API that wasn't yours and, instead, used the data at the edge, pulling only answers to your analysis questions?

This chapter discusses that type of distributed data. As you can imagine, this fundamentally changes the way you approach privacy, data collection, and your job as a data scientist. Let's explore why, when, and how this might work.

Why Use Distributed Data?

When you use distributed data as described in this chapter, you reduce your risk significantly. No data, no risk (or minimally, less data, less risk).

This is the fundamental theorem behind "Datensparsamkeit" (*https://oreil.ly/Dnkyg*), or data minimization, which is a core tenant of many privacy legislations, several privacy principles, and quite a few Privacy by Design frameworks. *Datensparsamkeit* is a German term that translates loosely to data-thriftiness. In English, you would interpret it as data minimization. Datensparsamkeit pushes you to decide what data you absolutely need and collect only that data. In reducing your data collection, you are not only preserving crucial privacy but also ensuring your data storage does not become a target.

When working with data in highly sensitive environments, you might not even be allowed to move data outside of the network or storage infrastructure. This is often true with highly sensitive data in on-premise systems. In those cases, you need to figure out how to either safely extract the data you need or work on those systems and export only the results of your analysis or processing. Here, federated analysis can help you by pushing the processing to these secure centers, rather than extracting data from more secure to less secure environments.

This is often the case when working with massive datasets across multiple data centers or data storage systems. For processing across large distributed systems or clouds it is often expensive and time- and compute-intensive to transfer all data to a centralized or set of centralized services. It makes much more sense and is far less expensive in computation and cloud costs to ship the analysis to the data instead of the other way around.

There are legal reasons to think about working with data on devices and on the edge or where it already exists. One compelling reason is the challenge of transatlantic data flows. Max Schrems (*https://oreil.ly/q3EYO*) is a privacy activist and lawyer, leading several significant lawsuits to defend European residents data rights that are violated by nonconsensual data flows to the US.[2] He has already won several decisions, and it is likely that these lawsuits and further enforcement will continue. Should he succeed, it could mean a fundamental restructuring so that European data no longer enters the US.

Additionally, pressure from politicians around data sovereignty is increasing in many locations around the world. Although one can argue about the validity of the concerns, many politicians are focused on how data from their country and citizens is moved and the implications of that movement. If there is more pressure to ensure a nation's data remains in that nation, it certainly will change how multinational companies use data.

Finally, some recent concerns have arisen from the changing Supreme Court interpretations of law and rights in the US. If your company collects data that could be used to prosecute a person, you could offer more protection for those people by not collecting that data. If you don't hold the data, you cannot be required to reveal it.[3]

 There is also a local-first push from software and research that includes investigating ways to make software friendlier to people who would rather use things offline and with local-only resources. I recommend taking a look at Martin Kleppmann et al.'s work on principles for local-first architecture and software design (*https:// oreil.ly/JHKj0*).

When you look at the possible benefits (privacy, legal, security, and computation and storage costs), it just makes sense to collect less data. How might analysis work if the data isn't actually on your servers or in your cloud?

How Does Distributed Data Analysis Work?

If you are using Hadoop, Spark, EMR, or Kubeflow services, you are already using one type of distributed data analysis—where the orchestrator is managing distributed compute nodes and abstracting this away from your interface. For example, when you run a Spark query, that query actually gets mapped to a plan that runs on separate machines or, at least, separate virtualizations with different physical storage locations. The interface may feel like you are interacting with a single source of data— e.g., your resilient distributed datasets (RDDs), datasets, or dataframes—but this

---

2 You can read more about his work via his organization NOYB (*https://noyb.eu/en*), which fights for privacy rights for all EU residents and for privacy activism and awareness globally. You'll also learn more about this and related issues in Chapter 8.

3 For example, Signal's stance on holding as little data as possible about its users and its activities can be well seen in their page on Big Brother requests (*https://oreil.ly/5w08g*).

abstraction is a logical construction that spans distributed storages, as demonstrated in Figure 6-1.

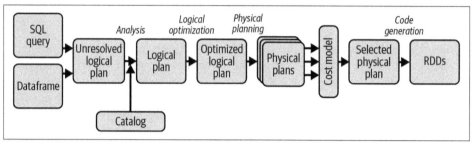

Figure 6-1. Apache Spark under the hood

Figure 6-1 shows how the DataFrame or SQL query translates to the actual computers and data storage. You can see that, first, your program is compiled into a logical plan that uses a catalog to map how the query could function. Then, that plan is optimized and translated into a physical plan—this is where the query first gets mapped to actual distributed storage. Based on a cost model, the best physical plan is selected, compiled into code, and run. For further detail on this process, take a look at the Databricks blog post that outlines the process and diagram further (*https://oreil.ly/ FWEif*).

This is also the process for many abstractions where you are running many nodes or microservices in the cloud or on-premise and using software to connect, orchestrate, and run analysis. Most of the time, these services run the data across local networks between those nodes. Often the data or results are traveling over the network or kept in local compute memory until the process is complete.

To create privacy-first distributed data, extend this network to the edge and restructure the software and queries so that, instead of moving the data from the edge to a centralized compute node or centralized storage, you move the compute to the data!

Let's walk through a potential workflow in Figure 6-2. You have three edge nodes representing different types of storage you might see in a distributed data analysis workflow, such as smartphones, Internet of Things (IoT) devices, and robotic hardware. Note that these are not controlled by you or your network, but you do have access to them over a public-facing internet connection or a securely connected network tunnel and an interface via software or hardware on the devices. You'll see a few examples of software you can use to get started later in this chapter.

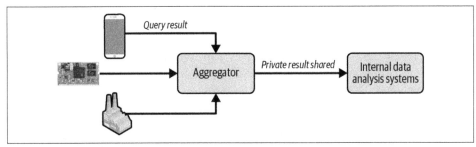

Figure 6-2. Distributed data analysis

When you run analysis or queries, you want to ship that query to the edge devices. This requires two things: first, each of these devices needs to run the query locally, and second, they must be online for your analysis to succeed. The query result is collected and sent back to the federated aggregation points. At that point, the aggregator can calculate the final result based on all of the intermediary values from the devices and send that result to the query generator. The result is the same as it would have been if you had collected and centralized all the data, but without the risk of storing the data on your own services. This method is much more privacy-aware.

When moving from a centralized notion of data analysis to a distributed or federated one, there are a few things to keep in mind. First, the devices might have different analysis capabilities, making some computations easier to manage than others. You may need to organize or sequence queries creatively to get the intended results. These devices or edge nodes also need to have the same software, likely the same software versions, that you ship so that they can run the local queries consistently. There is also a chance that a device is tampered with by an outside party—potentially damaging the data on the phone itself or tampering with the software. This threat is difficult to detect even when data is centralized and is something you should discuss with your security team to adequately address.

Second, the data at each of these nodes might be quite different from or inconsistent with each other. This happens in your centralized analysis as well, when you see your population or distribution shift, known as *model* or *data drift*. In a distributed or federated analysis context, this can be harder to identify because you are not looking at individual data points. If you are familiar with the concept of independent and identically distributed (IID) random variables (*https://oreil.ly/hs8_M*), you can see how this might make some parts of analysis tricky.[4] In real-world datasets, data is often

---

4 A collection of random variables is considered IID when the variables are identically distributed, meaning they are sampled from the same probability distribution and this distribution does not fluctuate, and they are independent, meaning they do not influence one another.

not IID. In a distributed data analysis setting this is also true, yet you must run this analysis to produce a result that can be used for decisions or conclusions.

An example will help make this clearer. Say you want to run an object recognition algorithm on local devices and collect details on what types of photos people take on their smartphones. The steps you need to go through are:

1. Ship an image recognition model to each smartphone. This means that the user's smartphone has to be able to run this model—which might exclude some older smartphones or you might choose to send it only to users with a particular version of Android or iOS software.

2. Run the image recognition model on the smartphone's photos. This means you need to ask permission to see the photos on the phone, including an explanation of what you plan to do. You should also consider when to run this—maybe overnight when the smartphone is plugged in so that it doesn't disturb the user's normal use of their smartphone.

3. When results are ready—or when you have decided how to sample and send partial results—they will need to be collected at the aggregation endpoint. For this, the phones need to have a stable internet or mobile connection.

4. When the aggregator accepts the updates from all of the models, you can then run data analysis on the results and answer the question you had in mind.

However, if one user has only cat photos and another user has only bunny photos, this will skew the results, causing you to assume all users have a mixture of cat and bunny photos. It could also be a problem if most users have a small number of photos and a few superusers have millions of photos. These superusers will be massively over-represented, also putting their privacy at risk. The data is non-IID, so you must account for that in your analysis. Be careful what assumptions you make. If necessary, find privacy-preserving ways to preserve some mapping of users to their results or aggressively downsample outliers.

It's now clear to you that even distributed data analysis can leak privacy and expose outliers. As you learned in Chapter 2, outliers and superusers will have much more privacy loss than others—even when you do not collect the data centrally. If you look at your analysis running in step 4, what are possible attacks to re-identify individuals, based on your knowledge from Chapter 4?

First, an attacker could gain access to the aggregator and observe the results as they come in. This would very easily let them log IP addresses or other information as updates are sent to the aggregator. This would mean they can also see each individual analysis result from each smartphone, degrading any privacy guarantees.

Second, the attacker could run the analysis before one user joins and then after to compare the analysis results. This differencing or singling-out attack makes it easy for anyone with access to the analysis queries and results to get information about a particular user's data.

Finally, as you know from the core theorem of differential privacy, even without access to the aggregator, aggregate updates and results do not actually guarantee privacy if no differential privacy mechanism is used.

For this reason, privacy-preserving distributed queries and data analysis often combines several approaches to give strong privacy guarantees users expect.

Privacy-Charging Distributed Data with Differential Privacy

You already know many privacy-preserving and privacy-enhancing techniques and technologies. To create a secure and privacy-first aggregator, you must ensure it is well-secured software and hardware, with few people having access. Use encrypted network communications and assess if encrypted computation can help (more in Chapter 7). Then, when you run the aggregations, use a differential privacy mechanism. This means bounding the number of contributions per user, which will actually have a nice effect on the IID problem—though it means you won't learn much about the outliers.

How might this look in your architecture? Figure 6-3 shows an overview of how the system might be organized at a high level, where devices connect and send updates or query responses over a secure connection to the aggregation points. Note that you could have multiple aggregation points to serve different zones or geographies (see Figure 6-5), but to have centralized results, those must be aggregated or harmonized somewhere.

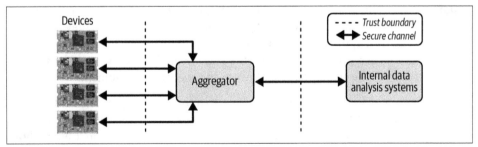

Figure 6-3. Securing federated learning architecture

As shown in Figure 6-3, the aggregation point needs to be properly secured with very little access. This is similar to Apple's local differential privacy and Prochlo (see Chapter 3), where access to these systems violates the privacy and security guarantees by directly leaking contributor information.

After the query is securely and privately aggregated (see Figure 6-4), it can then be revealed to the analyst team. Typically, the updates are sent from the aggregator to the normal analysis system or software. These two systems must have a trust boundary to ensure the privacy guarantees, as the aggregator will have additional information on the individual contributions.

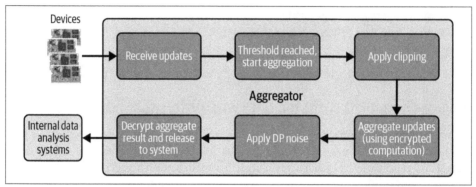

Figure 6-4. Federated learning secure and private aggregation

Zooming in on the actual aggregator itself, let's examine what is happening inside the aggregator. Figure 6-3 shows that the updates come in from the endpoints where the data is stored and are collected at the aggregator. Depending on the level of trust in the system, these updates can also come in encrypted form and be computed together (averaged, summed, etc.) using encrypted computation (see Chapter 7). A threshold must be chosen as there will be some participant dropout—if the device loses connection or has another error. Once that threshold is reached, the aggregation computation begins. The initial computational step, to meet differential privacy guarantees, is to perform clipping or bounding, either on the device before collection or on the responses. You can then aggregate them using encrypted computation if they are encrypted or apply normal plain-text aggregation mechanisms. Once they are aggregated, you can then apply centralized differential privacy noise as you know the sensitivity. If using encryption, this is when the result would be decrypted. The result is then released from the aggregator and flows to the analysis environment.

These systems add some complexity but have extremely strong privacy and security guarantees when compared with centralized data collection systems. Many of these approaches originate from the field of federated learning, which you'll learn about next.

Federated Learning

Federated learning is the process of using a distributed data architecture—like the one described earlier in this chapter—for a machine learning process. Instead of sending queries to the endpoints, you send models and training updates. Each edge node or device helps train a shared model using their local data without sending that data to a central location.

Federated Learning: A Brief History

Federated learning was first implemented at scale by Google to learn from data on mobile phones without centralized data aggregation. Google outlined its approach in a 2016 paper (*https://oreil.ly/wYv3S*) called "Federated Optimization." Once it hit the Google AI blog (*https://oreil.ly/t8HAs*), it was called *federated learning*, and this is the term used in industry today.[5]

Google had just released TensorFlow 1.0 (*https://oreil.ly/SerDa*) around this time, and its distributed workflow contributions were open sourced as TensorFlow federated (tf-federated). Google wanted to improve GBoard keyboard suggestions using federated learning. Keyboard usage leaks quite a bit of private information, and the goal was to see if they could train a performant model without centralizing user keyboard input data.

Shipping a small pretrained machine learning model (in this case, a model trained to perform text recommendation and completion) to every device meant training could run directly on the device. The keyboard data would not be sent to a centralized Google storage—keeping the data more private and protected. For each training round, only the gradient updates were sent to the aggregators, which then performed the averaging of those gradients and sent out that training round's final aggregate update to all devices, beginning the next round of training.

Figure 6-5 visualizes this process. In the initial step, the circle—which represents the model—is shipped to all devices. At that time, each device has the model and performs local training and generates a few local updates to improve the model (shown in Figure 6-5 as step A). Those updates are then sent to an aggregator shown in Figure 6-5 as step B. The diagram shows that some of the updates are for the same layers and weights; other updates might be singletons. The updates for use are selected and then averaged and simplified to a single update or series thereof—shown in Figure 6-5 as step C. This update is then sent to all devices to update the device's local model, and the process can continue for as many rounds as necessary. This entire process and several use cases and related concepts are depicted in Google's Federated Learning comic (*https://federated.withgoogle.com*).

---

5 To review clever uses of federated collaboration that came before federated learning, see Shokri et al.'s 2012 paper on hiding location privacy via device collaboration (*https://oreil.ly/6RKdh*). There were also new possibilities on SQL-based distributed data and federated analysis, like Microsoft's research on federated search (*https://oreil.ly/EpUhi*). Additionally, Snips home assistant (*https://oreil.ly/38Qg_*) deployed differentially private data collection and analysis and experimented with federated learning use cases in 2016, as described in its research (*https://oreil.ly/nW-AN*).

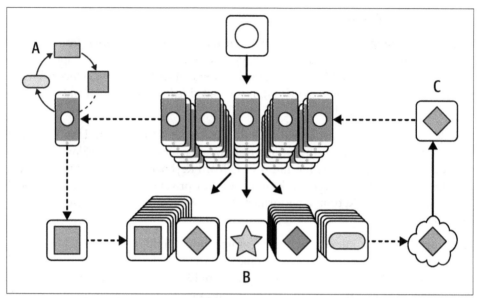

Figure 6-5. Federated learning workflow

In Chapter 5, you learned how gradients can be unbounded and leak privacy. This is still the case with federated learning! In the initial implementation, Google did not account for this; however, now it is common for federated learning and analysis services to also implement differential privacy as part of this aggregation. Instead of averaging the gradient updates and sending that average out to all phones, the aggregator clips them, averages them, and then adds a differential privacy mechanism scaled with the appropriate epsilon.

 Many of the production implementations of federated learning use deep learning architectures; however, there is also research and implementation for other models, including gradient boosted trees (*https://oreil.ly/xZKHi*). IBM's federated learning library (*https://oreil.ly/6Nti7*) includes several interesting implementations, including boosted trees and naive Bayes.

Another important consideration is the selection of devices, especially to manage non-IID data in a federated learning scenario. When Google first used federated learning, it did not send out the model to every single Android phone. Instead, it used a selection criteria that prioritized phones that were not actively being used, had a power and internet connection, had the latest Android software, had a particular hardware level (i.e., not too little memory), and had specific default keyboard languages. This avoided user disturbance and interruption of users due to memory or network bandwidth issues.

The non-IID data problem and several similar data issues (*https://oreil.ly/ztxbK*) continue to challenge machine learning scientists and engineers. In "Example Deployment" on page 152 you'll learn more about these concerns and ways to address them. In general, these problems are still open research issues and can be only partially addressed via better analysis, planning, algorithm design, and software engineering. Therefore, depending on the data you plan to use and the task at hand, federated learning might prove challenging or impossible.

Since Google's initial federated learning deployment, several other big players have released federated learning in production settings, including Apple (*https://oreil.ly/IRKAw*), NVIDIA (*https://oreil.ly/YXk1C*), and Amazon Web Services (*https://oreil.ly/e2kGc*). There are also an increasing number of federated learning open source libraries, startups, and companies incorporating federated learning into other machine learning offerings. Let's explore what problems federated learning addresses and how to use it.

Why, When, and How to Use Federated Learning

Federated learning is a good fit in several scenarios, where collecting data centrally is not possible. The primary use cases are:

Sensitive data
Where persons would rather have their data kept locally instead of collected centrally

IoT data or edge data
Where it is cumbersome to maintain massive scale datasets with ever-changing device and hardware support

On-premise data
Where systems have security or confidentiality rules about the data leaving the location or storage infrastructure

What these use cases have in common is that the data should—whenever possible—remain on the local infrastructure or device. These use cases apply when central data collection either violates specific policies, regulations or privacy or creates unreasonable performance and storage considerations.

By pushing computing to "the edge," you can reap the benefits of data analysis and machine learning without the risk of centralized data, which must be monitored, maintained, and administered. Optimizing by pushing compute to where the data lies offers new possibilities and allows more time for actual data analysis, rather than data management.

Moving computing to edge nodes and devices is, however, no small feat. It presents several new technical challenges to address, outlined in Table 6-1.

Table 6-1. Benefits and challenges of federated learning

Benefits	Challenges
No central data collection	Data standardization on device
More diverse data	Unevenly distributed data
On-device and/or offline machine learning	Shared model
Privacy protection	Dependent on implementation

Federated learning, unlike its counterpart in traditional machine learning systems, does not centralize data in one place. This offers more data privacy and can reduce data collection infrastructure costs and support. One challenge this presents is that you then need data to be standardized at the edge and organized in a way for you to train. This means all preprocessing must happen on device and the data must be aligned before training begins. The training data can be vertically partitioned, where you are joining columns across devices, or it can be horizontally partitioned where you are expanding the training and testing dataset by adding samples from all devices. You must be able to line up the datasets and run calculations on them. For this, the data needs to be in the same format or to be manipulated into the same format across all the edge devices. You can see why it is appealing to use edge devices or hardware with a standard data setup, such as devices that all run the same software.

Assuming the data is not data you could collect centrally due to security and privacy issues, these systems have an additional benefit of larger reach and user input, which helps in de-biasing the model by opening up a broader population. This diverse data is by definition non-IID and brings the analysis and debugging problems discussed in "Federated Learning: A Brief History" on page 147. One possible solution for this problem is to be extremely picky about your selection criteria and to run some EDA beforehand to get a better idea of disparate user populations. You can also architect logic into your aggregators to group or cluster users to an aggregator based on their data qualities. Know here that you might end up overexposing their information if your groups become too small!

Learning on device also allows for speedier model responses and offline uses. In situations where managed IoT or connected devices will be offline when WiFi or mobile internet drops, those devices can still use the local model and data to make decisions. The downside is that the model must be shared to all devices (see Chapter 4 for potential privacy and security risks). You need to be sure that shipping the model (or a version of it) to each device is compliant and secure—and keep in mind that someone likely can and will pull it from their device and inspect it.

Privacy for individuals increases when the data is kept on the device but, as you know from Chapters 2 and 5, this can vary greatly depending on the implementation because gradients and intermediary values can also leak quite a bit of private information. You need to assess what these risks are and adopt appropriate controls, like adding differential privacy mechanisms to your aggregation points.

Structuring your machine learning in a federated model or system means adjusting your normal data science workflow. First, you likely won't have the EDA step of your data analysis; you'll be working with significantly less data understanding and access than normal. You can often use federated learning software to run distributed queries to get an idea of the overall population, but you won't be able to see the data directly. As you can imagine, this makes debugging a malfunctioning model challenging.

The model architecture and data splits need to be defined and implemented. In federated learning with tabular data, you can choose vertical or horizontal splits—meaning that the data is split between the different participants on either a "row" (horizontal) or "column" (vertical) basis. If you aren't working with tabular data, you can still leverage these splits should you need to in order to match labels with input. In order to decide on splits, you need to know what type of data your devices will have—are they simply more examples with appropriate labels? Are the labels on some devices and the input features on other devices? Are the input features and variables split across multiple devices? Depending on how the data is distributed, you need to structure your model, keeping in mind that some setups are easier than others. Horizontal splits where each device has training data and labels are easier to manage with the federated learning libraries available today. Support is growing, however, for vertical splits where labels and/or input features might be split across devices.

There has also been some interesting research on learning multitask models (*https://oreil.ly/dhBjt*) in a federated setting, where the data is heterogeneous and each model might be optimizing for a different task. This is still mainly a research topic, but the promise of knowledge transfer in these heterogeneous settings could unlock new federated and distributed learning architectures. Not only that, these advances could find new methods to learn tasks when specific task data is lacking but related data exists.

There are other interesting federated learning structures, such as split learning (*https://oreil.ly/Eh_06*), personalization of models on device (*https://oreil.ly/oJNGk*), and meta learning (*https://oreil.ly/QA86F*). I'll cover a few of these in the rest of the chapter when they address specific questions or issues. The field of federated learning is still quite young—and therefore many of these ideas have been proven in research but not necessarily deployed at scale. I highly recommend reading more on the latest of any unique architectures that fit your use case to see if they have been deployed and to evaluate if they've been recently optimized or improved in research or practice.

A large part of "how" you will train federated learning models depends on closely working with the infrastructure, software, and DevOps specialists at your organization. To start the conversation, you'll need to learn what architectural and deployment concerns should be addressed and how you can help support your colleagues in making these choices.

Architecting Federated Systems

Architecting federated systems is no small task, given the variety of constraints and performance requirements in these deployments. In this section, you'll review information to keep in mind when architecting a federated or distributed data system and what to consider when designing and deploying software that keeps data as far from the centralized service as possible.

Example Deployment

In federated learning or distributed data analysis systems, you will have several essential components. They are:

- Communication channels between devices (and a centralized service if used)
- An aggregator, or several aggregators, or a coordinated aggregation process
- Software that supports this coordination and analysis deployed on all devices

First, you'll need to figure out how the devices coordinate and send results. There are several different ways this can be done, as shown in Figure 6-6:

Classic
> Devices connect to a centralized aggregator. That aggregator or a connected service is in charge of selecting the devices, coordinating the training rounds or analysis, and performing the actual aggregation step. The end devices send the updates to this central service, usually over a secure network connection (such as HTTPS or via VPNs).

Clustered
> You decide to split your analysis or learning across several aggregators to service varied devices based on their software, or because your current system architecture is distributed, or for network performance optimizations. Again, the connections should still be over a secure channel, and the edge devices would still talk to their assigned aggregator. These separate aggregators also need to coordinate with one another if they are to produce one aggregate model.

Fully distributed
> Each of the prior setups relies on centralized pieces in architecture that must be maintained and operated by an organization or group of people. But what about actually decentralizing this process? While possible, it requires quite a bit of extra coordination and communication between the devices themselves. They must take on the actions and responsibility of the aggregators (i.e., selection criteria,

coordination, as well as aggregation). Practically, this is not yet feasible at scale, but for a small proof of concept or as a new product or software offering, I think this has some really interesting privacy and decentralization properties! You'll also learn more about architectures like this in Chapter 7.

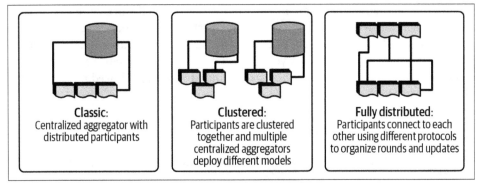

Figure 6-6. Federated learning aggregator architecture options

In addition to determining the federated and aggregator architecture, you'll need to develop a sensible selection criteria. Here are a few questions to help you make that choice:

Device connectivity
What connectivity does the device have to the internet? Can you trust that it will not lose connectivity in the middle of the analysis? What happens when a particular number of devices "drop out" of a round? Setting a threshold on when to continue is a good idea.

System memory and load
What is the current state of the device? Is it actively under high load due to other running processes? How much memory (RAM) is available for an analysis or training round?

Power and hardware
What are the hardware specifications of the device? Is the device connected to power? If not, what is the battery state, and how much battery is necessary to run the analysis or training on the device?

Software and data access
Is the device running a current software version? Does the software running support the analysis? Does the device have local data that fits the training and analysis, such as user consent and access?

Data distribution

Does this device and the data fit into data science requirements for your analysis? Are there particular selection criteria you'd like to use to ensure success, such as regions, languages, user type, etc.?

These decisions cannot be made in a vacuum. Instead, you'll work closely with your data colleagues as well as your peers in infrastructure, operations, system reliability engineering, and/or DevOps. Those teams will likely deploy, monitor, and maintain the infrastructure and devices for your learning or analytics system. It is not easy to run these types of computations successfully and at scale. You'll need their guidance on how to organize, test, deploy, and learn as you go.

Ideally you have some infrastructure and operations colleagues who are interested in these types of architectures. Evolve your thinking on these systems by learning from decentralized identity systems (*https://oreil.ly/yvdJu*) and zero-trust architecture (*https://oreil.ly/9oS83*). These approaches are not the same, but they do address similar problems in architecture design and distribution of trust.

To decide how to test, roll out, and (potentially) roll back your software and distributed analysis, start a coordinated conversation that leads to a communal decision. The last thing you want to do is crash your edge devices because the memory usage exceeds what the devices have available or introduce software bugs that degrade user experience or even introduce errors in the federated analysis. You should develop a comprehensive and robust CI/CD pipeline, integrated test suite, and a battery of test devices that you can use as a "staging" environment.

You'll also want to perform distributed debugging on data that you cannot see. This is about as difficult as it sounds! Here are a few priorities to keep in mind to get this right:

Maintain privacy

If privacy benefits are the primary motivation for moving to a federated architecture and analysis, ensure that your debugging actually respects those requirements. This might slow your debugging, but in the end it creates robust systems that can both maintain privacy standards and guarantees and perform distributed analysis and learning. There is no point in building all of this infrastructure to just copy the data centrally to debug it or to log sensitive details centrally.

Test often and develop error metrics

Developing a small device lab for local testing speeds up your debugging. You can inspect both ends of the problem and identify bugs and errors quickly. In doing so, it's a good idea to also develop metrics and safe error codes that can be collected without leaking sensitive or private information. Remember, avoid collecting information that identifies a particular user or device. Instead, find basic metrics that point to the problems at hand. If you find that the metrics you need contain sensitive details—such as summary statistics of the data or user location—you should build differential privacy aggregation into your collection of these metrics. This means if you don't see this error across many devices, you won't see this error at all.

Push debugging to device and identify patterns
Similarly, the closer you push debugging to the device, the better the data you will have available. Use those metrics and/or safe error summaries and identify patterns where problems are occurring by comparing across devices, and you'll have systemic ways to identify problems.

My advice, having worked on distributed systems that maintain privacy (*https:// oreil.ly/UrKbf*), is to be patient and spend sufficient time experimenting and debugging before moving to production. In the following section, I'll share some hard-earned lessons regarding building and maintaining distributed computation systems.

Security Threats

You've already looked at a few concerns and considerations in this chapter, including deployment choices, device capabilities, debugging options, and potential data problems. Unfortunately, this is not a comprehensive list just yet! You will also need to think about the security of the model itself as you ship it to the devices.

As you learned in Chapter 4, there are few ways to protect against reverse engineering a model—particularly if they have a local copy of it. One method to mitigate this is to split the model (called split learning (*https://splitlearning.mit.edu*)) at a particular layer, shipping only some layers (fine-tune or base) to the devices. While this does not prevent exposing what the model does, it avoids sending the entire model to all devices.

 For a comprehensive research-focused review of advances and challenges in federated learning, I strongly recommend reading "Advances and Open Problems in Federated Learning" (*https:// oreil.ly/s79IZ*), a paper written by multiple scholars and practitioners on the state of the field.

Another security consideration is the possibility that a user "breaks" the centralized model (either maliciously or erroneously). Data poisoning is one type of adversarial attack—where a user or group of users submit false data to influence the model toward a particular or incorrect prediction. In a federated setting, this could be one user or a group of actors participating together in a round of training. Data poisoning attacks in a federated machine learning setting are also called *Byzantine poisoning attacks* (often shortened to *Byzantine attacks*).[6]

To overcome this threat, you can use an evolved selection criteria and train several candidate models in parallel, evaluating them with separate users as a test set. You can also sample data given to the model and assume data that is displaying very large gradients is odd and either reject or clamp those contributions. This might, however, prevent your model from learning or converging in cases where the data is not actually malicious.

Other methods recommended for data poisoning and adversarial attacks include transforming examples to be closer to the manifold (*https://oreil.ly/icwSq*) or training with adversarial and poisoning attacks in mind (*https://oreil.ly/QN4Ip*). None of these will eliminate the possibility completely, but they should reduce the influence of a small group of actors in a large distributed machine learning process.

One final concern—if the users, themselves, expect their data to be backed up somewhere, how do you ensure that the important data is properly secured if you are not centralizing it? You could ask the user to identify the data they would like stored centrally in a user-friendly manner or offer backup options they might already be using, such as cloud storage options via their connected accounts.

Here, you still need to evaluate a privacy-first, consent-driven, and secure option for your users. In the field, there are plenty of examples where assumptions are made on the user's behalf that are unlikely to be true for all users (e.g., stale chat messages from years ago or content users believed was ephemeral are saved longer than desired). When in doubt, talk with users directly!

Use Cases

Federated learning and analytics opens up completely new use cases that are not a good fit for centralized data collection. Edge devices that generate large quantities of data are poorly optimized for submitting data to a centralized service due to connectivity and memory issues. As compute and memory power for edge devices increases, new possibilities emerge to ship compute to these devices instead of centralizing data that you often don't need or want.

For example, aggregate IoT data is often not useful—particularly because it is difficult to link with interesting data sources, such as weather and location data, malfunction and error data, or other situational data that is accessible only to someone near the device. If this data remains on the edge and at the device level and the statistical

---

6 There is quite a bit of research on adversarial learning (*https://oreil.ly/z9DOq*) in federated and nonfederated settings, as well as several interesting code implementations (*https://oreil.ly/8UvHt*), should you decide to explore this topic further.

analysis and/or training can be pushed to meet the data at the edge, these systems could more quickly discern actual cause and effect for problems such as predictive maintenance or warning systems.

Because of the extra privacy and security controls, federated learning can open new options for cross-silo learning or analytics tasks—where different parts of a single organization that normally don't share data can build a model or analyze data together. This can enable multi-organizational or intra-organizational data projects— such as between parent and daughter companies or different companies that can see different parts of a task, such as industry partnerships in logistics, operations, or tele-communications.

At its core, federated learning is a way to share models more democratically with users. As you are using their data to train the model, giving them more access and participation seems like a fair trade. This has the added benefit that you can rethink personalization. What if you wanted to offer more personalized models by allowing local models to diverge from the central model? Users could then have a personalized model—better fit to their data, presuming they have all features and labels available locally. It also means you don't hold a copy of this model—aligning with your privacy guarantees while still adding value to the user's experience.

This also aligns better, in my opinion, with users' perception of how their data is stored and used. Headlines exposing how machine learning systems work (i.e., that humans will see and label training data, that the data is stored centrally in a place not under control of the user directly, etc.) demonstrate the lack of transparency and responsibility the industry has developed as the industry has developed. It is clear we have far to go to regain trust. Building systems where users are actually in charge of their data, with fine-tuned consent and local-only storage options, would help repair the damage and underscore the value of privacy in that particular product, software, or service.

If you've decided federated learning fits your particular use case or you are motivated to enable more privacy and data minimization, you'll first need to figure out how to deploy the software and configure the aggregation and orchestration infrastructure to support the first steps.

Deploying Federated Libraries and Tools

To deploy federated learning at scale, you must choose the type of architecture and maintenance that works for your organization. Although I am personally excited about fully federated and decentralized solutions, most of the robust frameworks take a semi-centralized approach.

This means you'll need to work closely with the DevOps, infrastructure, and/or platform teams at your organization to coordinate and deploy supporting architecture. If you already deploy software to edge devices, this will be simpler than you expect.

Here are a few leading questions to start that conversation:

- If we wanted to implement or utilize open source software at our nodes, how might that work? What deployment capabilities do we have to push new libraries to the edge?
- What is the connectedness of our edge nodes/devices?
- What is the memory and compute capacity of our edge nodes/devices?
- When we need to debug, how would we safely and securely collect logs and error messages from the nodes?
- What information do we have about our running processes on the devices to help us debug and monitor the computations?
- How might we set up continuous integration where a smaller group of nodes get software or training updates first? Could you show me how node selection would work based on data criteria?
- Where should we set up aggregators in our architecture? How would you advise securing these parts of the architecture?
- How would the aggregators communicate properly with our data science infrastructure and services?

Make certain your team has support in testing and rolling out federated infrastructure, as it is a complex operation and you'll need to work cross-functionally to get the initial deployment working. Remember that even things like logs and error messages from the devices contain highly sensitive information and should be treated as PII.

 Don't boil the ocean—try a beta-test with a smaller number of devices that have better connectivity, better compute power, and better data for your task. Prioritize with the best outcome in mind and see if it works. If you run into any expected or unexpected problems during your development, deployment, and training, starting with the optimal situation can speed up debugging and determine next steps.

If you're not already running federated analysis, start with open source software before deploying or building your own. In the next section, you'll learn about one open source library to try your initial deployment.

Open Source Federated Libraries

The open source community as well as many larger technology companies and start-ups have truly embraced the notion of distributed data analysis. There are many open source, well-supported, and well-maintained libraries for implementing federated computations and learning.

If the machine learning library you already use has a federated approach, just use that one. For example, if you are already using TensorFlow, it makes a lot of sense to just stick with tf-federated (*https://oreil.ly/siJyK*).

In this chapter, you'll learn Flower; it's an interesting and useful library maintained by Cambridge researchers. It also has the ability to change machine learning back-ends with support for TensorFlow, PyTorch, Hugging Face, and more.

 Libraries and functionalities and open source offerings can change quickly, so please determine what works best for your use case and architecture. Federated learning is an active area of research and practice, so evaluating what new libraries are available can also open new possibilities.

Flower: Unified OSS for Federated Learning Libraries

Flower's goal is to create one user interface for several different federated learning backends including TensorFlow, PyTorch, Hugging Face, MXNet, and scikit-learn. Flower also exposes iOS and Android emulators and works with Ray (*https://oreil.ly/CMMTH*), a library and community focused on distributed data analysis, analytics, and machine learning.

Flower can also support basic queries, enabling you to pull particular values from nodes. You can see more of their examples and several Google Colab notebooks in their documentation (*https://flower.dev*).

You can find the full notebook and scripts for using Flower in the book's code repository, which uses a slightly different setup than the code demonstrated here. This code is from one of the many helpful examples in the documentation, showing how to set up strategies for managing your federated training using the built-in class:

```
strategy = fl.server.strategy.FedAvg(
    fraction_fit=0.1,
    min_fit_clients=10,   # Minimum number of clients to be sampled
                          # for the next round
    min_available_clients=80,   # Minimum number of clients that need to be
                                # connected to the server before a training
                                # round can start
)
```

Let's walk through these parameters for a better understanding:

- `fraction_fit` determines the percentage of clients that are selected. Here 10% of clients will be chosen.

- `min_fit_clients` determines the number of clients that will be sampled in the next round to see if the loss function is working.

- `min_available_clients` determines the number of clients that the server needs to have connected before a training round can begin.

The strategy in this code example is a federated averaging strategy, which was the original algorithm proposed in 2017 by Google researchers (*https://oreil.ly/xTH_4*); it has since been implemented in many federated libraries. This algorithm takes gradient updates from each of the client models—usually after a few rounds of local training—and aggregates them via the aggregation server, which averages the updates to produce the federated average gradient. This gradient is then sent to the devices to continue the training rounds.

There are many algorithms worth evaluating to improve this basic approach, including Federated Averaging with Client-level Momentum (*https://oreil.ly/JX6HS*), Byzantine-Robust Federated Averaging (*https://oreil.ly/y9oUk*), and several novel ideas in the "Advances and Open Problems in Federated Learning" paper (*https://oreil.ly/YUtFw*). There is significant ongoing work on aggregation algorithms that provide differential privacy and encrypted computation guarantees, which are often referred to as *private* and *secure* aggregation. You'll learn more on this in Chapter 7.

Walking through the strategy tutorial (*https://oreil.ly/_s9RA*) will help you learn more about strategies and creating your own `Strategy` class.

Flower also has a simulation module that can help you debug potential issues by simulating them first, shown in the following code:

```
fl.simulation.start_simulation(
    client_fn=client_fn,
    num_clients=NUM_CLIENTS,
    config=fl.server.ServerConfig(num_rounds=100),
    strategy=strategy,
)
```

Here the simulation method requires a few key arguments, including a function to instantiate a client, the number of clients to start, the server configurations, and the strategy. Note that you need to run many simulations to figure out what looks most similar to your actual usage—and to leverage the built-in library tools if you would like to simulate Android, iOS, or embedded devices.

When running this code, a Ray-based simulation is created in the background. Ray has its own way of managing clusters, which you can read about in the documentation (*https://oreil.ly/2s-_X*), but Flower abstracts this away, which is great for local simulation and testing. You will want to take a deeper dive into these abstractions before you run Flower in a staging or production environment.

After running several simulations, you'll be ready to run Flower with a set of connected devices. If you are a mobile application developer, you might use a service for this or even have your own lab of devices.

To run Flower on devices, you first set up a server deployed within your architecture and available to clients via SSL. There is some basic documentation (*https://oreil.ly/wA2pL*) on this, but have your infrastructure and software team ensure the server is set up securely, with robust processing and memory power and a load-balancing strategy, if you expect high load from the connected devices.

You'll then need to install and deploy Flower to the devices, making sure that the client-side starts and is available for at least the minimum number of devices in your strategy. To do so, ensure the federated clients integrate well into the software you are already running on the devices. To get an idea of how this could be configured, read the client documentation (*https://oreil.ly/UCYyq*) and the architecture diagrams (*https://oreil.ly/FcrRS*).

At that point, you're ready to actually run your first production analysis or learning. Once your first analysis or model is successful, you'll have the confidence and learnings to continue, iterate, and experiment. With each model or analysis, you are reducing privacy risk and growing knowledge on how to do data science with less centralized data.

As mentioned, Flower is just one of many newer federated libraries emerging to provide distributed data science and federated learning. This space will grow significantly in coming years—creating not only more open source libraries but also the potential for reorganizing data to better fit the real-world problems data science hopes to solve.

A Federated Data Science Future Outlook

I strongly believe that distributed data science, analytics, and machine learning represent our future. Let's look at a few examples to see how data analysis and data science at the edge can help address today's problems.

Cities, counties, and states could manage crops and food distribution with intelligent farm equipment, which can ask and answer questions about average yield per plant per season. This data can then be aggregated to answer the larger question, "Will we have enough food?" Instead of this data going to a centralized agriculture giant, it could go to the local or state government or farmers' collective for better planning and coordination.

The COVID-19 pandemic demonstrated that smaller local data, such as small embedded devices in hospitals, can report spikes in new infections. This data can identify potential outbreaks and stop the spread of the virus using intelligent modeling to guide public health recommendations and regulations. This gives better information to health authorities while also preserving the privacy of those affected.

Ever-expanding climate emergencies could be better addressed with connected weather and water sensors to provide better situational reporting, leading to early detection and warning systems powered by federated data aggregation at the edge.

These examples are just the beginning. If data is more local, it opens up new possibilities for collective ownership of data. If data is collectively owned and operated, use cases emerge that have nothing to do with centralized profit and control. If users, communities, or even disparate data providers are empowered to help each other analyze problems with data and figure out how to train their own models, via better and more user-friendly interfaces, then a completely different picture of how machine learning can be used appears.

Shifting to a collectively owned and operated way of thinking about data fundamentally changes the constraints into possibilities. Limited compute power becomes a useful tool where communities design and work together on local problems. Those communities network together and transfer knowledge without ever centralizing or handing over data ownership. The world is already shifting to more edge devices; I hope we can use that as an opportunity to ask and answer better questions for ourselves and our world.

Summary

In this chapter, you learned about distributed data analysis and federated learning and how they might apply to your particular use case or problem. You also explored the challenges and opportunities of such technologies—including how to increase privacy guarantees by combining federated approaches with concepts you already know, such as differential privacy and trust boundaries.

You explored how deployment and architecture of federated systems can and will affect your use cases, and you had a chance to explore an open source federated library to see how it might work in a real-world deployment. You also, ideally, began thinking about how federated learning and distributed data analysis open new possibilities that can fundamentally change the way you manage and think about data.

In the next chapter, you'll learn about encrypted computation. As I mentioned in this chapter and several others, this technology can help enforce stronger privacy, secrecy, and security guarantees and change how trust is designed in distributed systems.

## CHAPTER 7

Encrypted Computation

Encrypted computation is a subfield of cryptography that allows you to compute on encrypted data without decrypting it. First discovered through research in the 1970s, it has grown and developed since then, offering secure ways to compute in insecure settings. In this chapter, you'll learn several foundational concepts in encrypted computation, along with how to determine if and when this technology is a good solution for your data science needs.

What Is Encrypted Computation?

At first, the idea that you can compute on data without decrypting it seems impossible. After all, you would think that you'd need to crack an egg before cooking it, right? In actuality, it's possible to boil an egg with its shell still on, and it's possible to compute on data without decrypting it. In fact, there are many protocols and methods to carry out this encrypted computation. You might have heard of some of them already: homomorphic encryption (HE), secure multiparty computation (MPC), garbled circuits, or related methods like zero-knowledge proofs (ZK-proofs).

Much of encrypted computation relies on interesting mathematical properties to maintain correctness while processing on encrypted data. This chapter will provide a solid introduction, which you can build upon with more learning after this book.

Cryptographic protocols are used to encrypt, transmit, compute, and decrypt information. A protocol is a plan and way to exchange information—usually between multiple computers or parties—to communicate or compute together. When you browse the internet, you are utilizing several encryption and networking protocols at once, including TLS, DNS, and HTTPS.

If you have used tools like GitHub, you're probably thinking about encryption in a public-private key-pair way. Turns out, there are many more ways to encrypt than just that! As you read this chapter, avoid trying to fit these protocols into a familiar context because, chances are, the mental model doesn't fit. Learn these building blocks and tinker with the notebooks in the book's repository to build a new understanding.

Encrypted computation solves a security issue when multiple parties want to compute together but don't want to compute using unencrypted, or plain-text, data. These scenarios have varying levels of trust between the players. To better control and increase trust, you use encrypted data, allowing you to control what is decrypted and by whom.

A classic problem in encryption is Andrew Yao's millionaires problem (*https://oreil.ly/47-jZ*). This problem describes two millionaires who want to figure out who is richer in order to decide who will pay the bill at dinner. They don't want to reveal their net worth to each other but are happy to learn who is richer. Yao solved this problem using an early implementation of encryption protocols you'll learn in this chapter (namely, secure multi-party computation).

Encrypted computation is useful in many settings where decrypting the data is not desired or even allowed. Let's review when encrypted computation adds trust and security and enables new ways of collaborating with data.

When to Use Encrypted Computation

Encrypted computation is a great fit for use in situations where you might not trust the participants or the entire setting:

Insecure cloud environments
> Let's say you would like to compute in a cloud environment using on-premise data but you don't trust the cloud environment. Encrypted computation can ensure the data is never decrypted in the cloud.

Computing with third parties
> What if you want to compute with others but you don't want the others to see your raw data? Encrypted computation allows you to compute without revealing the plain-text data. You can also determine who can see the final result and how it will be revealed before you start computation—providing each party with appropriate security and privacy protections before processing begins.

Computing on encrypted data

You might want to compute on highly sensitive data—like evaluating a photo for a cancer diagnosis—but the patient or user might not want to have their data revealed. Encrypted computation provides the security and privacy a user expects—letting you compute a result on encrypted data and return it to them to decrypt.

Comparing data across parties

Sometimes you want to ensure a new business venture is mutually beneficial. Imagine you are running a marketing department and you'd like to know if a particular service is of interest to your users before you work on a new collaboration. What if you could compare user bases beforehand to see how many users overlap? With encrypted computation, you can compare datasets across parties without revealing the plain-text values of either dataset. This process is advantageous for the user privacy and collaboration.

Distributing data or secrets

There are times when you might not trust the storage environment or compute environment in which you are working—or you might want to take zero-trust architecture to the next level. To address these challenges, you can store your data or secrets encrypted and decentralized. If someone gets access to part of the data, they cannot decrypt or use it unless they get access to the other pieces of the secret or data. This thinking is also reflected in zero-trust architectures, where you might rethink how credentials and secure storage work and distribute these checks and controls. As a concrete example, Unbound Security (*https://oreil.ly/ Z8hJP*) managed distributed keys to offer better security for cryptocurrency wallets and other high-value assets.[1]

Guaranteeing collaboration and distributing control

Encrypted computation can be used to create algorithms or models that require multiple parties. Because of how the protocols work, the computation cannot be run successfully without reaching a certain level of participation. This participation threshold ensures there is some democratic control over the execution between a small or larger group of parties. For certain computations—such as auctions, elections, or committee or community decisions—encrypted computation provides an online mirror for how trust works in the real world. Encrypted computation can maintain vote secrecy, while also implementing requirements like achieving a quorum before a vote can take place.

---

1 The company was acquired by Coinbase to better secure user wallets for an undisclosed sum in November 2021.

Encrypted computation reduces liability for legal and security teams in the same way that encryption at rest demonstrates a "best effort" for keeping data safe. If your organization uses encrypted data when high-risk data is accessed and processed, this emphasizes that you are reducing risk and potential exposure should auditing and regulatory authorities ask. In addition, you are fulfilling more stringent internal infosec policy, which appeals to security teams and reduces the organization's held financial liability.

There are many other applications of encrypted computation—such as private and secure matching, inference, and search—but you've now gotten a sense of the more commonplace uses of this technology. There are several major benefits of using encrypted computation, which mimic the benefits of encryption in general. It provides security and secrecy for data, while still allowing data use for important insights, analysis, and decision-making.

To determine when to use encrypted computations, you will need to understand some core principles of encryption—including the distinction between privacy and secrecy and how to model the problem to determine the appropriate threat level. With these building blocks, you'll be ready to begin applying encrypted computation to real problems.

Privacy Versus Secrecy

In this book, you've learned rigorous and scientific privacy definitions via the guarantees of differential privacy. When cryptographers talk about privacy, they are usually referring to secrecy. Let's cover the differences and ensure you know how to evaluate both when making decisions about how to process data.

Privacy, as you've come to understand, is the guarantee that information about an individual is not leaked or revealed without their consent or awareness. If you want to protect the privacy of individuals in the data, you have to, first, be aware of how information might leak and, then, modify how you handle that information to prevent catastrophic leakage. You would also consider the context in which they have provided the data and the expected and desired level of privacy, given governance information like policies and consent.

Privacy in cryptography is the ability to decide and guarantee what data is revealed to whom. There are no assumptions, as in differential privacy, about the leakage of that information once it is revealed. This property is also called *secrecy* because it communicates that the values remain secret so long as they are encrypted. However, just as in computing with sensitive values, computing on secret values can leak private information. While the data is encrypted, it is also private because the information is hidden via the encryption mechanism. But this is not the case once you can see the decrypted result.

In a distributed trust setting, you might actually care only about secrecy, not privacy. If you are coordinating a computation across parties, as described in Chapter 6, they might want the result without noise but still not want anyone to see their exact input. In this case, encryption offers the right benefits (accuracy) and secrecy for the parties involved.

You need to make decisions about secrecy and privacy when you use encrypted computation. Choosing when to encrypt and decrypt is important; this provides the secrecy guarantees for the encrypted computation and determines who can see the results. But there are also privacy guarantees to consider. This might mean applying differential privacy before revealing the final result—or at some point during the computation. If you are primarily concerned about secrecy but not about privacy, then encrypted computation itself should provide the guarantees you seek.

Threat Modeling

To determine when, where, and how to apply encrypted computation, you must first understand the threat model. As you learned in Chapter 4, threat modeling is used by security professionals to determine the appropriate actions and mitigations to take, given the current status of the architecture, software, and threat landscape.

When you are asked to threat model for encryption use, you need to determine who is involved in the computation and how that fits the security model.

You'll evaluate two security models to make that decision, shown in Table 7-1. As you have seen throughout this book, the choice involves trade-offs. Although a malicious security model will give you the strongest level of security, it also means a slower and more resource-intensive protocol. Some protocols will not have a malicious security option.

Table 7-1. Security models in encrypted computation

Security model	Description
Semi-Honest (a.k.a. Honest but Curious or Passive Security)	You assume that parties will follow the protocol but will try to learn more information about the others' secret inputs if they can easily do so.
Malicious (or Active Security)	You are assuming at least one party will actively try to manipulate the computation by not following it, modifying intermediary values, aborting the computation, or colluding with others to reveal information about the inputs.

When choosing a cryptosystem, which is a system defining a particular cryptographic protocol and several related methods, you must also consider with whom you are computing and, based on that, select your security requirements. For example, if you are participating with other companies that will benefit from continued collaboration, the likelihood of malicious activity is much lower. In these cases, violating the protocol might be considered a violation of the contract or agreement. Particularly for companies that currently share plain-text data with each other, the addition of encryption under a semi-honest model would be a benefit for the privacy of the individuals and the secrecy of the company data. Evaluate security models often, with a focus on what fits the current use cases and security requirements.

When you run threat modeling for cryptographic protocols, you are most interested in the trust and relationship between parties. As shown in Table 7-1, this involves determining what assumptions you are willing to make about the other parties involved. You must also consider external factors to assess the probability of malicious behavior. The implications are quite different when collaborating within a small, and regular, group rather than a huge anonymous crowd.

In cryptographic theory, there is an understanding of different levels of security guarantees—information theoretic, statistical, and computational security—that you will consider as you model the problem and potential threats.

When a security protocol is first designed, it will be assigned one of three theoretical secrecy guarantees, as outlined in Table 7-2.

Table 7-2. Security guarantees in encryption protocols

Security guarantee	Description
Informational-theoretic	An attacker with unlimited computational power cannot break the encryption scheme.
Statistical	Given unbounded computational power, there is a small statistically measurable chance of recovering values or learning something.
Computational	An attacker with unlimited computational power has a chance of learning something or even recovering a value, but it is bound by the computational power available.

The highest level of security guarantee is information-theoretic security. It is the so-called unconditional or perfect security that is completely secure against a malicious adversary, even one with unlimited computational power.[2] One example of this is a one-time pad, which is a way to perfectly secure a string by XOR-ing it with another equally long, randomly generated key. An XOR operation is performed at the bit level and returns 1 if the two values are different and 0 if they are the same.

Statistical security is the next level down. This security is often how information-theoretic protocols are practically implemented. For example, a protocol might need to use a pseudorandom number generator, which does not provide pure randomness. There are often statistical security parameters in implemented protocols to tune the security of a particular method using extra information for your particular use case or threat model.

---

2 Yes, this includes quantum computers; however, theory and implementations can diverge, so be careful about claims unless the implementation is also proven to have information-theoretic security and be quantum-safe. More on this in Chapter 10.

Computational security is the final level—guaranteeing that the protocol can be broken only by a motivated attacker given time and access to large computing power. You can think of this as making the problem quite expensive as it would require potentially years of compute and large compute instances to crack a single key or message. Many relaxations of information-theoretic security fall under computationally secure guarantees. In fact, the public key encryption systems used to secure all web traffic, email communications, and so forth are all computationally secure.[3]

 When you look at implementations of these protocols, they often depend on underlying network security implementations. This means that information theoretic security is often downgraded to computational security, because it depends on network security protocols like TLS that use a generation and exchange of keys using a public-key encryption protocol.

Types of Encrypted Computation

You'll learn two types of encrypted computation in this chapter: secure multi-party computation, sometimes also called secure computation, and homomorphic encryption (HE). You should understand these as you make choices for your use case.

Secure Multiparty Computation

Secure multiparty computation (often SMPC or MPC for short) is a subfield of encrypted computation that involves multiple parties agreeing to compute together but only if the data is encrypted. Many MPC protocols are information-theoretic secure with various guarantees regarding expected behavior from those parties. Thinking through your security model is an important step with MPC.

MPC was first developed in the late 1970s to theoretically design fair online games for multiple players. Those initial theories were shortly thereafter named as "Mental Poker" (*https://oreil.ly/rqkng*).[4] One fun artifact of this history is that the involved parties in a computation are often called *players*. Since that time, MPC has expanded—in theory, to practical use and protocol design—powering real-world use cases and secure computation for decades.

---

3 Computational security is much of what cryptographers use in implementations today, and there are protocols that are also quantum-safe within this category. Note that quantum computing itself doesn't change these categories; it just means using a different, more expensive computer.

4 Fun fact: some of the first MPC protocols were developed by the same cryptographers who developed the RSA algorithm that you have likely used at some point to generate a public-private key pair for your computer.

A typical MPC setup involves several parties (or players) who want to compute and evaluate a function or series of functions with one another. They don't fully trust one another and/or they would like secrecy for their inputs. They do trust each other enough—or are incentivized enough by the potential outcome of collaborating—to compute something together and reveal the output to one or more of the parties. There are many possible use cases for this, such as two or more companies sharing data to solve a common problem or other multi-player scenarios such as voting, auction, and private data sharing like when evaluating matches for dating or DNA.

The typical steps of an MPC scheme include encrypting the input data via clever mathematical transformations and then sharing the encrypted data across multiple parties. The parties then cooperate and exchange intermediary values until, ultimately, the final result is revealed via a set of decryption mechanisms and interactions.

MPC provides interesting secrecy properties. The parties involved in the computation would like to keep their inputs secret and ensure no other player learns much about their input information. Therefore, the protocols must be designed such that intermediary processing steps or function evaluations do not reveal anything about the inputs. Only when a certain number of parties are ready for the final step is the information revealed, as part of decryption of the final result.

MPC protocols and schemes are accurate and resilient. Some protocols require a particular number of parties to decrypt the end result—often called a *threshold*. MPC protocols should provide the same result as if you computed with all plain-text inputs. This is guaranteed, based on the mathematics built into the encryption method, which you will review in a specific protocol in the following section. A few protocols opt for speed or performance, accepting a small possibility of error insertion, but none of the protocols highlighted in this chapter make that trade-off.

MPC has a wide variety of protocols—hundreds, if not thousands—and is an active area of continued research, discovery, and development. If you want to explore some of the interesting ones, take a look at the protocols in the MP-SPDZ library (*https://oreil.ly/ZFPXz*) or the SCALE library (*https://oreil.ly/9Au0-*), which is led by top researchers in the space, including Nigel Smart's group (*https://oreil.ly/g-ZaQ*) at KU-Leuven in Belgium.[5]

---

5 Nigel Smart also has a fun and informative introductory Q&A about MPC recorded for the OpenMined privacy course (*https://oreil.ly/dpkuy*), which covers his introduction to the technology and relevant use cases from his many decades in the field.

To better understand MPC and how it works, let's walk through a popular approach called *secret sharing*.

Secret Sharing

In secret sharing, a secret value is divided into shares (or pieces) of that value. For example, you might have a number that you would like to contribute to a computation, but it needs to remain encrypted.

You could encrypt that number by adding a randomly generated number to it. That randomly generated number is now the key and should remain confidential so that no one else can decrypt it. When you want to decrypt the result, you simply remove the randomly generated addition. This is not, however, a useful scheme for data science, as it would destroy the ability to actually compute something with it!

You could also design a scheme that divides the noise and secret into many pieces, requiring that all pieces be recovered to decrypt the result. This would be useful, for example, if you wanted a specific threshold of players to decrypt or if you want to distribute these values across a number of people (like a committee or board) or across a number of computers (like in a distributed architecture). One of the powers of MPC is that it distributes trust across these parties—which also mirrors ways people distribute trust in the world.

If you do this naively, you could take several numbers at random, using them as a one-time pad by subtracting them from the value you want to encrypt. Here, the value you want to encrypt is x:

```
x = 45
keys = [100, 22, 43, 56]
enc_x = x - sum(keys) # enc_x is -176

# to "decrypt" you can add the keys to the "encrypted" value
enc_x + sum(keys)
```

In this case, you can then distribute the keys and enc_x to the different parties. Everyone needs to put those values together to decrypt the x.

But this naive scheme has a nasty side effect: it leaks information about x. By looking at the sign of the encrypted value (here: enc_x) a curious participant could determine information about the size of x (i.e., whether it is a large or small number).

You could devise better ways to generate "keys" or other clever ways to hide this information, but basic cryptography offers a superior method, called a *finite field* (*https://oreil.ly/ggFH9*). When the field is created over a prime number, it allows you to immediately solve this information leakage:

```
Q = 431
x = 45
keys = [100, 22, 43, 56]
enc_x = (x - sum(keys)) % Q
```

 This is a modulo (%) operator, which returns the remainder of a division operation. For ring or field operations, this ensures the results "wrap around" and
remain inside the field or ring.

Now enc_x is 255 instead of –176. The field allows numbers to "wrap around," hiding
the size of x in the field itself. For the field arithmetic to work, the keys also need to
be within the field—they need to be less than Q. Here's how you might go about
ensuring this:

```
num_players = 5

shares = [randrange(Q) for _ in range(num_players-1)]
shares += [(x - sum(shares)) % Q]
```

When I ran this, the resulting shares were [260, 163, 120, 82, 282], but if you
run it yourself, your values will be different. You could then distribute these shares to
the five participants. Only when they combine them with one another can they reveal
your secret value. This means they must collaborate and agree on the computation—
hence distributing the trust among them.

But the best thing about this scheme is that these encrypted shares can be added with
other encrypted shares from other participants, as long as they use the same field.
This can then be used to create encrypted sums, averages, and counts across all of the
parties, which can be decrypted by combining all of the shares together. The answer
will be the same as if the computation was in plain text. This is the most basic
approach for secret sharing—called *additive secret sharing*. You can play around with
this scheme in the related notebooks in the book's repository.

 One neat property of operating in a finite field is that there are
many possible explanations for the encrypted share values that are
all equally probable if an attacker has no outside information. In
fact, each element of the field, meaning all numbers between 0 and
the field size (Q), can be a possible explanation! Secret sharing
therefore provides information theoretic security. For a deeper dive
into these methods from an expert in the field, see Morten Dahl's
secret sharing series (*https://oreil.ly/hKtu-*), which also has accompanying notebooks (*https://oreil.ly/-md4f*).

Let's take a look at another scheme that lets you multiply shares and get the accurate
result when decrypted.

Say you want to multiply two numbers, A and B, but you don't want to share those values in plain text. You can use secret sharing to do so. Initially, you would divide the shares in the same way you did with the additive shares so that each is in three shares. Then, you can distribute these shares so all parties must collaborate to calculate the multiplication and reveal the solution.

Let's evaluate how this works:

1. Players 1 and 2 each divide their secret into additive shares (a_1, a_2, a_3) and (b_1, b_2, b_3), respectively, using the same finite field (Q).

2. A third player is added for the computation, and shares are distributed. Player 1 owns A and keeps a_1 and a_2 and receives b_2 and b_3. Player 2 owns B and keeps b_1 and b_2 and receives a_1 and a_3. Player 3 has no data but participates in the computation to provide secrecy. They receive a_2, a_3, b_1, and b_3. The players are now ready to compute and, unless they cheat by sharing shares outside of the protocol definition, they cannot learn anything about the secret with the shares they have received.

3. Each player runs part of the computation. Player 1 calculates $c_1 = a_1 b_2 + a_1 b_3 + a_2 b_2$. Player 2 calculates $c_2 = a_1 b_1 + a_3 b_1 + a_3 b_2$. Player 3 calculates $c_3 = a_2 b_1 + a_3 b_3 + a_2 b_3$.

4. Via factorization you can see that adding $c_1 + c_2 + c_3$ equals

   $a_1(b_1 + b_2 + b_3) + a_2(b_1 + b_2 + b_3) + a_3(b_1 + b_2 + b_3)$, which also equals

   $(a_1 + a_2 + a_3)(b_1 + b_2 + b_3)$ or $A * B$!

   However, because they already have seen some shares in step 2, trading the intermediary values (c_1, c_2, c_3) would leak information. To avoid this, each player can hide their intermediary value by adding a random element from the finite field (r_1, r_2, r_3). Player 1 receives $c_2 + r_2$ from Player 2 and calculates $c_2 + r_2 - r_1$. Player 2 receives $c_3 + r_3$ from Player 3 and calculates $c_3 + r_3 - r_2$. Player 3 receives $c_1 + r_1$ from Player 1 and calculates $c_1 + r_1 - r_3$. Since the players do not exchange the random values, they cannot reveal extra information unless they collaborate.

5. All players can now safely combine their results without leaking extra information and calculate $A * B$. As you can see, they could do so by trading all of the values with one another or by sending these final values to only one party who can reveal the result. This is determined beforehand and agreed to by all parties.

For a walk-through of how this works in code, please refer to the book's repository (*https://github.com/kjam/practical-data-privacy*).

You might be thinking, "So what? If I know A and I know A times B, then I know B." This is true! But, often, when you use MPC, you are modeling a larger computation, of which multiplication is only one piece. The building blocks in this chapter demonstrate how these protocols work but are not meant to be implemented and used directly. Instead, use a well-vetted cryptography library.

You can see that this is a fairly simple protocol, given the security guarantees that the parties and their secrets receive. However, it is a semi-honest or passive model of security—you are trusting that each party follows the protocol outlined and does not introduce arbitrary values, trying to learn more or disrupting the computation. In addition, you are trusting that the parties will not deceptively collaborate by sending the shares they received to one another. Finally, you trust that the parties will send the final results as expected to compute the result and not abort before the computation completes.

Notice that this protocol involves three players, but only two players have inputs. Numerous protocols have different numbers of players and contributors. Some also require a *crypto provider*, which is a role that either a trusted party can play or that can be addressed with other encryption methods. The crypto provider generates material to maintain secrecy guarantees and accelerate intermediary computations. For performance improvements, this material is produced before the computation starts in a so-called "offline" phase. This expedites runtime by reducing interaction rounds between the parties.

But the magic isn't over yet! These operations can be inversed to allow for subtraction or division. In a finite field, these properties exist in the field inverse. You can calculate the subtraction inverse for each field element as follows:

$$(x + y) \mod Q = 0$$

where y is the inverse and Q defines the field. So for a field with $Q = 5$, you would eventually calculate these results, which are shown in Table 7-3.

Table 7-3. Additive inverse for Q=5

ring-element	additive-inverse	proof
1	4	$(1 + 4) \% 5 = 0$
2	3	$(2 + 3) \% 5 = 0$
3	2	$(3 + 2) \% 5 = 0$
4	1	$(4 + 1) \% 5 = 0$

Just as these elements have additive inverses, you can also find the multiplicative inverse to perform division operations in the field.[6] This is found as follows:

$$(x * y) \mod Q = 1$$

I won't go through the entire multiplicative inverse table here, but it could be fun for you to take a few minutes and calculate it yourself. Notice the power of operating in a field!

To use the additive or multiplicative inverse, you can apply the ring inverse of the share instead of the share itself. The book's repository (*https://github.com/kjam/practical-data-privacy*) has several examples, should you be curious to see it in action.

 The examples in this chapter operate in a finite field or Galois field, because it holds special properties. These fields are defined over a prime, usually a large prime, to give more room for the intermediate and secret values. If you chose a non-prime Q, you could still do some operations, based on ring properties (*https://oreil.ly/IGsyT*), but they do not hold for all operations possible in a field. To see this, try calculating multiplicative inverses in a ring (i.e., Q=4 or Q=6).

There are several other secret sharing mechanisms that are more efficient and flexible than the additive scheme you've seen in this section. For example, Shamir's secret sharing allows you to set a threshold, so when some players exit the protocol, the remaining players can continue and reconstruct the secret. Selecting the threshold determines the minimum number of parties necessary to reconstruct the secret and decrypt. Once that is decided, you create a polynomial of degree $t - 1$ where t is the number of players required to decrypt the secret. The coefficients are chosen at random, and the secret is stored in the y-axis intercept when $x = 0$.[7] To distribute the secret shares, each player gets a point on the function—also chosen at random but with no possibility of choosing $x = 0$.

To reconstruct the secret, at least t persons must reveal their shares to one another. Then interpolation (*https://oreil.ly/1srCK*) is used to reveal the resulting polynomial and its secret.

---

6 Note that to support division for the shares, there are more steps than just the multiplicative inverse. To see a walk-through on what is involved, take a look at the "Secure integer division with a private divisor" paper (*https://oreil.ly/9HeuQ*).

7 This isn't the only way to hide the secret in a polynomial. For a more complete review, see Morten Dahl's secret sharing series (*https://oreil.ly/hKtu-*).

Security models in MPC

When you are using MPC, you decide how you'd like to distribute trust across the parties and define what to do if parties cannot be equally trusted. In the examples you have seen so far, you are using semi-honest or passive security. You expect the parties to attempt to learn what they can from what they are given, but not actively deviate from the protocol or maliciously alter inputs as a way to reveal extra information.

It is possible, however, to provide active security for secret sharing using protocols that support testing for cheating and aborting should a cheater be found. One way to do this is to implement Verifiable Secret Sharing (VSS) (*https://oreil.ly/LCddy*), which provides active security against malicious participants. There are several protocols to implement VSS; typically the party distributing the secret also sends a related value used to validate that each of the shares is properly formulated.

Depending on the protocol used, there are additional ways to both locate and correct cheating shares—allowing the computation to continue without the cheating party. For example, error checking and correction codes exist for Shamir's secret sharing. These variants also frequently have a threshold to allow other parties to continue without the cheating players. Morten Dahl's blog post on these corrections (*https://oreil.ly/Pt815*) demonstrates this protocol in action.

Factors to consider when using MPC

There are several performance, architecture, and trust factors to consider when you are ready to use MPC. These choices affect protocol and scheme selection and can be dependent on the implementation. The number of implementation possibilities grows each year, as MPC moves from labs to production settings.

The actual computations you would like to run are a significant factor in protocol choice and performance. You'll need to determine if these are easy or challenging with the MPC library you would like to use. Some operations are easier than others, depending on the protocol. For example, comparisons like "greater than" or "less than" are complex in secret sharing, but easier using methods like garbled circuits (*https://oreil.ly/j3D3T*). There is no simple, all-encompassing choice or way to easily map MPC protocols to computations. Libraries or frameworks should own these decisions—choosing ways to optimize operations and even switching low-level protocols based on high-level computation. Ideally, these act like a compiler to help your human-readable code become machine instructions with optimizations already built into the compilation steps.

Evaluating Encrypted Computation Trade-Offs

Many different factors can affect the speed of your computation, including networking optimizations and setup, computing power, algorithm design, encryption scheme, and library choice.

There are often trade-offs between usability and performance, which is why sometimes a slower but easier to use protocol is chosen because it is more understandable and maintainable.

To navigate these decisions, consider who will be using the software and for what use cases, and define any hard constraints, especially on runtime and user experience. It is worth taking the time to compare a few frameworks or libraries and to build small examples to evaluate. Getting the first few deployments right and making them useful for your users is key to building sustainable use cases where privacy technologies can shine and gain wider acceptance.

Another factor to consider relates to properties when you are operating in a field. In a field, you are operating with integers. For data science use cases, with many mixed types, this requires not only converting everything to tensors or numbers but also moving from floating-point arithmetic to fixed-point arithmetic. As a result, you may need to think about precision as part of your algorithm or function design. Good libraries (like what you will use in this chapter) should make this change relatively painless. If you need to work with very large integers or very small floats, however, you should implement a scaling factor before processing your data in an encrypted computation.

In addition, you want to evaluate the speed and efficiency of your computation. This will depend on the protocols used and whether there are any available optimizations. As mentioned in "Secret Sharing" on page 171, there is a role called a *crypto provider* that can help provide optimizations and offline steps for computations. There are also ways for the parties to do some of this themselves in a more active security setting. If you are interested in reading more about protocols that support this, please reference Dahl's MP-SPDZ blog post (*https://oreil.ly/-3C6V*) and the OverDrive paper on SPDZ improvements (*https://oreil.ly/RIVhS*).

There are ways to optimize MPC protocols to exploit parallelization and timing. When you are working with multiple parties who need to send each other values, you want to reduce the time players spend waiting for intermediary results or values sent by the other parties. Optimizing these computation graphs to maximize parallelization can have significant performance improvements. Ideally, these optimizations are also left up to the library or framework.[8]

Additionally, you must determine robustness—choosing whether there can be participant dropout and, if so, how many parties can drop out yet still have the computation successfully complete. Choosing an appropriate threshold may require some trial and error at first, particularly with largely distributed parties. You first may need to try this across a smaller sample, experimenting with the dropout threshold, similar to what you learned from Chapter 6. If you are operating in a smaller group, you may need to require more shares be distributed across the parties for redundancy.

Server-Aided MPC

Another optimization for MPC protocols is to utilize server-aided MPC. In the same way an aggregator assists federated analysis and learning, servers can also act as intermediaries or meeting points for MPC algorithms and computations.

In these setups, servers can be placed strategically and provide robustness as they will always be reachable. To achieve appropriate security requirements, these servers need to be placed directly into the computation as players, and the algorithm must support server-aided MPC.

There are several interesting implementations of server-aided MPC, including one from Microsoft Research that uses garbled circuits (*https://oreil.ly/f5EEx*).

Finally, you should always use a well-reviewed and audited library. As with differential privacy (Chapter 2), finding an open source and audited library is essential for being able to trust that these protocols were implemented properly. In cryptography, open source is more trusted than proprietary code because protocols and algorithms are peer-reviewed by the entire field and not just a small group of internal employees or auditors.

Given that each party needs to send data to one another at multiple steps, you can see why MPC is called *interaction-heavy*. However, as data concentrates in cloud computing and networking and more investments are made in optimizing networking cross-connections, the costs of interaction decrease. Secret sharing isn't the only MPC scheme of note, but, clearly, it can provide a full suite of operations (addition,

---

8 If you are interested in learning about these problems more specifically, take a look at an introductory post to implementing MPC as part of dataflow programs (*https://oreil.ly/CKVpr*), which addresses several of the challenges of implementing these protocols for Google's TensorFlow library. To see some results comparing several libraries with real data-science use cases, check out Moose and MP-SPDZ benchmarks for tensor operations and logistic regression (*https://oreil.ly/F_mlp*).

subtraction, multiplication, and division) with a fairly low cost across multiple parties.

You'll experiment with MPC later in the chapter when using Moose to perform encrypted computation, but, first, let's investigate other approaches to encrypted computation that require less interaction but more computational power, such as homomorphic encryption.

Homomorphic Encryption

Homomorphic encryption (HE) is another subfield of encrypted computation with protocols and schemes that are different from MPC. HE, like MPC, computes results without ever decrypting the data. HE does this via special cryptosystems that maintain homomorphic properties, allowing encrypted arithmetic operations on the data. Homomorphism is the ability to map algebraic structures, such as groups or vectors, to one another while maintaining the mathematical properties for certain operations, like addition or multiplication. In this case, the ciphertext and the plain text are homomorphic, allowing you to accurately perform mathematical operations on ciphertext.

Compared to MPC, HE is very computationally and memory intensive, requiring much more processing power to perform the computation. It also does not require the involvement of more than two parties, so it works well when there is one data owner and one processor but the data owner wants the data to remain encrypted during processing. It is therefore a good fit when a user would like to send one encrypted piece of data and receive an encrypted response that they then decrypt locally.

Protocols for HE are labeled as either partially homomorphic encryption (PHE) or fully homomorphic encryption (FHE). PHE supports only one mathematical operation; you can run additive or multiplicative operations but not both. FHE means that you can run arbitrary mathematical operations of any circuit depth (*https://oreil.ly/ 1Gvs3*).[9] There are a few protocols that enable leveled fully homomorphic encryption, which limits the number of circuits that can be modeled.[10]

HE utilizes homomorphic properties of the underlying cryptosystems. The cryptosystems that support HE operations create homomorphic relations on ciphertext when the same key is used to encrypt the data. This means you can multiply values encrypted with the same key together and get an encrypted representation of the product of those values. You can also perform operations with plain-text values and receive

---

9 You probably don't often think about circuit depth of your operations. You can think of this as graph or function complexity. Circuit complexity or depth happens at a lower level but has similar properties and computation implications.

10 OpenMined has a useful deeper dive into these distinctions on YouTube (*https://oreil.ly/rUZYW*).

accurate encrypted results. These values can only be decrypted using the same key pair with which they were encrypted.

Unlike many MPC protocols, there is usually a need to reduce inserted randomness at intermediary steps, as these cryptosystems insert randomness as protection against statistical attacks. The breakthrough in HE systems came in 2009 with Gentry's method for bootstrapping (*https://oreil.ly/l1uyS*), which allowed HE to begin computing more complex operations, gates, and algorithms. Before then, there was no way to remove the additional randomness that built up as homomorphic operations were performed on a piece of ciphertext. Eventually, this noise would grow too large, and the decrypted result was incorrect.

Gentry demonstrated that the secret key could itself be encrypted and then used to "decrypt" the value in the encrypted space. Think of this as a double encryption. This step reduces the additional randomness in the ciphertext without revealing anything about the data itself. HE can complete more operations than before because this reduction in randomness can be performed as an intermediary step. When noise grows too large, the bootstrapping step is performed and then normal HE operations continue. This method is still in use today and is part of many protocols for FHE.

Let's take a look at a simple homomorphic encryption protocol so you can see how the homomorphic properties work.

Paillier encryption

Using the Paillier cryptosystem (*https://oreil.ly/dE5xv*), you can perform additive homomorphic encryption—adding numbers together while they remain encrypted. A review of the cryptosystem itself highlights its homomorphic properties.

To create a public and private keypair, you choose large prime numbers with a particular property and compute dependent values with an additional random number. You end up with a public key that has two values (n, g) and a private, or secret, key that has two values (λ, μ).

To encrypt a message (m), you calculate $c = g^m r^n \bmod n^2$, where r is randomly chosen with some constraints.

Note the homomorphism as you review the encrypted message properties. Let's use two messages m_1 and m_2.

If you encrypt these two messages with the same key pair and multiply them together, you get $\left(g^{m_1} r_1^n\right)\left(g^{m_2} r_2^n\right) \bmod n^2$.

You can reduce this to $\left(g^{m_1+m_2}(r_1 r_2)^n\right) \bmod n^2$, which you can then see is the encryption of $m_1 + m_2$. Pretty neat!

To decrypt the new result, you need to have the secret key, meaning that as long as these are kept secret, the security properties hold.

You can take a look at this in code, within the book's code repository (*https://github.com/kjam/practical-data-privacy*), which is implemented in Python classes. The notebook defines the functions required to generate the keys, in order to encrypt and to decrypt.

First, you'll want to generate the keys and encrypt a message:

```
ek, dk = keygen() #ek is encryption key, dk is decryption key
r = sample_randomness(ek) # randomness required as part of the encryption
msg = 4
ciphertext = enc(ek, msg, r)
print(ciphertext)
```

You should see a very large integer! If you run the cell again, your result will be different because your keys and randomness will be different.

To decrypt this ciphertext, you'll use the decryption method in the notebook:

```
dec(dk, ciphertext)
```

which properly reveals the input 4.

You probably already know systems that encrypt and decrypt messages. What makes this system special is its homomorphic properties. You can define functions that use field properties like you used in secret sharing. Here are some functions from the notebook for adding and subtracting ciphertexts. Note that ek.nn is a field, which is how these properties exist:

```
def add_cipher(ek, c1, c2):
    c = (c1 * c2) % ek.nn
    return c

def neg(ek, c):
    return inverse(c, ek.nn)

def sub_cipher(ek, c1, c2):
    c = add_cipher(ek, c1, neg(ek, c2))
    return c
```

If you use these on two encrypted values, you can see that adding and subtracting ciphertext works, and when you decrypt the result, you get the same result as if you had run the operation in plain text. This is homomorphic encryption at work:

```
msg_one, msg_two = 45, 234
c1 = enc(ek, msg_one, r)
c2 = enc(ek, msg_two, r)

result_addition = add_cipher(ek, c1, c2)
```

```
assert dec(dk, result_addition) == msg_one + msg_two

result_subtraction = sub_cipher(ek, c1, c2)
assert dec(dk, result_subtraction) == msg_one - msg_two
```

You can also add, subtract, and multiply encrypted values with plain-text values. See the notebook for all the methods described in this section and try it yourself. This implementation does not support homomorphic multiplication, which would grow the randomness more quickly and eventually require bootstrapping to remove the randomness before continuing the computation.

 You wouldn't usually "roll your own crypto," or write cryptographic protocols from scratch; this is just an example notebook to show you the properties and let you play around and learn more about how these systems work. If you want to use Paillier HE at scale, look at libraries that support these protocols and cryptosystems, like python-paillier (*https://oreil.ly/SCjOX*) or Intel's Paillier (*https://oreil.ly/DllcL*).

As cool as Paillier is, most folks in cryptography are moving away from this system as it does not have today's hardness assumptions and is quite slow compared with other methods. Paillier uses factorization as its hardness assumption, but today's most performant and secure FHE schemes are based on other hard problems, like the learning with errors problem.

Learning with errors

Learning with errors originated out of lattice-based cryptosystems and breakthrough work between lattice approaches and probabilistic noise.[11] Before you dive further into this, let's define a few of these terms.

A lattice is a mathematical structure with particular properties—it defines a basis for a complete set of linear vector combinations that could have many possible bases as explanations. In cryptography, lattices are an alternative to older public-key cryptosystems such as RSA, Diffie-Hellman, and elliptic-curve cryptosystems, which are generally not quantum-safe due to their reliance on factorization. Lattice cryptosystems use lattice properties to create special base lattices, which prove useful in structuring hard problems that are believed to be quantum-secure.

One of these hard problems is the learning with errors problem. This problem can be simplified into a few equations.

---

11 One of the initial pieces of research on this was co-developed by Cynthia Dwork (*https://oreil.ly/MJ5O2*), who you first heard about in Chapter 2 due to her fundamental contributions to differential privacy.

In the original paper by Oded Regev (*https://oreil.ly/weWz4*), you'd like to generate an encryption key and secret so that others can decrypt your encrypted messages. You start by sampling randomness from a field over q—perhaps as a n-dimensional matrix (A). This matrix functions like an encryption key and is sampled from a field that you will use to ensure hardness and homomorphic properties.

You then have a tensor with your secret s. You take the inner product of your matrix with your s tensor and add relatively small errors from a Gaussian distribution ($\langle a_n, s_n \rangle + e_n$). The resulting values modulo over your field will be close approximations of your secret, but this fact will be very hard to determine without definitely knowing your A. The final key generation step looks like $s^\top A + e^\top$.

To actually encrypt the data, you prepare the message by breaking it down into bit-wise vectors calculated by $\lfloor \frac{q}{2} \rfloor \cdot (0 \ldots 0b)^\top$, which you save as $\vec{b}$. You can then take the generated keys and secrets and encode the message by sampling randomness like you sampled error and by calculating $\vec{c} = A\vec{r} + \vec{b}$. To decrypt the message, you compute $\langle c, s \rangle \mod q$. Because of the added error, you take the absolute value of the decrypted value and output 1 if it is greater than $\frac{q}{4}$; otherwise, it is a 0.

The homomorphic properties are retained by the field, as in the other methods you've learned. But this time, the addition of randomness must be taken into account. For example, let's say you have two ciphertexts and two secrets, as defined earlier. If you add them together and take the modulo over the field, you will essentially be getting $\lfloor \frac{q}{2} \rfloor (b_1 + b_2) + randomness$. This adds more noise because it is not just one sampling of the error: it is two samplings! The error must stay below $\frac{q}{4}$ in order to properly decrypt the values.

> To explore how this works for multiplication, first review Ring-LWE via Stephen Hardy's illustrated primer (*https://oreil.ly/Zgjme*) to build understanding of ring operations in a polynomial modulus. Then refer to Shai Halevi and Tal Malkin's lecture introducing the scheme and its properties (*https://oreil.ly/cBnZj*). For a code implementation of Ring-LWE, take a look at Bill Buchanan's implementation (*https://oreil.ly/a3Cx3*) or Ring-LWE implemented by Ayoub Benaissa on OpenMined (*https://oreil.ly/B-Rwx*).

How does this relate back to lattices? The security of this scheme is based on the hardness of lattice problems, as it reduces to certain problems at the core of security assumptions for lattices, like the Short Integer Solution (*https://oreil.ly/8CofL*) and the Shortest Vector Problem (*https://oreil.ly/M3nP1*). To learn more about the hardness of this problem and how it relates to other problems in cryptography, start with Chris Peikert's Lattice-Based Cryptography introduction (*https://oreil.ly/-ok5y*).

In this example, your *A* operates as a key that must scale with your message size, meaning the key size grows very quickly. While there have been many improvements on this factor, it is assumed that larger keys are going to be a part of post-quantum-computer life.

Basic LWE has been expanded into several cryptoschemes that support HE operations. Ring-LWE and TFHE (*https://www.tfhe.com*) both provide fully homomorphic operations with better optimizations. For example, torus-based HE has more efficient bootstrapping— typically the most expensive step in homomorphic frameworks. Ring-LWE builds some polynomial reduction into the computations themselves, which reduces bootstrapping steps.

Lattices and other post-quantum cryptography are already appearing in actual implementations as companies prepare for a future when quantum machines are larger and more readily available. Google has used NewHope for some time in its BoringSSL library (*https://oreil.ly/jmK7D*) and Microsoft has tested Ring-LWE schemes in its research group (*https://oreil.ly/KkXH-*). Note that MPC schemes are also quantum-safe as long as the network between players is secure.

If you are evaluating FHE for your use case, take a look at Zama's Concrete library (*https://oreil.ly/Y8NuB*), which has a NumPy-like API. There is also an interesting Microsoft's SEAL library (*https://oreil.ly/FTt3h*) and IBM's HElib (*https://oreil.ly/XBvcs*), which have several protocols available.

Factors to consider when using HE

If you want to use HE in production systems, it's recommended that you think about specially designed hardware, which will significantly accelerate processing time. Some have attempted to speed up HE systems by using field-programmable gate arrays (FPGAs) to optimize computation (*https://oreil.ly/H_UFy*) or specially designed optical systems to accelerate FHE search (*https://oreil.ly/gtUdG*).

Trade-offs can be made between expediency, performance, and accuracy. Some of the optimized protocols for FHE rely on not always removing the randomness inserted as part of the process. CKKS (*https://oreil.ly/EFqlf*) is a protocol that allows a reasonable amount of randomness insertion to bypass the bootstrapping step. As in differential privacy, there are many data science problems where randomness insertion is expected from the data itself. If you can accept an approximate rather than exact answer, these protocols offer more speed.

Another factor affecting your HE implementation is the data and computation size. Some optimizations work only if your data is quite small, such as 8- and 16-bit values. Other computations can be performed by a smaller circuit—avoiding expensive steps like bootstrapping. These optimizations are evident to seasoned HE engineers and cryptographers; you are not as likely to identify them immediately. In the future, frameworks are likely to support these optimizations as part of the compilation step. For now, just be aware of potential optimizations if your data or your computation is smaller.

Finally, keep an eye on libraries, research, and work in this space—it has come a long way in the past few years. There is always a possibility that evolving computing power or algorithm and hardware design create a breakthrough—shifting HE to the core of everyday computation. Stay up-to-date with new developments in research and implementation by following the work of Zama (*https://www.zama.ai*) or Microsoft SEAL (*https://oreil.ly/qfECd*).[12]

> There's not enough space in this chapter to cover every area of encrypted computation, so I've omitted garbled circuits and oblivious transfer (*https://oreil.ly/4p-bA*). These can be used in libraries and frameworks you've learned about in this chapter as subprotocols; they offer optimizations for particular operations. If you want to learn more about them, see *A Pragmatic Introduction to Secure Multi-Party Computation* (*https://oreil.ly/zraeM*).

Validating HE computations via zero-knowledge proofs

There is no easy way to find and validate potential cheating in an HE operation—unlike secret sharing and MPC schemes. You can, however, leverage another cryptographic method called *zero-knowledge proofs* to do so.

Zero-knowledge proofs are based on an unequal distribution of information, where the prover has access to secret information. There is also a verifier, who would like to validate that the prover indeed has this information. The prover would like to demonstrate that they know or have the information without revealing the information itself, and the verifier would like to ask for the proof as many times as they need until they are sure that the prover is not falsifying the results. These proofs can be interactive—both parties are online and answering in real time—or noninteractive (i.e., offline, or signed proofs posted in a public place). These proofs can be used for a variety of other use cases, such as validating personal information online or proving you hold particular data.

In an HE use case, one party could perform extra computations on the encrypted data—particularly if they might benefit from these changes. Imagine that you are uploading an encrypted value and the other party provides a service to you based on

---

12 Pascal Paillier shared his own predictions (*https://oreil.ly/7dpFA*), recorded for OpenMined's privacy course. He now leads Zama, which gives him a close-up view of the challenges and opportunities ahead.

the underlying value of data, such as a recommendation or optimization if the value is too low or high. What keeps them from changing the computation to incentivize you to use the service? Or, in a group setting—such as an auction or an election—what prevents someone from copying your input, performing operations with it, and submitting it as their own?[13]

Zero-knowledge proofs can be added to these scenarios as an audit trail. They can also be used to prove that you hold the original encrypted value and the encryption key. For machine learning, zk-ml (*https://oreil.ly/jwX8X*) used zero-knowledge proofs to prove that a model was trained properly and to validate the results. Another related implementation using MNIST (*https://oreil.ly/PeXsy*) looked at validating both the model and its inputs.

For a non-ML computation, you could imagine posting a noninteractive signed proof or an endpoint for an interactive proof to validate that you hold the inputs or the processing used in the computation. For those providing the computation, you could also provide an audit trail of the processing as a ZK-proof. These would function similar to signed software binaries so that interested parties can validate the inputs and processing.

With your basic understanding of encrypted computation, let's explore real-world use cases to move from theory to practice.

Real-World Encrypted Computation

To review real-world encrypted learning problems and solutions, you'll look at private set intersections, private joins and encrypted computations, secure aggregation for federated learning (Chapter 6), and encrypted machine learning.

Private Set Intersection

Private set intersection (PSI) is a common computing problem where two or more parties would like to figure out how their data overlaps and identify the intersection of their datasets. This could be user-related data, potential customers, or confidential business data, but, for whatever reason, they do not want to compute this in plain text.

To compute this in a safe and secure manner, they decide to use PSI, allowing them to join the datasets in encrypted space and choose how to decrypt and reveal the intersection. There are also methods for continuing the compute in encrypted space

---

13 MPC is always the preferred choice for group settings, as it is more secure and performant for these shared operations.

instead of decrypting the intersection, which you'll learn in "Private Join and Compute" on page 189.

How does private set intersection work? A variety of methods and protocols are available. You'll review a simple one that, while not very efficient, is easy to understand.

Diffie-Hellman for PSI

The Diffie-Hellman key exchange can be used for PSI (*https://oreil.ly/hPv0Y*). Let's walk through how it works and how you can leverage it for PSI.

In Figure 7-1, you can see an initial setup. Alice and Bob would like to create a shared key that they will use to encrypt messages and communicate without others being able to read their messages.[14]

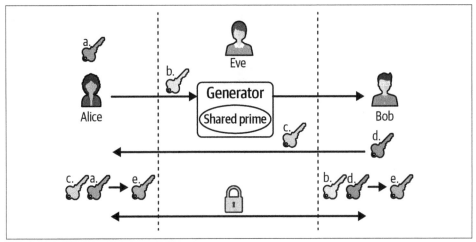

Figure 7-1. Diffie-Hellman key exchange

To build a shared key securely, they need to exchange a few pieces of information. First, Alice will send Bob a generator and prime. These must be agreed upon before any other steps are performed and are sometimes predetermined by the software used. Next, Alice will generate a public-private key pair locally and send the public key to Bob. She will keep her private key private during the entire exchange.

Bob will use the information received from Alice regarding the generator and prime as input to generate his own public-private key pair and send Alice his public key. At

---

14 Alice and Bob are commonly used characters in cryptography (*https://oreil.ly/K5i-6*)—along with a myriad cast of side players like Eve (for eavesdropping, get it?). They help cryptographers and security analysts understand what problems the protocol is addressing by setting up the use case. It also makes for fun jokes (*https://xkcd.com/1323*).

this point in time, they can both use their private key pair with the public key from the other party to generate a shared key.

You can see Eve in the middle, who is the malicious adversary, trying to listen in on the network traffic and deduce what the shared key will be. Even with the information Eve collects listening in on the network, Eve cannot deduce the shared key without access to one of the two private keys (or several other pieces of information, such as many examples of plain text and the ciphertext output using the same shared key). Therefore, this protocol is secure against a bounded computational adversary.

But how can Alice and Bob use this protocol for PSI? Well, as part of the shared key generation or even as part of the initial protocol, they can combine a representation of their values in a hash form with their private keys to find matches. The step-by-step sequence is outlined in Will Clark's blog post (*https://oreil.ly/9DDUO*); essentially, it involves adding a hashing step and a few more interactions using the private keys between Alice and Bob. This adds extra interaction steps and increases the message size when compared to the simple shared key protocol shown in Figure 7-1.

 It's always a good idea to take a look at the latest research as more efficient and faster protocols are developed each year. Many improvements can be made by understanding the two datasets— are they the same size or vastly different? Later in this chapter, you will use a library that implements a few different options, but research is optimizing this problem each year.

You might be wondering if this is secure—couldn't a party lie about their input data? Indeed, there are ways that one of the parties could change their initial dataset to find out if a particular ID is in the other dataset. One of the parties could even create a dataset representing all possible variations, completely revealing the other party's data.

This protocol, therefore, is secure only in semi-honest settings. This suits the problem, since you don't want to intersect data with a known adversary. It also means the choice of a mutual ID is important. You want to ensure the search space is adequately large or that all parties are trusted to follow the protocol. When PSI is used in production systems, it's usually internal to the business, across a multinational company or with a partner—greatly reducing the chance that someone will violate the protocol to learn more.

There are other setups with increased security, such as Google's implementation of Private Join and Compute. Let's explore it to see its additional benefits.

Private Join and Compute

Google's open source Private Join and Compute (*https://oreil.ly/WcRf5*), based on research conducted in 2019 (*https://oreil.ly/l5_VB*), takes a PSI protocol and, instead of returning the intersection to the parties, computes a sum based on those values. This is used in a special part of Google Ads to calculate the number of transactions that a merchant receives from Google Ads.

In this model, Google does not want to show the merchant all users who saw an ad because this would be a violation of user privacy and of Google's corporate secrets (i.e., how users are selected). The merchant does not want to send all shopping transactions to Google. This would also violate user privacy and provide too much information about its customers and business. However, they would both benefit from knowing the amount of money generated by advertising to optimize ad spending, content, and budget allocation.

The private join and compute works as follows. First, a modification of a Diffie-Hellman PSI is done—involving a hash function that maps the identifiers to a group in a field. This is used in conjunction with private keys, similar to the Diffie-Hellman protocol in "Diffie-Hellman for PSI" on page 187. Here, the shared data points are the user identifier or the ad identifier that both Google and the merchant have.

Next, the merchant, who has the amount of money a particular user spent in a given time period, will encrypt the per-user spend using an additively homomorphic cryptosystem (here: Paillier) and attach that to the encrypted identifiers. These values are sent to Google, where it will be aggregated appropriately based on the intersection (per user, per ad, per targeting group, and so forth).

The final result will then be sent to the merchant to be decrypted, using the merchant's private key. At this point, the merchant has learned only the aggregate values of what customer groups purchased after viewing a particular ad campaign. Google has not learned any additional information about users not included in the intersection set.

Google chose a protocol based on the original Diffie-Hellman key exchange, despite it being less performant. This was, in part, due to the simplicity—software developers understand it, ensuring that it will be securely implemented. It's important to keep this in mind when architecting and designing systems of your own. Whenever possible, choose a design that can be understood by others as long as it still meets the requirements of the task at hand. If the task is too complex or requires an advanced protocol, consider the trade-offs you are making, realizing that many people will not be able to update, change, or debug the system.

Now that you've been able to evaluate a simple setup where HE helps two parties calculate private sums, let's take a look at how encrypted computation can help machine learning problems.

Secure Aggregation

As mentioned in Chapter 6, federated learning and analytics can benefit from encrypted computation by providing additional secrecy. One way to implement security for the model updates or gradients received from the different participants is to introduce MPC or HE as the core computation for the updates. For example, the inputs from each of the edge devices or end users arrive encrypted and are decrypted only after differential privacy is added at the aggregation point. This adds a stronger guarantee that the aggregator learns very little about the individual inputs and that, if the aggregator was compromised, it could not decompose the individual points.

To analyze how this might work, look at a diagram of an example process in Figure 7-2.

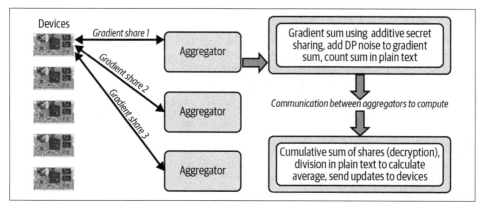

Figure 7-2. Secure aggregation using secret sharing

Assume every device runs their local training and now has an update they would like to send. This is happening across several devices (as shown on the left in Figure 7-2).

When they are ready to send the update, rather than sending it in plain text to an aggregator, they can send secret shares of their gradient to several aggregators. The aggregators can collect these encrypted shares, along with the number of players who have sent them shares. Each gradient must be clipped at the device level, before the gradient is encrypted, but the differential privacy noise can be added via the aggregators as part of a noisy sum. The aggregators can combine either noisy sums or noisy averages to get a federated average, as you learned in Chapter 6.

Note that special precautions are needed for dropout because the shares need to be complete. Additionally, this architecture requires some extra engineering and additional randomness. This additional noise can help, or hurt, the model training depending on the data and the task at hand.

This architecture ensures privacy and secrecy for the updates, while also allowing for accurate updates. It also enables system design and architecture flexibility and ensures the security of the updates as they are now distributed across multiple aggregators, making them less vulnerable to a simple malicious aggregator attack (where an aggregator is compromised and therefore reveals all gradients to the adversary).

 This is just one example of secure aggregation. Jason Mancuso and the Dropout Labs team introduced the first open source implementation for TensorFlow secure aggregation using HE with the Paillier cryptosystem. You can read about their approach in a blog post (*https://oreil.ly/Judux*) and test or review the code in the repository (*https://oreil.ly/o31Vl*). This setup creates one extra server and a few steps for key generation and sharing, making it quite efficient when many devices participate.

If you can perform gradient updates in encrypted space, can you also train an entire model on encrypted data? Yes, you can! Let's take a look at the exciting field of encrypted machine learning.

Encrypted Machine Learning

Encrypted machine learning is a promising area—moving advanced research methods and protocols from encrypted computation into practice by enabling machine learning on encrypted data. What if you could train solely on encrypted data and keep sensitive data secure and secret during model training? This would open new use cases, where data currently cannot be used as it cannot be shared decrypted. This would empower new collaborations and data sharing use cases. Hospitals could work with one another to train cancer detection algorithms. Governments could train together to fight climate change. Competitors in sectors like transportation, logistics, internetworking, and security could join together to optimize systems made of multiple data owners.

A number of researchers in encrypted computation proposed ideas for encrypted learning as early as the 1990s, but the first paper with an open source implementation was from Microsoft Research called CryptoNets (*https://oreil.ly/9pLU9*) in 2016. Microsoft Research implemented the network using homomorphic encryption, based on the Microsoft SEAL library. The simple MNIST CNN proposed in the paper was successfully trained using the library, and you can review the implementation on GitHub (*https://oreil.ly/3KVv6*). Although it was an optimization of previous work, each prediction took about four minutes on a basic laptop. They then optimized the prediction by allowing batch predictions so that multiple inputs could receive predictions at the same time.

Since then, several real-world MPC applications have brought encrypted learning out of the labs and into practice. I had the pleasure of working with the Dropout Labs team, which built the first widely used encrypted learning library, called tf-encrypted (which stands for TensorFlow Encrypted) (*https://oreil.ly/bfH1_*).

How does tf-encrypted work? It uses the MPC basics outlined in "Secret Sharing" on page 171—but with extra layers of protection for additive sums using masking and adding randomness, which is later removed. It enables encrypted multiplicative and division tensor operations and several machine learning optimizers such as ReLu.[15]

One of the stumbling blocks encountered by the Dropout Labs team was a way to validate that each party is running the computation as expected, as well as a way to reason about the computation across parties. Before each protocol is run, the parties must agree on what should be computed and trust that the computation meets their expectations and requirements. To ensure all parties are following the protocol and to help optimize the protocol compilation and implementation, the team needed to build a secure runtime—which could take high-level instructions easily understood by a data scientist and execute them in MPC protocols, which could be validated by a cryptographer.[16]

This was no small task, but the results are now open source and available for use by anyone who wants to run computations in a distributed and secure manner. In the next section, you'll learn how to install, run, and execute your own encrypted computation using the secure runtime (called Moose (*https://oreil.ly/ih1lw*)), as well as the higher-level language built for data science (pyMoose (*https://oreil.ly/dsJ6Z*)).

Getting Started with PSI and Moose

Moose is a secure runtime that takes high-level computational graphs (or directed acyclic graphs [DAGs]), compiling them down into MPC protocols and into an actual physical execution plan. Like the inner workings of Spark shown in Figure 6-1, Moose takes the high-level NumPy-like code and compiles it into code that can be validated by a cryptographer. It can then further take that code and compile it into a logical plan and a physical plan to be executed on running nodes.

It was designed specifically to enable data scientists to work together, creating encrypted dataflow graphs, without the assistance of a cryptographer. Should there also be a security or cryptography team—or if the data scientists would like to audit the computation using an external security provider—this can be done by showing

---

15 You can read the full implementation paper (*https://oreil.ly/NJ32W*) for performance metrics, protocol details, and an overview of the initial design and motivation. At launch, it had a modified SPDZ-protocol (*https://oreil.ly/-3C6V*). Later, the Alibaba security team added support for the ABY3 protocol (*https://oreil.ly/xdz7i*), which optimizes several operations for machine learning tasks.

16 Although not implemented at this point, this runtime could support active security protocols, making the computations verifiable.

the library, compiler, and generated MPC protocol to the security provider or having the provider compile the graph themselves using Moose.

To see it in action, let's walk through how two parties can use a combination of homomorphic techniques and MPC to calculate results together securely. Suppose you work at a consumer goods company that wants to compare purchase data with another firm to identify potential product and marketing collaborations. Each company will categorize purchases in known and shared groupings, such as home furnishings or sports clothing. To identify possible collaborations, the companies will compare user bases and find shared customers. Then, they'll compute how these shared customers spend their money across categories to see if there are interesting patterns. To maintain privacy and secrecy guarantees, they will not reveal the total spending per category, but instead use a calculation to see the percentage of spend in a category for any given user. Of course, you must also obtain user consent for these computations.

The initial step uses Facebook Research's Private ID library (*https://oreil.ly/rNzel*), which allows two parties to find a private join between their values. The library is built in Rust and will require you to compile several pieces before you can run all commands. You can follow along with this code and run it yourself by using the book repository code (*https://github.com/kjam/practical-data-privacy*).

After installing Private ID, each party creates a CSV file with the identifiers they want to compare for the computation. They must agree on a common data element that is a unique personal identifier. In your example, this is the customer email address, but it could also be a combined token, using elements such as name, email, birthdate, and so on, as long as each party has this information.

Each party runs a Private ID server. Note that it is critical to find a way for these servers to talk to one another. The library implements a few ways to do this, along with several protocols that can be used depending on dataset size. As advised in Chapter 6, architecture and security teams should be involved in these setups when deploying into production and even testing environments where real data might be used.

For this example, you'll run the servers locally. Here, there is also a folder in the working directory titled `data`, and the generated CSV file with identifiers is `alice_id.csv`:

```
env RUST_LOG=info cargo run --bin private-id-server --
    --host 0.0.0.0:10009
    --input data/alice_id.csv
    --output data/alice_keys.csv
    --no-tls
```

The other party will run the same command using their data. To simulate this, you run both on your localhost, connected over your local networking. If you wanted to simulate or run this in production, you would need to set up several machines and allow them to network via TLS. The servers need connectivity and discoverability to route the communication.

When you run the code, you will receive an output file at the address you designated. This file will have an encrypted value in one column and your ID column. For each of the rows where no match on your side was found, the ID column will be null. The protocol used for this particular example returns all encrypted user IDs in the same order, a necessary data preparation step for the encrypted computation later.

Now each party will prepare the data for the encrypted computation with Moose, using the matches found in the Private ID file. This is done by matching the encrypted IDs to other data sources and adding the required data for the encrypted computation as extra columns. In practice, you can do so in a file, in SQL, or in Python. In this example, you will also create an extra column that is a Boolean value representing whether the ID exists in your system. This column is based on the Private ID file.

You're now ready to develop your Moose computation. As mentioned, you can do this using a NumPy-like interface that ships as part of the pyMoose package. Let's take a look at the syntax of your computation:

```
import pymoose as pm

FIXED = pm.fixed(14, 23)

alice = pm.host_placement(name="alice")
bob = pm.host_placement(name="bob")
carole = pm.host_placement(name="carole")
rep = pm.replicated_placement(name="rep", players=[alice, bob, carole])
mirrored = pm.mirrored_placement(name="mirrored", players=[alice, bob, carole])
```

At the beginning of the computation, you set a fixed-point definition. A suggested default is provided, with 14 integer precision and 23 decimal precision. You may want to scale or tune this, depending on your setup and data.

Next, you set up placements, which represent each of the players in your computation. Because Moose uses replicated secret sharing to support multiplicative and division operations, you will need three placements. You set them up here as Alice, Bob, and Carole. Next, to define the replicated or encrypted placement in the computation, you pass these participants to the `players` parameter. Here, you are also using what is called a *mirrored placement*—allowing you to share plain-text constants for use in local or replicated operations:

```
@pm.computation
def psi_and_agg():
    with alice:
        x_a = pm.load("x_a", dtype=pm.float64)
        user_id_available_a = pm.load("user_id_available_a", dtype=pm.bool_)
```

You can then tag your encrypted computation, using the decorator @pm.computa tion. Usually, you'll want to define the computation as one big function, using the namespaces you generated earlier to define which players do what steps. This helps for transparency and ensures that all players understand what will be computed and where. If you wanted or needed to break this down into smaller functions with unit tests, you could do so in nondecorated functions and then use those functions in the decorated function.

In the example code, the data is being loaded and cast into fixed type. The pyMoose library loads data using the load method with a declared NumPy dtype (*https:// oreil.ly/G7K-s*) and fixed-point value:

```
with bob:
    x_b = pm.load("x_b", dtype=pm.float64)
    user_id_available_b = pm.load("user_id_available_b", dtype=pm.bool_)

    # Compute logical and between user_id_available from Alice and Bob.
    # If it returns 1, it means the User ID was in Alice and Bob's datasets
    exist_in_alice_and_bob_bool = pm.logical_and(
        user_id_available_a, user_id_available_b
    )

    # Filter Bob's feature to keep only records where
    # exist_in_alice_and_bob_bool returned 1
    x_b_sub = pm.select(x_b, axis=0, index=exist_in_alice_and_bob_bool)
    x_b_sub = pm.cast(x_b_sub, dtype=FIXED)

with alice:
    # Filter Alice's feature to keep only records where
    # exist_in_alice_and_bob_bool returned 1
    x_a_sub = pm.select(x_a,  axis=0, index=exist_in_alice_and_bob_bool)
    x_a_sub = pm.cast(x_a_sub, dtype=FIXED)
```

Bob also performs these preparations and then calculates the intersection between the sets using a logical and operation on the Boolean columns from each player. Because Private ID returned the same encrypted IDs to each user in the same order, this confirms that all the rows match up properly. Once they have just the intersection between their datasets, they can perform the actual calculation:

```
with mirrored:
    ten_percent = pm.constant(0.1, dtype=FIXED)

with rep:
    # Aggregation: average ratio between sum of x_a_sub & x_b_sub
    spend_per_category = x_a_sub + x_b_sub
    spend_per_user = pm.sum(spend_per_category, axis=1)
    category_percent = spend_per_category / pm.expand_dims(spend_per_user, axis=1)
    res = pm.greater(category_percent, ten_percent)

with alice:
```

```
    res = pm.cast(res, dtype=pm.float64)
    res = pm.save("agg_result", res)

return res
```

First, you set up a mirrored plain-text constant of 0.1 that will be shared with all participants. This will be used later to preserve the privacy of the users and the secrecy of the results.

The actual computation then uses the replicated namespace. Within this namespace, the data and all computations will be encrypted. The pyMoose library has similar functionality to NumPy and supports many nd-array operations. The core difference is that these computations run in Rust and as part of encrypted protocols in a ring!

Here, you are using normal vectorized operations as you would with NumPy, calculating the spend per category, total spend per user, and then the spending percentage of each category per user. You return a Boolean result, where each category shows 1 if the spending represents more than 10% of the total spend. This increases the privacy for the users but still shows meaningful overlap. You could, of course, adjust this value to best fit the partnership or product requirements as needed.

At the end of this particular computation, only Alice gets the results and is able to cast them back into a float value to save on her computer. If you'd like both parties to get the result, you would define another block of code allowing Bob to receive the result also.

Now that the computation is defined, you can run it when you have Moose installed. Moose also uses Rust to build the computations:

```
executors_storage = {
    "alice": {"x_a": x_a, "key_a": key_a},
    "bob": {"x_b": x_b, "key_b": key_b},
}

runtime = pm.LocalMooseRuntime(
    identities=["alice", "bob", " carole"],
    storage_mapping=executors_storage,
)

runtime.set_default()

_ = psi_and_agg()
```

You can find installation instructions in the Moose repository (*https://oreil.ly/ih1lw*).

To run the computation in Python, define a dictionary with each party's inputs to show the data location. Moose currently support CSV and NumPy files, which you can easily create from Pandas or NumPy objects. To start the local executors and runtime, you define the players, their storage, and then run `set_default` to initiate the runtime.

Once you run this cell in the book's example Jupyter Notebook, the computation will run and print the final output because you returned it in the computation. You can compare this with the plain-text output in the following cell and confirm the numbers are the same.

This computation is running each placement on your own computer as separate processes for ease of testing and debugging. Obviously, in real encrypted computation these would need to be distributed. In the Moose repository documentation (*https://oreil.ly/MnvNP*), you can see how to set up multiple players and how to set up networking between the different hosts.

When running in a production setting, you must ensure the hosts are located as strategically as possible to reduce latency and data transfer costs. For example, if all players have a presence in a particular cloud, it would be good to use the same cloud networking and if possible the same region. This will speed up the computation, particularly for large and involved computations such as training a model.

If you wanted to use or test a variety of protocols, you can also take a look at other available MPC and HE libraries. I recommend following the curated awesome-mpc (*https://oreil.ly/6DAM-*) and awesome-he (*https://oreil.ly/BnuHX*) GitHub repositories for an updated view on the best frameworks, libraries, and protocols available. I can also recommend the CarbyneStack project (*https://oreil.ly/gcnm5*) from Bosch research, which aims to make MPC protocols easy to set up and use for software developers.

Moose's compiler takes your high-level representation in Python and compiles it down to a low-level representation to execute. Several passes are implemented to make this translation. At any of these passes, the computation can be inspected by one or more parties to validate that the protocols and plan function as expected.

For an idea of how this looks, review the side-by-side comparison of a simple dot-product graph at a high level and at a low level in Figure 7-3, where all cryptographic protocols and network activity is also shown. You can see both up-close and learn how to visualize your own graphs in the Moose example post for graph generation (*https://oreil.ly/kTmq-*).

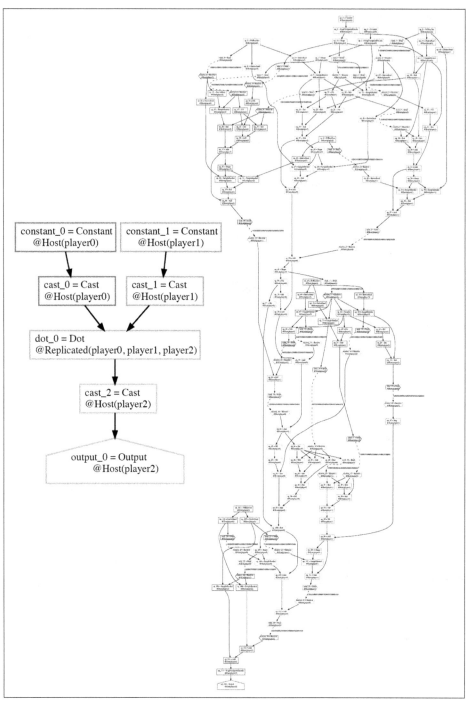

Figure 7-3. Moose compilation graphs: high level to low level

In the future, compilers like Moose will be able to optimize computations for particular privacy and secrecy guarantees and performance.

 To see both MPC and HE in action for private inference, where the model and values remain encrypted, take a look at the Zama + Hugging Face notebook (*https://oreil.ly/pVPxs*) and the Yann Dupis's Moose + Hugging Face notebook (*https://oreil.ly/K49M7*). Because both of these libraries support NumPy-like code, there is much potential to use and expand these use cases.

Imagining a World with Secure Data Sharing

I hope this chapter has stimulated your thinking about how encrypted computation can help real-world data science problems. Encrypted computation has been the most inspiring technology of my career—and something I firmly believe can, and will, change data sharing as we know it.

Today, companies share large quantities of data in plain text—developing complex data sharing agreements that attempt to place legal restrictions on data use, replication, and expiration. Although placing legal restrictions is a good idea, they can never be fully enforced. As you might have seen from your own experience, the practice of taking third-party data and mixing it with core business data is all too prevalent. Without stringent data lineage and governance systems that have formally validated rules and privacy-enhancing technologies, it's difficult to ensure shared data complies with the legal agreements and stringent measures, protecting individual privacy and keeping data secret.

Encrypted computation—particularly areas like MPC—allows you to do data science with accurate results in a shared setting but keep data more secure and confidential. Instead of storing third-party data, you create secure and encrypted processing, with no change in accuracy. Instead of relying on contractual obligations and legalese you might never read but need to understand, you could rely on actual cryptographic protocols and techniques to ensure data is safe.

Distributed and encrypted computation—like what MPC offers out-of-the-box— opens up new possibilities such as those reviewed in Chapter 6. This fosters new collective, collaborative uses of data by creating new distributed ways extremely sensitive data can be shared yet remain secret. MPC is already based on a communal and distributed understanding of trust—one that maps well to the real-world trust people experience as citizens, residents, and community members. In current data science implementations, this trust is transferred to a few powerful parties via vast data aggregation. Instead, this trust could remain close to the user context and wishes, promoting user-driven collaborations and forming computations that benefit the users directly and contribute positively to their world and societies.

In combination with techniques such as federated analytics and distributed data processing, encrypted computation inspires new ways to ensure data remains secret and secure, decrypted only on the user's preferred storage system or as a result of an agreed-upon computation. This can fundamentally change the way data is processed, shared, and used, ensuring that corporate data breaches never release private details about individuals and that the processing is verifiably secure and confidential.

Summary

In this chapter, you learned the fundamental protocols and primary cryptographic principles in encrypted computation. You have a better idea of use cases where encrypted computation can help, including the ability to share, understand, and process data across multiple parties using MPC or to process and return an encrypted piece of data to the user for decryption using HE. You explored different security modeling to better understand how cryptographic protocols offer users truly secure data processing.

You also analyzed some real-world use cases and investigated how to build your own encrypted data processing using open source libraries like Moose. Ideally, you're now open to the possibilities when encryption could add more privacy and security to data science use cases. In Chapter 9, you'll start thinking more holistically about all of the privacy technologies you've learned thus far—figuring out how to look at your problem to evaluate the best fit for your use case. But, before that, in Chapter 8, you'll dive into the legal aspects of privacy to learn how to assess privacy risk and align organizational and regulatory requirements.

## CHAPTER 8

Navigating the Legal Side of Privacy

You've learned so much about privacy definitions and technologies in this book so far. As you apply them in the context of your work, you'll inevitably find this requires understanding the legal aspects of privacy.

Legal factors are not the only reason to apply privacy—nor do I see them as the driver of privacy-first data science. For some, however, they are the primary impetus for implementing privacy-enhancing technologies (PETs). In many large organizations, privacy is first understood as a compliance problem and then later implemented in technology. Even if you consider yourself a privacy champion and want to lead initiatives based on the technology and social aspects of privacy, teaming with the legal or privacy team makes sense. You can use their knowledge and guidance to convince the business of the value of privacy initiatives.

This chapter explores two very different pieces of privacy legislation: the European Union's General Data Protection Regulation (GDPR) and California's Consumer Privacy Act (CCPA). This review will help you understand how to translate regulations into technological decisions and how to review and audit those decisions for compliance.

You'll then take a look at contracts, privacy policies, internal guidelines, and policies to understand how regulatory needs are translated into the organization. Sometimes these are written by internal counsel, other times with external legal assistance, which means you may have access to the people who wrote them—or not! Understanding them to determine how to implement privacy at your organization can be a challenge. You will also learn how to engage with the legal teams at your organization—or at a client's organization—to translate their needs into technological decisions.

Finally, you will revisit governance. You've learned how to define and implement governance in your data science and engineering work, but can you imagine governance in an ideal world? I hope to inspire your thinking on how governance could work if people and their data rights were at the center of our data architectures and implementations.

GDPR: An Overview

GDPR is the European privacy regulation that set a bold global example of privacy and data rights in 2016, when it was finalized. The legislation itself was fairly well understood four years earlier, as teams of EU working parties formulated recommendations that became the basis of the law.

You might know about GDPR from the third-party cookie messages you now see on most websites. I don't think that was how the initial regulators imagined it. In this section, you'll explore the fundamental data rights upheld for people under GDPR and compare those to the ways compliant software has been designed and deployed. My challenge to you is to reimagine ways to deploy compliant software using the knowledge you have learned in this book.

GDPR also isn't settled yet. Case law in Europe during the writing of this book shows that enforcement authorities are beginning to review and rule on new types of cases. This case law changes how GDPR is interpreted and what is considered compliant. These newer cases show a broader understanding of GDPR's reach, calling some business models, like personalized advertising (*https://oreil.ly/q2eKd*) and machine learning on scraped personal data (*https://oreil.ly/xmh6e*), into question. In coming years, the GDPR rights described in this chapter will approach the reality as enforcement expands.

GDPR has also inspired other pieces of legislation, such as the LGPD (Lei Geral de Proteção de Dados Pessoais) in Brazil and several US state legislative proposals. GDPR will surely have longer-term impact in the coming years.

Fundamental Data Rights Under GDPR

GDPR guarantees eight fundamental rights for EU residents and their data, outlined in Table 8-1.

Table 8-1. GDPR data rights

Data right	Description
Right to be informed	People must be informed on how their data is being used, processed, collected, and so forth.
Right to access	People can access what information is held about them.
Right to rectification	People can correct information that is false or misleading.

Data right	Description
Right to deletion/erasure	People can ensure companies delete their data.
Right to restrict processing	People can opt out or restrict how their data is being used and processed.
Right to data portability	People can take their data with them—to use themselves or to try competitor services.
Right to object	People can object to the usage of their data for particular uses (like marketing, research, and several other use cases).
Right to opt out of automated decision making	People can opt out of automated decision making processes, such as algorithmic or machine learning systems.

These are some powerful rights, and they might differ from what was implemented at your organization, or in services you use. These rights apply to EU residents, even when they are not in the EU, although enforcement is easier and more straightforward within the EU.

Each company has a legal team or advisor responsible for interpreting GDPR and defining internal policies, processes, and guidelines, to comply within the operating model of the business. Some companies decided simply to not comply with GDPR and to take on the financial risk that they could be fined. Others went for fairly lax implementations in hopes that it would be enough and that they wouldn't garner attention. As enforcement broadens, the financial risk GDPR poses—up to 4% of global revenue—will likely mean internal policies adapt to better reflect the rights in Table 8-1.

Enforcement—and fines—are the responsibility of local authorities across the EU. For example, in Germany, the local implementation of GDPR is called the Datenschutz-Grundverordnung (DSGVO). Each country has its own version and its own enforcement. Legal communities are well aware of which countries are stricter or more lenient in their interpretation of GDPR. Germany is known to have a stricter interpretation for use of personal data—requiring a double opt-in for all email marketing. France is also quite strict, bringing continuous fines against large tech companies like Google and Facebook for illegal data collection and products that violate GDPR rights.

If you are a European resident and would like to exercise your GDPR rights, take a look at noyb's Exercise your Rights guide (*https://oreil.ly/IWYEe*). noyb, which stands for "My Data is None of Your Business," is a nonprofit organization run by Max Schrems, famous for the Schrems I and Schrems II European lawsuits that invalidated data flows from Europe to the US due to the NSA's snooping on internet activity in the US.

There are many tools, lots of software, and plenty of vendors offering to assist you with compliance. Many companies have built these controls directly into their software and data management systems. You may have been involved in a GPDR compliance migration or retrofitting, which often has to do with ensuring that these rights are semi-automated in data management systems. As you learned in Chapters 1 and 3, knowing where your data comes from and having it properly documented and understood is critical when upgrading your systems for GDPR. Like the example of the consent-tracking pipeline in Chapter 3, these rights are much easier to enable if you know your data, its lineage, the user consent, and what processing it has gone through.

You might also notice some of these rights would require technology or new processes that you don't have right now. Imagine, as part of your governance initiatives, how your data infrastructure would have to change to allow people to automatically port their data, opt out of machine learning systems, or specify what processing they will allow for their data. This might change several parts of your current architecture—and it would be a stimulating team or group activity for a workshop. At the end of such an activity you would have a privacy-first data architecture plan.

> Since this book is focused on privacy technology in data science and not GDPR compliance in data management, I won't go into all of the details of how these rights can be implemented in your systems. There are several good resources for the data management and basic compliance controls, including the EU's GDPR compliance guide (*https://gdpr.eu/compliance*) and *Data Privacy* by Nishant Bhajaria (Manning, 2022) (*https://oreil.ly/s1qhE*).

Implementing these rights requires understanding where your organization and your data processing operates under GDPR. One important distinction is to determine if you are operating as a controller or processor.

Data Controller Versus Data Processor

GDPR outlines two primary data processing roles. The data controller is usually the one with a direct relationship to the people whose data is being collected. In most cases, the controller initially collects the data and its consent. The data processors are companies and services, used by the data controller in this collection, storage, usage, and processing, but they are separate legal entities with their own processing infrastructure—not under purview of the controller.

For example, let's say Amazon web services (AWS) is used by a controller who directly manages, designs, and deploys their data collection infrastructure on AWS using their AWS account. Amazon is a data processor for that company, but the controller is responsible for how the service is used and takes on the liability of using the service compliantly. In many cases, the processors hold the responsibility of appropriately building compliant architecture and data flows, because the controller can often only influence small parts of these choices. When this happens, the controller must perform due diligence to ensure that the processor adequately complies to the controller's needs and requirements under GDPR.

Due Diligence for Data Processors

Usually there is a person or team responsible for performing due diligence on data processors for a company, and you should always check with that team when exploring new vendors or services you want to use, even if they are free or open source.

Consult this team or person early and often, as there might already be an approved vendor or tool for your use case. They can also inform you of assessment requirements and steps that the vendors or open source tools will need to undergo for use in your organization.

If you design an architecture or product around a third-party service and then later find it's not compliant, this will be a hassle not only for you and the entire engineering team but also for the privacy folks who are trying to ensure your company upholds the rights outlined for your customers.

There are very clear roles and responsibilities for these two entities under GDPR. The data controller owns the legal and financial risk and, therefore, has the most at stake in enforcing GDPR and enabling controls in its own software, infrastructure, and products. The data controller sets up a data processing agreement (covered later in the chapter) that outlines how the data will be managed compliantly but does not take on responsibility for the GDPR data rights and compliance decisions.

Your role as a data professional and privacy engineer depends on whether your company is a controller or a processor. If you are working at a place that has a direct relationship with individuals and you are making the strategic decisions about data use, you are likely a controller and hold the responsibility for choosing how to manage that risk directly. If you work for a processor, such as a business-to-business company that helps other companies process personal data, you hold risk differently via the agreements that you make with the controllers.

 As a data processor, you still have obligations under GDPR—like raising your concerns if you believe GDPR compliance is not being followed properly. Depending on your role with the controller, the lines can get blurry. For example, if you are a consultant providing architecture guidance or privacy advising, this could be interpreted as crossing a line, as these are key risk and decision areas for any controller. Get legal advice if you are an independent consultant providing these services.

Regardless of your role, you should never provide legal or compliance advice unless you are a privacy advisor. If a situation gets too confusing or the lines get blurry, the best idea is to get the responsible folks together and outline as a group how to proceed.

In the next section, you'll see how the privacy technologies you've learned in this book can help with GDPR rights and their implementation in running software and data systems in either type of firm.

Applying Privacy-Enhancing Technologies for GDPR

GDPR has several requirements regarding PETs—and more are likely to emerge as case law examines particular approaches to determine their compliance.

Like most privacy regulations, GDPR doesn't name specific technologies in the law. Instead, most regulations try to steer clear of prescriptive remedies (i.e., use this technology and it will be considered compliant) and instead offer higher-level legal language around expected outcomes.

Let's first review one mention of anonymization in the GDPR—outlined in Recital 26:

> The principles of data protection should apply to any information concerning an identified or identifiable natural person. Personal data which have undergone pseudonymisation, which could be attributed to a natural person by the use of additional information should be considered to be information on an identifiable natural person. To determine whether a natural person is identifiable, account should be taken of all the means reasonably likely to be used, such as singling out, either by the controller or by another person to identify the natural person directly or indirectly. To ascertain whether means are reasonably likely to be used to identify the natural person, account should be taken of all objective factors, such as the costs of and the amount of time required for identification, taking into consideration the available technology at the time of the processing and technological developments. The principles of data protection should therefore not apply to anonymous information, namely information which does not relate to an identified or identifiable natural person or to personal data rendered anonymous in such a manner that the data subject is not or no longer identifiable. This Regulation does not therefore concern the processing of such anonymous information, including for statistical or research purposes.

Let's review it piece by piece. First, it outlines that pseudonymized data is not anonymized data. Then it mentions that pseudonymized data can be used with "additional information" to identify a person—you know this from Chapters 1 and 4!

Then, it specifies that, to determine if a person is identifiable, all "reasonable means" should be used such as "singling out" (which you know about from Chapter 4 as well). It outlines several factors that should be considered—costs, time, technology, and processing improvements. This starts sounding a lot like ideas of differential privacy as well as informational theoretical security (Chapters 2 and 7). And then it tells you that if your data has been appropriately anonymized by meeting those guarantees, the data is outside of GDPR and can be used for processing.

 Legal texts and legislation use lots of words to say something that might, in the end, be fairly simple. One tip I've found helpful is to look for the action-oriented parts of the sentence and rephrase them to make them more active. For example, "To determine whether a natural person is identifiable" can be interpreted as "To identify a person…." It helps to read slowly because, often, there are many ideas in one sentence. Obviously, your interpretation will not be a legal one. If in doubt, speak to a lawyer.

Pseudonymization, which you learned about as part of basic privacy methods in Chapter 1, is also recommended throughout GDPR as a way to implement more privacy-friendly systems and to develop with Privacy by Design. If you have customers or services in Europe, it is often recommended that you think about who needs to see what data and use pseudonymization as a way to mitigate accidental exposure of personal data.

Although GDPR does not prescribe a method for anonymization, it does specify how to review methods and compare their security. Interpretation of what is considered a reasonable attempt to anonymize will evolve due to processing and technological developments. As you learned in Chapter 4, the research continues to push forward the boundaries of anonymization methodology.

I've received advice from multiple lawyers; differential privacy is seen as the "gold standard" of anonymization within legal circles. To determine what your organization's take is on anonymization, build a relationship with the legal team, should you have one, or lawyers who are interested in privacy and technology. Later in this chapter you'll learn more about working with legal professionals.

If you employ differential privacy and you've cleared it with legal advisors on your project or at your company, data after you've apply differential privacy mechanisms is no longer subject to GDPR. This is critical for many businesses, as they want to retain information about customer behavior, buying patterns, and other insights even after the customer requests their personal data be removed. But, how does this work when you know that applying differential privacy to individual data points (local differential privacy) is error-prone and very noisy?

Most organizations do not think through *what exactly* they would like to retain and why. This often leads to haphazard solutions and old, broken ways of "anonymization" where only certain parts of the data are removed or hashed (such as customer ID), but all other information is retained.[1] You can do better than that!

To apply anonymization effectively and in a future-friendly manner, you must decide—with top stakeholders at the organization—what data is important to summarize and how. Hoarding data introduces privacy and security risks and avoids clarifying data collection goals and related business needs. At organizations with strong data hoarding you will often find dysfunctional data initiatives lacking clear business goals.

This book isn't about data transformation or how to implement a functional business strategy. There are some great books covering that, including *Good Strategy, Bad Strategy* (Rumelt, 2011), *Competing against Luck* (Christensen et al., 2016), and *Playing to Win* (Lafley, 2013). Certainly, a clear business strategy and a unified vision for data and data value at the organization make it easier to identify the type of analysis and which artifacts to retain regarding your customers, your product, and your market.

 Regardless of GDPR, data retention makes sense only if the data remains valuable to the organization. Talk with your privacy team about what retention schedules are already set. If the data is too stale or your customer population has significantly changed, holding onto old data will not help you achieve business goals. In fact, it might, instead, harm you! As mentioned in Chapter 5, determine how much history is needed to achieve expected performance results. Anonymize or remove data older than that.

Once the data deletion and anonymization requirements are clear, set up regular analysis and artifact creation using differential privacy mechanisms. This should mean the analysis is outside the bounds of GDPR and can be retained when a customer removes their data, but please check with a lawyer! Automate this to be regular and you won't have to run it every time you get a removal request. That person will be represented in prior analyses and artifacts but gone from future ones. The company will benefit from insights about interested and active customers rather than uninterested, passive ones.

Other privacy technologies you learned in this book can guide you to create more privacy-friendly systems from the start. Federated data analysis and federated learning can keep data out of your hands but still provide value. Then you only have to

---

1 The practice of removing IDs, linkage keys, or PII but keeping all other attached person-related data seems to be trending, sometimes referred to as *data decapitation*. Please don't hurt the data; just properly anonymize it! As you already learned, removing these identifiers does nothing for anonymization other than make your life harder when you choose to apply it, as you then need a new way to determine individual contribution.

evaluate the outputs for potential privacy leaks. Technologies like secure computation can help determine who can see the data and ensure confidentiality. In combination with differential privacy, these tools are extremely powerful and allow you to build compliant and secure systems.

But, how can you evaluate whether the system is actually GDPR compliant? This involves communication between your software, data, infrastructure, and legal teams. Luckily, GDPR has some advice on how to best coordinate this conversation via data protection impact assessments.

GDPR's Data Protection Impact Assessment: Agile and Iterative Risk Assessments

The GDPR's Data Protection Impact Assessment (DPIA) is an assessment performed by an organization's technical and legal experts. The goal of a DPIA is to identify potential harms introduced by a use case involving sensitive information and to evaluate ways to potentially reduce or mitigate those harms. At the end of the process, you'll have a decision on whether to move forward and an action plan on how to do so in a privacy-aware way.

This process should remind you of some of the risk assessment and modeling you might have been exposed to as a technologist or when working with security professionals. The major steps in any risk assessment—data protection or otherwise—are outlined in Figure 8-1.

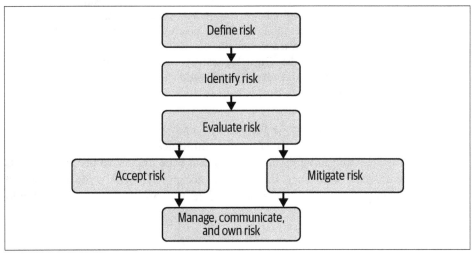

Figure 8-1. Risk assessment process

You begin by defining risk in your context. What do you consider a risk given the setting, participants, technologies and data used? One neat thing about doing these exercises with a multidisciplinary team is that different people will see risk quite differently. You may—after this book—be more cautious about privacy risk than privacy professionals because you now understand the potential for information gain at a technical level.

Next, the team will move on to identifying risk. Once risk is defined, a particular use case is reviewed. Where can you see risk? At what points in the processing or data usage is privacy risk present? How? Why? Having this conversation also builds risk empathy—the ability to see what others define as a risk. This is a superpower in your work and will help you learn more from other skill sets on the team.

Once risk is identified, you'll need to evaluate the risk. If the risk is not addressed, what is the impact? How dangerous is this risk to the users of the service or the people whose data is being processed? And what is the likelihood of this risk occurring? Evaluating privacy risk in a technical way—for example, via definitions like differential privacy—can be enlightening for the team.

This evaluation step is also where your data science skills can help. Breaking the risk down into smaller and more easily measured bits makes it an analysis problem. Does data exist that can help you calculate the probability of the event occurring? The more clearly and precisely this risk is defined, the more likely it is that you can use data at hand or collect data to evaluate if and when this is risk is present.[2]

 Arriving at a common evaluation of risk is a team effort. It's unlikely that all stakeholders will evaluate risk the same way. Here is where risk empathy helps you understand and effectively navigate these conversations. Building psychological safety (*https:// oreil.ly/HTuvX*) on teams that manage risk is absolutely critical to properly evaluate risk. Once that safety is ensured, the team can use critical listening and careful conversation to come to a common evaluation.

After risk is evaluated, you reach a fork in the road. You need to decide either to accept the risk and properly document and communicate it or to mitigate the risk and re-evaluate after that mitigation. If the risk has little impact on people or results from a highly unlikely occurrence, then you can accept it. If a risk is more likely or if it has a large impact on the people whose data you are processing, you should

---

2 One great example from security risk history is the research that exposed Rowhammer (*https://oreil.ly/ PAXEG*), a privilege escalation vulnerability in dynamic RAM; many believed it almost never occurred, but, with experimentation, it was shown to occur fairly regularly. When discovered, it wasn't disclosed if this vulnerability was being actively exploited, but it was managed as an urgent vulnerability by many data center providers.

mitigate that risk. The entire team, of course, should be in agreement on these factors as they are examined in the evaluation process.

There are multiple mitigation strategies if that is the decision, including technologies discussed earlier in this book. Look at easy options as well, such as collecting or processing less data and therefore holding less risk. It's important here that you choose something that is easy to implement, easy to use, and easy to understand given the current systems.[3] This book has focused on accessible methods and libraries so that you have a variety of tools in your toolbox.

Once mitigations are suggested and evaluated, choose which mitigations make the most sense for the organization and the particular data processing at hand. You will also need to communicate the risk and mitigation to the teams involved. Since this risk will leave the initial group and be carried on by the group implementing the processing, they need to properly understand the risk and be able to reason about it as they are working on the software and systems. If you are operating as a privacy engineer or advisor, you will also work alongside them during the implementation to answer questions and to help implement and ensure the implementation is correct.

Regardless if the risk is mitigated or accepted, it needs to be documented and communicated for review from any interested parties and people at the organization. This means breaking it down for a variety of audiences, like you learned in communicating governance standards and work. It is particularly important that the teams holding the risk—with or without mitigation—understand the risk at hand. Here is one nice rule of thumb on communicating: if everyone on the team cannot explain this jointly held risk at some level, you still have some work to do.

At the end, the plan needs to be implemented! This involves choosing what library and tooling to use; choosing the appropriate parameters, which may mean some experimentation and trial and error; and actually writing the code to put mitigations in place. You may be asked to advise this team even if you are not actually implementing the mitigations.

Be sure to review how the system is working, monitoring that things are functioning as expected. This might be as simple as setting up a check in two months from now, or it might mean actively logging and monitoring the system when it hits production for several weeks to ensure everything works as expected. You've ideally already built a relationship with the infrastructure, operations, and monitoring teams to ensure you can access a dashboard or set up alerting, in case you need a thorough analysis of the system.

---

3 Google chose the Paillier-based protocol for Private, Join, and Compute and not a more complex and efficient one. Why? So that software engineers with no experience in cryptography could safely use the helper libraries without additional education.

It doesn't stop there! As you have already learned, the technological and legal landscapes around data privacy are continuously evolving. If a risk assessment is made only once, it likely doesn't have the most up-to-date interpretation of these contexts. Assessment should be performed at regular intervals as part of an agile and iterative cycle.

You will still want to have legal, compliance, infosec, and privacy experts as a core team involved in subsequent DPIA risk assessments. The scope, purpose, and context of the processing are weighed against the privacy risks. GDPR guidance and data subject rights assist the team in determining whether the processing is legal and compliant.

 There are several excellent guides and examples for running a DPIA, and if you work in the EU, you might want to look up one in your local language. These are often prepared by the regulatory authorities and are a great example and conversation starting point for the initial assessments. Here are two good examples in English:

- ICO's DPIA template (*https://oreil.ly/Tjkvk*)
- IAPP's DPIA template (*https://oreil.ly/4werw*)

If you aren't processing data under GDPR, running regular risk assessments and implementing stronger privacy protections inside your organization are still sound ideas. They will help your security team better understand and manage risk, help the privacy team feel comfortable approving more processing, and help your technologists and product teams grow more mature in how they think about and manage sensitive data. It can also help financial liability held by the organization, especially in a changing threat and regulatory landscape.

Beyond DPIAs, GDPR prescribes other changes and obligations for data processing and management. Not all are within the scope of this book, but the right to an explanation brings some interesting and challenging issues for data scientists.

Right to an Explanation: Interpretability and Privacy

The GDPR includes a hotly debated "right to an explanation" when an automated decision is made, discussed in recitals as part of the right to opt out of automated decision making. The goal of this right was to provide some transparency and information for the users so they could decide if they would like to opt out of this type of automated decision-making process.

This right was heavily discussed in machine learning circles as providing an appropriate explanation for a model decision is still an active area of research. Putting aside the complications of providing interpretable explanations for model predictions, it also opens up some interesting questions about privacy.

As you learned in Chapter 4, some explanations are known to leak private information—particularly for outliers in the datasets. In fact, you might be able to find your own information in models that "show" their training data. Have you tried asking GPT-3 if it knows who you are (*https://oreil.ly/ggSRo*)?

Keep in mind that machine learning models contain massive amounts of person-related information. Most people did not think text they wrote online 10 years ago would end up in a future chat model. In the Preface, you read about social aspects of privacy and the context that is often lost when moving from real-world spaces to online spaces. I believe this context loss also occurs online. The social and online setting of a comment, a blog post, or a tweet is lost in massive machine learning training iterations. What does the right to privacy mean in the current machine learning community norms, and how does it affect how you communicate transparently about training data decisions? These types of questions were what the authors of GDPR were trying to address and are worth pondering as you use your privacy engineering knowledge in the field.

GDPR isn't the only law talking about data rights. To establish a global and varied view of privacy regulations, let's examine a more recent California privacy law.

California Consumer Privacy Act (CCPA)

In 2018, California passed the CCPA (*https://oreil.ly/y42GM*), which aims to protect consumers from unwanted data usage. This state law outlines several data rights, including the right to be informed about what data is being collected and how it is used, the right to delete personal information collected, the right to opt out of sale of personal data, and the right to nondiscrimination, which means if you exercise your rights, you should not have a worse experience as a consumer than those who do not. These rights are offered to California residents, even when they are outside of the state of California.

Like GDPR, the intention of the law is that these rights are automated or semi-automated, allowing things such as easy opt-out and deletion requests. Unfortunately, the actual implementation in many software stacks leaves much to be desired—often resulting in the same type of cookie-banner-spam that was seen during the rollout for GDPR.

Unlike GDPR, the CCPA does not have large fines attached to it or the ability to sue for a violation that does not involve a data breach. It is still fairly new legislation that will likely evolve as enforcement continues. There have been several critiques from privacy activists for changes made via lobbying groups.

This led to the creation of the CPRA (*https://oreil.ly/gmqne*). This law passed by ballot proposition, and enforcement begins in 2023. It modifies several aspects of CCPA, including expanding the definition of sensitive data use, establishing a separate authority for enforcement, removing the time period to correct violations without a penalty, increasing some of the fines, and adding new avenues to how privacy lawsuits can be brought against companies. Since it is not yet enforced at the writing of this book, it's difficult to understand how it will change in normal operations—but it does clearly show that sensitive data processing and use will change quickly.

CCPA has some case law, but not much—as plaintiffs can bring lawsuits against companies only if there is a data breach due to insufficient protections and there is no dedicated state enforcement body. Beyond changing the normal consent and usage flows, it is not yet clear how CCPA will affect data protection in the US. Some of this uncertainty will clear only as CPRA goes into effect—and the state's authority begins investigating sensitive data usage.

Applying PETs for CCPA

CCPA has different specificity around PETs and privacy measures than GDPR. The law does not mention anonymization but instead defines de-identification.

> "De-identified" means information that cannot reasonably identify, relate to, describe, be capable of being associated with, or be linked, directly or indirectly, to a particular consumer, provided that a business that uses de-identified information: (1) Has implemented technical safeguards that prohibit re-identification of the consumer to whom the information may pertain. (2) Has implemented business processes that specifically prohibit re-identification of the information. (3) Has implemented business processes to prevent inadvertent release of de-identified information. (4) Makes no attempt to re-identify the information.

Let's break down this part of the legislation and compare it with GDPR. You can see that de-identified data might be similar to the definition for anonymization, in that it cannot be used to "reasonably" associate with, link, or "directly or indirectly" identify or describe a particular person. What CCPA doesn't have is examples of what might be part of a reasonable test, which GDPR outlined.

What CCPA does have is a specific list of requirements for de-identification—including technical safeguards against re-identification, business processes prohibiting re-identification, release of that information, and/or re-identification by the business. Here, business processes refers to both technical processes and policies to prevent those behaviors such as access control restrictions. If a business can prove the data is de-identified, it no longer is defined as personal information and therefore falls outside of the legal obligations for processing data.

Perhaps you have noticed that this description is very high level and doesn't map easily to the techniques you've learned in this book. This is one of the criticisms of the legislation by many privacy activists. What exactly is an attempt to re-identify the information? For example, could a targeted advertisement based on my location and gender be a re-identification? Legal advice around CCPA has mentioned the law is kept vague purposefully, allowing for a broader understanding of interventions that permit weaker standards than GDPR.

CCPA advice often focuses on basic privacy measures, such as pseudonymization and tokenization as a technological safeguard against re-identification. Based on this interpretation and advice, it appears that older, broken methods of anonymization like k-anonymity on its own—even without l-diversity and t-closeness—would be considered valid de-identification methods.

This means that in comparison to the bar set by GDPR, CCPA currently accepts much weaker privacy technologies than you have learned in this book. Over time, however, case law and clearer definitions will evolve this legislation and enforcement. It is likely that the basic measures you learned in Chapter 1 are enough to prepare your organization for CCPA enforcement. Automating those measures as outlined in Chapter 3 could also be useful for creating easier compliance so you can see consent workflows and automate deletion requests.

It remains to be seen how companies will implement CPRA and how the new California data protection authorities will choose to view the law. Thinking future-forward and approaching almost all legislation as possible to change or open to interpretation are good starting points.

CCPA, GDPR, and CPRA aren't the only players; there is much more legislation already in the works and passed in recent years. Let's review a few more to give a more expansive view.

Other Regulations: HIPAA, LGPD, PIPL, and More!

CCPA and GDPR are two regulations within a massive global landscape. Learning how to navigate this landscape can be intimidating, but from what you have learned so far, you can begin reading and understanding legislation and evaluate how the technologies you know might be applied.

Let's try your improved reasoning skills by looking at the US Health Insurance Portability and Accountability Act (HIPAA) (*https://oreil.ly/CPcBf*), which regulates how all health documents are treated nationwide. HIPAA outlines what types of health information are considered sensitive, appropriate protection for health-related data, and safe and compliant data releases. The law went into effect in 1996; as you can imagine, it is quite different from more recent laws.

For example, there are two different ways to release health data for safe usage under HIPAA. You might compare this with GDPR or CCPA advice on when data is no longer subject to compliance requirements.

Under HIPAA, you can release health data to others if you can prove that it meets "Safe Harbor" (*https://oreil.ly/cGeZ3*), requiring de-identification of certain fields containing PII—things such as hospital admittance date, release date, patient birthday, gender, and so forth. The general advice is to remove those data points entirely. However, as you know from the attacks outlined in Chapter 4, this does not prevent singling-out attacks or other inferences an attacker could make based on the data that is released. For example, if a disease or medicine tends to affect one part of the population more than another, an attacker might be able to infer the gender, age, or race of a particular patient. If there is external information available, such as travel details to and from treatments from another data processor, then this information could be linked using techniques like those used in the Netflix prize attack.

Under HIPAA, another method for releasing data is called an *expert determination* test. Here are the steps for performing that test:

1. You must identify a person with appropriate statistical and scientific knowledge of and experience in rendering information not individually identifiable.

2. That person then applies those principles and methods, and they conclude whether the privacy risk is small enough. To do so, they consider the data alone and in combination with other available information and determine the difficulty to identify an individual in that data.

3. They must document the methods and results of the analysis that justify such determination.

As you can see, this requires reasoning about what information an attacker might have rather than thinking about the properties of the data protection mechanism. It also puts the determination in the hands of a party that may or may not know about technologies such as differential privacy or may not think those technologies apply to HIPAA. This could also create quite a bit of variance in expert ratings, as seen in security expert ratings from Chapter 4.

Following the use of either method, the data is considered "anonymized" and can be released. It is obvious that this is a more lenient understanding of data privacy compared with GDPR.

Let's review another law. Brazil has one of the most stringent data protection laws, the Lei Geral de Proteção de Dados Pessoais (LGPD) (*https://oreil.ly/q3Km3*). The law, which was passed in 2018, went into effect in 2020 and is heavily modeled after GDPR. Most of the concepts covered in "GDPR: An Overview" on page 202 apply to LGPD, including data rights, the role of processor versus controller, and the impact assessments. Therefore, if you are collecting or processing data in Brazil, you'll want to treat it just as you do EU data. Yet to be seen is how this will be enforced over a longer time frame, but your legal team can provide more context.

There is also the Chinese data protection law, the Personal Information Protection Law (PIPL) from 2021 (*https://oreil.ly/Z36ld/*). Although there haven't been many public examples of enforcement, the law defines anonymization as "a process in which the personal information is processed so that it is impossible to identify a certain natural person and unable to be reversed." If understood literally, this is a significant bar to achieve and might mean using stronger differential privacy mechanisms or destroying more information to guarantee that the process is compliant.

The global legal sector is heating up for data privacy and protection regulations and individual case law. Because this book won't reflect the latest legal news, review articles from the International Association of Privacy Professionals (IAPP) (*https://iapp.org*) and regularly talk with your legal team to keep your understanding up-to-date.

In addition to regulatory requirements, there are often internal organizational requirements for data privacy and security initiatives, guidelines, and obligations. While some of these are derived from regulations and how those are interpreted for a particular company, others are specific to how a company plans to use, manage, and implement data privacy and security controls. It is important to learn how to read internal policies and contracts and ask for help from your legal team as you consider applying technologies you have learned from this book.

Internal Policies and Contracts

Reading internal policies and business contracts can be the hardest part of understanding and implementing privacy initiatives at most organizations. These internal policies are often a mixture of advice from legal, business, and technical leadership at an organization. This mixture can sometimes mean that the policies or contracts are difficult to implement and interpret.

That said, these are critical because they contain your organization's direct advice for adherence to compliance requirements in regulations. These policies may also outline specific rules leadership has set to reflect the business needs relating to privacy and security. Some organizations might have additional requirements due to contractual obligations. For example, an organization that works directly with a government is likely to have specific security and privacy requirements based on those contracts and the nature of the work.

You might have already read many internal policies and contracts or been through required trainings. If so, that's great because you already have an idea of how your organization thinks about privacy and security, technological implementations and guidelines, and what types of data your organization considers sensitive. Sometimes, though, these trainings are high level and don't answer the specific questions you might have about the actual text of the policies or guidelines or how those are interpreted in relation to your data science work. Actually reading the policy can help you better orient your work.

Reading these policies, contracts, and legal texts can be daunting, and you should always use legal support to figure out what exactly is intended. You'll learn more about how to work with legal professionals on these questions later in this chapter. But first, let's see how to use the skills you've learned so far to investigate company legal documents related to data privacy and security.

Reading Privacy Policies and Terms of Service

Reading your own company's privacy policy and terms of service can be quite enlightening as it might show you a different side of your organization's take on privacy by showing how the company communicates privacy to users. This exercise builds user empathy and understanding, showing how difficult it can be as a user to understand how your data is used and how to exercise your data rights. The length and the complexity of the text can significantly impact users' ability to understand what they are agreeing to, how their data will be used, and how to exercise their data rights.

The *New York Times* ran a study of more than 150 privacy policies and provided an interactive feature (*https://oreil.ly/fEHgR*) for investigating the complexity and length of those policies over time. According to the analysis, some policies took hours to read and a doctorate degree to understand. That has since changed. They concluded that GDPR significantly reduced the time and effort required to read privacy policies. One of GDPR's major goals was to set clearer expectations of privacy and more user-friendly privacy controls.

Let's analyze an easy-to-read privacy policy from the Signal app, the encrypted messenger service (*https://oreil.ly/IUZQC*):

Information that is used and collected
Here Signal outlines what types of information are collected or used by the application in user-friendly language. In the sections, they provide clear examples of the protections applied to that data with links to more documentation on how these protections are implemented. They give real-life examples of when that data is used and how it is used. You might notice a reference to private joins in how Signal finds other contacts who use Signal, which you now know about from Chapter 7.

Information that is shared
Here Signal outlines third-party providers and what data they receive and for what purposes. Unfortunately, they do not clearly list those third-party providers, but the policy may have changed by the time you read this. A better list of third-party providers, their use, and their location is included in the Hugging

Face Privacy Policy (*https://oreil.ly/EjH8y*). Signal also then outlines when the data might be shared in abnormal conditions—like when a law enforcement agency contacts them with a warrant or subpoena.

Updates, terms, and contact information
The other recommended fields for a privacy policy are included here, so readers know how and when policies are updated, what the terms of the service are, and how to contact the privacy team with questions.

That's it! Not all privacy policies are so clear and simple. You can absolutely find examples of long and convoluted policies within the services you use. GDPR is thankfully making privacy policies more legible over time. Perhaps your company has already implemented this user-friendly approach.

The terms of service are often also attached in the privacy policy and are frequently full of legalese. There are some boilerplate texts or sections that are commonly used to protect the company against lawsuits, such as the disclaimers and limitations. GDPR has inspired many terms of service to provide references to the privacy and protection of data when using the service though these are often also covered in the privacy policy itself. Terms of service will also generally describe how to legally use the service and what the service will do if you violate the terms. This can include both direct examples or specific outlines regarding correct usage of the service. Most of these don't apply to your work as a data scientist or privacy engineer.

The shift toward understandable privacy policy also created pages explaining how people can toggle privacy controls, better evaluate how their data is being used, and change consent options. This has led to privacy policies like the BBC's example—with clear question and answer sections written in plain language (*https://oreil.ly/wXdSW*). Many companies with managed consent options have created helpful guides for users on how to check their current settings and easily change them.[4]

Examples of customer-friendly walkthroughs of privacy policies and private data collection toggles are often found where companies have been under public scrutiny to provide better privacy settings. For example, Facebook's Privacy Checkup tool (*https://oreil.ly/AG7_z*) and Amazon's Alexa Privacy Center (*https://oreil.ly/OF41v*) are fairly well-thought-through pages with clear examples and easy how-tos. As you learned in Chapter 1, fine-grained consent options are essential for Privacy by Design.

---

4 Although this is a step along the path to Privacy by Design, the safest way to ensure users are protected is to provide safe, secure, and privacy-aware defaults. Many users never check these setting or alter them unless directly prompted to do so.

Some privacy policies also outline data processors that the company uses. This is particularly relevant if your company operates as a data processor instead of a controller.

Reading Data Processing Agreements

Data processing agreements (DPAs) are legal agreements between a data controller and a data processor under GDPR that outline compliant data processing requirements for both parties. You may have seen these before when you've signed up to use a data processing service.

A DPA will normally outline how a processor should treat personal information during the processing and allow the data controller to provide that information to the individuals who might be affected. For example, if you are a data controller who provides an e-commerce storefront to your customers, you probably collect payment information and use a payment service like Stripe or PayPal to process payments. A DPA would outline how that personal data is sent to that service and how Stripe or PayPal can use that data.

In practice, smaller companies have little influence over DPAs and must accept the DPAs offered by the services. Let's take a look at an example DPA from Mailjet, an email sending provider (*https://oreil.ly/Exm6Z*), to see how this works:

Definitions
> Like many legal documents, most DPAs start with a definition of terms used throughout the document. This will include definitions for important terms like *controller* and *processor* and references to regulations and other common terms used throughout the document.

Details and scope
> This is the most important section to understand as a data person. This section outlines the details of the data processing and bounds the scope as best as possible. Like in this Mailjet example, it usually outlines the type of personal data processed, how and why that data is processed, and the responsibilities of the controller and processor. These sections can be filled with jargon, so go through each sentence and reword it for yourself in easier language. Should you have difficulty understanding a sentence or section while reviewing services for your data work, consult your legal department for clarity.

Controller and processor roles
> As this agreement is explicitly between a controller and processor, there are usually long sections around the roles and responsibilities of these entities.

Security and privacy controls and compliance with privacy rights
> If there are particular security and privacy controls provided by the processor, these are outlined in one or more following sections. A quick scan can show you which sections might be relevant for your work or if you are curious and evaluating several processors and want to compare their privacy and security maturity.

Other legal sections: transfers, subprocessing, termination
> There are a number of other required sections, and these are likely to change over time. The transfers section can be a fun read to see how the company is complying with transatlantic data flows after Schrems II, but most of these sections are not relevant for your work as a data scientist or privacy engineer.

If you are a data processor, your legal and privacy teams should be able to tell you what DPAs your company is actively supporting and walk you through how the controls outlined in those documents are best understood. These may also point to other internal policies and contracts or have ripple effects for internal guidelines. It's essential to understand these, as they might contain the overall approach to data processing, data risk, and regulatory oversight.

Reading Policies, Guidelines, and Contracts

Internal privacy principles or guidelines give you the best start in understanding how privacy is implemented at your organization. These are often used by companies to aggregate the vast array of data protection requirements, creating a single summary for employees.

As with any document of principles or guidelines, don't expect these to describe *how* to actually implement privacy controls. For that guidance, you should talk to the infosec team; they often have a list of appropriate controls for security and privacy measures.

These principles or policies show how your privacy team talks about privacy and gives advice. The privacy team will also outline the baseline for the organization on how privacy is treated and implemented. This could define acceptable uses or describe assessment processes for use cases. You might have already been through a use case assessment process if you had to write a memo to the privacy team outlining a particular use case and justification for the data usage.

If your company has other important internal contracts, such as agreements with third-party services or providers, these should be referenced somewhere in the other documents. It doesn't hurt to ask explicitly for guidance should you want to better understand the risks and responsibilities for these third-party providers.

If you are interested in reading longer frameworks and ways to approach data privacy from a technical and legal point of view, here are a few longer reads:

- Germany's Data Ethics Commission report (*https://oreil.ly/UglA8*)
- The ICO's Anonymization Decision Making Framework (*https://oreil.ly/QFTMK*)
- The annual reports from France's regulatory authority (CNIL), currently available only in French (*https://www.cnil.fr*)

Getting advice and guidance directly from the privacy team for anything not outlined in these principles or standards is always helpful. In the next section, you'll learn how to nurture your working relationship with the privacy team into an effective and informative one.

Working with Legal Professionals

When you work in data governance, you are working very closely with legal professionals. Working with legal and compliance staff might seem difficult, but that's primarily because their area of expertise is so different from your own. Their legal language is just like your statistical language—understandable to those in your field and completely unintelligible to those outside. You don't need to get a law degree, but try to learn enough legal jargon to have a productive conversation about data privacy risks and potential remediation or solutions for those risks.

A corporate lawyer responsible for data privacy and data use will generally be taught to think about a problem as a risk probability exercise. They are empowered to understand and interpret related laws and to evaluate what the company is doing to both comply and/or exceed the standards of the law. Think of them as data privacy referees; they know the rules, and they are watching the game and officiating. Some referees also know what it's like to be a player on the field, others not so much.

The technical understanding of these legal professionals will vary, but, again, technical deployment of privacy and governance policy is not their primary job. It is, however, part of your job. Here's where things can get interesting. If you can learn to approach them and their expertise inquisitively, you will often pique their curiosity about your work and domain expertise. Instead of viewing their "No, you cannot use this service due to privacy concerns" as the end of the discussion, treat that "no" as an opportunity to learn more about privacy risk. What exactly about that service is out of bounds? Are there ways to turn the "no" into a "yes" if you were to use a different service or if you were to prepare the data using techniques from this book? These are moments to collaborate and learn instead of turning away.

In the field of privacy engineering, a major part of the role will be helping legal professionals ensure that planned and upcoming privacy initiatives are followed, used, and championed across the organization. Most governance councils, boards, or entities are legal professionals, with some technologists and business professionals to ensure governance policy and measures match the organizational capabilities.

Getting to know more about their job and primary concerns offers a way to open a conversation. Legal professionals dealing with data management face particular types of problems. Let's review them so you have a general and basic understanding of the lay of the land.

Adhering to Contractual Agreements and Contract Law

If your company participates in data sharing, it is probably governed by a contract, and that agreement is subject to contract law and dependent on the other parties in the contract. Ideally, you are in a place where contractual agreements are standardized and not often changed so you can learn the basic rules and adhere to them. If not, you'll need to check with legal quite regularly to determine if the data you use or provide has new or updated restrictions.

Data sharing contract agreements usually have strict clauses around data use. This is particularly important for data science teams to learn. If that data can be used only in relation to one specific task or sets of tasks (for example, the data can be used only to update a shared service or model that all parties have access to), then using that data or even its artifacts in other areas of the team's work would violate the contract and potentially the data subject rights. Talk with a lawyer and get a clear idea of what parts of contractual law and what types of contracts affect your data and work.

Interpreting Data Protection Regulations

It's becoming commonplace for organizations to have legal professionals who specialize in data protection. These folks are absolute gold for your data privacy work. Network with lawyers specialized in these areas. Part of their job is to stay up-to-date on privacy issues, future legislation, and changes in case law and precedents around privacy. They often specialize because they really care about privacy, so they are treasure troves of interesting stories and examples!

For their daily work and concerns, legal privacy professionals must interpret how data privacy regulations in your jurisdiction(s) are followed and influence related internal policies. If you serve customers in an area without many privacy regulations, your organization's privacy staff are there to determine basic precedents and standards and might be primarily focused on cybersecurity. If you serve customers in multiple regions where at least one region has stronger regulations, these professionals are the person (or people) on the line for ensuring compliance. This means it is part of their job to say no if they believe that is the best way to adhere to the law.

For example, when Schrems II (*https://oreil.ly/-wuqR*) went into effect, it changed the legal understanding of data flows between the European Union and the United States. It essentially invalidated the way companies had been doing that for many years. From a data science perspective, this is like a global pandemic breaking all the deployed models, forcing everyone to scramble to put the pieces back together. Luckily, the European Court provided some guidance, and legal professionals were able to create new contracts that adhered to the new standards for now.

If your company deals with European data flows or serves European customers, then the data protection authorities are ensuring you adhere to GDPR. This means your organization can be audited at any time for data protection impact assessments, data processing agreements, and internal standards that outline compliant data management and processing. These authorities check with your privacy teams should it come to their attention that GDPR is not being followed or that users are unable to easily exercise their rights.

Since every company may interpret these regulations slightly differently and since case law and enforcement can vary from country to country, it's a good idea to collaborate with the data protection professionals at your company and build compliance into the way your team works. Your role as a data scientist who also knows advanced privacy definitions and technologies can be incredibly helpful for keeping data, business, product, and compliance goals aligned. That's likely one reason why you picked up this book.

Asking for Help and Advice

To build a solid relationship with legal professionals and understanding of the regulatory aspects that apply to your organization, talk to your privacy and compliance team. Spark up the conversation by asking for help and advice on a specific use case.

I had a chance to work closely with George Jones, a privacy professional at Thoughtworks (*https://oreil.ly/RPjhI*). One conversation stuck with me. He said, "Sometimes data or software teams don't come to us with problems, because they think they are going to wake a sleeping bear, and then that bear will come sniffing around and figure out what they are doing. But, actually, that's our job—and we're going to come sniffing around whether you ask us or not!" So, better to be proactive than reactive.

Most legal professionals know their specialty is not top of mind for technologists and have found ways to make the topic more digestible for data and technology specialists. Meeting them where they are by learning a bit about their field goes a long way. Did you know that data protection as a human right is outlined under the Human Rights Convention (*https://oreil.ly/d2BrP*), created after World War II? Gaining an understanding of the field and your team's concerns helps build rapport and alignment.

When meeting with privacy legal professionals, come prepared with questions and make sure you have already explored possible approaches. This will make the conversation more efficient and show that you respect their time and work. Getting their input on important data architecture and processing decisions can be instructive, especially at project or product inception, where you can more easily adapt and incorporate feedback.

Having regular conversations builds shared understanding, which is tremendously useful for your collaboration and proper implementation of privacy technology at your organization. You also need a shared vocabulary.

Working Together on Shared Definitions and Ideas

One of the jobs of the privacy and compliance team is to formulate definitions for important terms like PII, personal data, and confidential data. Your privacy team probably already has this glossary somewhere, and you can read it to become familiar with the organizational definitions.

For mitigations and privacy protections, they might already have clear definitions, or it might look more like the guidance provided by regulations. Whereas some companies might have a list of approved technologies or their understanding of topics like anonymization and pseudonymization, others might have definitions that describe the process, not the actual implementation. Those teams might, in fact, want to keep it general and not approve particular technologies as compliant or not. In any case, it is a conversation worth having now that you have a better understanding of these technologies and their uses.

Working with the privacy and compliance team to create some shared technical definitions and approaches can be rewarding and informative. This can help technologists de-risk projects early by incorporating approved technologies in their design. It can also help the privacy team better understand the data goals and provide more concrete advice. They might still want to review choices on a case-by-case basis, but these conversations clarify appropriate approaches for different types of data processing, and your knowledge can accelerate future decisions.

Starting this conversation might also mean you have a chance to teach them about privacy technologies and how they fit in your organization.

Providing Technical Guidance

Privacy professionals are usually very open for learning. Personally, I have yet to meet a privacy expert who doesn't want to learn more about the technical aspects of their job. If you are building a collegial relationship with your privacy professionals, they might start to come to you with technical questions as well.

What you might not expect is how much they already know about the data at the organization. Until you remember, this is part of their job! When providing technical guidance to these teams, have them first explain what they already know about data processing in question to use the time wisely and focus on more specific questions rather than speaking too generally.

Some privacy professions really do want to dive deeper into the way things work, for example, wanting to learn how machine learning algorithms train models, how encryption protocols work, and how differential privacy mechanisms function. This is where the knowledge you have from this book can shine. Teaching them about the standards in the field of data and privacy engineering can help them better see and understand risk and risk mitigation—likely making future data conversations much easier.

This provides better ideas and solutions when you are pitching new data ideas at the organization. How can you learn to "see" the privacy problems as a new data project or product is being developed? How can you then understand enough about the solution space to suggest useful interventions, changes, or mitigations? By regularly discussing these topics with the privacy team, you'll build that risk empathy muscle, coming up with better ideas each time.

This relationship is a reciprocal one. Helping them do their job more effectively and with more knowledge helps you, and vice versa. Treat this as a mutually supportive relationship and reap the benefits personally and for the entire team. Learning how privacy professionals see the world opens up new perspectives such as what data governance could look like in the future.

Data Governance 2.0

Reading this book has probably helped you realize that most companies implement governance without the benefit of the interesting research and technical accomplishments of the past 10 years. The processes might not even align with the rapid changes seen in privacy regulation, requiring "retrofitting" of policies and processes. Unfortunately, this can leave everyone more confused than before.

This is exactly why the governance process needs a rehaul. You've now learned innovative privacy technology and privacy engineering—and how to work with legal departments and regulatory authorities. The next iteration for governance, which I call Data Governance 2.0, is to approach governance with agile ways of working and an iterative scientific method. Governance needs ways to ideate, experiment, test, and incorporate new ideas that work as smoothly as possible. Instead of a cautious reactive mode, governance could be a proactive and explorative field—where legal, compliance, and risk specialists work with technologists to develop road maps and deliver technology with privacy built in.

To do this, governance needs to be something that all parts of the organization can grasp. It needs to be something that teams can talk about and integrate with their planning. To do so, governance needs to become more federated and less centralized. How could this work?

What Is Federated Governance?

As I joined Thoughtworks in early 2022, I first encountered the concept of data meshes (*https://oreil.ly/OQFFv*), a way to reimagine data via domain-driven design, product thinking, and multidisciplinary teams developed by Zhamak Dehghani. Regardless of your opinions on the entire philosophy and approach, I was fascinated by the concept of federated governance. It inspired a blog series (*https://oreil.ly/Z-gCz*) I wrote on privacy-first mesh and this small section of the book.

What is federated governance? In *Data Mesh* (Dehghani, 2022) it is actually called *federated computational governance* and aims to create data SLAs/SLOs and metrics to evaluate the data product quality. Governance is federated by being spread across domains that can be vastly different. The governance part of Dehghani's original idea (*https://oreil.ly/7Dbf7*) creates consistency, interoperability, and easier comparisons and oversight of the variety of data products.

As I read her book, I saw a different possibility. I realized that what I call *governance* (privacy- and compliance-centric) could be transformed into something more manageable, more proactive, and more agile. What if teams were able to experiment with privacy technologies and report their results? What if these successes could be built from the ground up instead of coming from a top-down policy that doesn't necessarily address the technologies that could or should be used? And what if this opened clearer lines of communication between these teams and the legal department themselves?

To me, federated governance is a way of incorporating expert-led assessments of critical governance issues into the actual day-to-day functioning of a technology company. Governance leadership still needs to play a strong role, including analyzing upcoming and changing regulations and the organization's relationship to its customers. This planning from the executive team can set an agenda that distributes a vision and priorities that spark bottoms-up team-led ideas to test and experiments to run. This process leverages team knowledge and competence and aligns business goals with day-to-day work.

From these experiments, there will be some that succeed and others that fail. These teach the teams as well as the leadership more about what works and what doesn't. From the successes, there is a path forward and an eventual iteration onto other pressing governance issues. Instead of retrofitting a large regulation like GDPR, teams could have been well prepared in the two years where the law was known but not yet enforced.

This process could look like Figure 8-2. This shows the same iterative cycle you might know from your data science work. It starts with an expert assessment to prioritize what governance needs exist. Then, it moves to teams that work closely with the types of data processing or data in question. Those teams can look at their own priorities and backlog and determine how to incorporate one experiment into their upcoming work. Your skills and others with similar skill sets will be needed to help experiment and integrate privacy technologies.

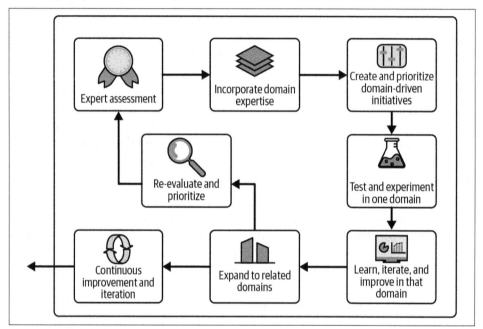

Figure 8-2. Agile federated governance

They actually then run the experiment and have results—either it was successful or a failure or they need to revise and repeat. At some point, they report back to the governance specialists as well as other leadership with a recommendation: should this experiment become the new way of doing things, or does it need changes to adapt to the way the teams function? What other teams might be interested to try it or to iterate on the ideas? This is also when platform and systems teams will need to imagine how to scale the solution.

If the experiment was a failure, there will still be learnings to share with related teams and governance stakeholders. The cycle then begins again with more ideation on what is possible and how to prioritize governance initiatives alongside technology and business needs.

For this process to succeed, the organization needs to be open to experimentation. If this isn't already the case at your organization, there are ways to jump-start the process.

Supporting a Culture of Experimentation

You are already familiar with cultures of experimentation. As a data scientist, you are asked to experiment, learn, and iterate as a daily part of your work. You are, therefore, likely to know if your current organization embraces this culture or sees it as a nuisance.

If your organization already supports iterative and incremental experimentation, you can skip this section and move onto the next one—hooray! If not, this section provides guidance on how you can create more willingness to experiment. This actually starts somewhere you might not have expected—with feelings!

In my own career, I have clashed with leadership that is unwilling to support research needs. Those conflicts made me realize that these leaders were simply afraid of the unknown. When you experiment daily, you learn to trust the process. Even if a particular experiment fails, you know you will eventually find something that works and that through those failures you will learn and grow. Many leaders, however, did not find success this way, and they may view this process as chaotic, disruptive, and uncertain. Why take an unnecessary risk when you can have the same success without those risks?

Psychological safety in teams means building empathetic understanding of the other person's needs (*https://oreil.ly/DBX3d*). If you find that a person in management or leadership is emotionally reacting to conversations around experimentation, ask yourself, why is this person reacting this way? What might they need, thinly veiled by their reactive language? How can you find a way to discuss the process and facts, rather than their reactive feelings? There are many approaches, but, for me, what worked is studying nonviolent communication (*https://www.nycnvc.org*), which states that all feelings come from unmet needs and teaches compassionate communication between individuals. You might find a different process or way that works for you, but the important first step is to build empathy and, via that empathy, psychological safety.

Once you've had the feelings conversations, you should notice a shift in the dialogue. Because folks are no longer reacting from fear, anxiety, or frustration, they will be more open to finding a compromise. You want to teach them to trust the scientific process. It might mean making compromises, such as timeboxing experiments or deciding when to call an experiment a failure and to move on. The critical outcome is a mutually agreed upon way to experiment and learn.

Up to this point, the conversation has been quite interpersonal. Ideally securing buy-in from those people allows you to shift the conversation to the organizational level. Working with experts in organizational change and psychological safety is a great way to accelerate this change, but you can also work incrementally.

In the end, you want a culture that embraces some level of experimentation, including the domains of privacy and governance. This reframes the governance conversation from one focused on old methods to one about forward-looking initiatives, including using privacy enhancing technologies and other techniques you've discovered in this book.

Documentation That Works, Platforms with PETs

Incorporating what you've learned into your daily work will mean helping put guardrails in place to enable easier usage of privacy technologies. How can you empower teams to document data as it is ingested? How can your company embrace PETs[5] and embed them in software and data system functionality?

If the industry is going to move to Governance 2.0, these technologies should be table stakes. Data teams should not have to know how encrypted computation works in order to use it, just as they don't need to know the internals of a Spark query to run one. For this reason, these tools need to be made more digestible and, if possible, built directly into platform systems they can use.

Building self-documenting systems, whose documentation is easy for humans to understand, is another large, unsolved problem space. Data lineage, tracking, and enforcement of policies are largely manual at many companies. For Governance 2.0 to be actualized, this must shift, and these features must be built directly into software and data workflows so that implementing data rights in software is simple and usual.

This is obviously a task for more than one person, which means that it's likely discussed as part of a company, software, or technology vision. If you are in a leadership team or have influence in the organization, you can help set this as an important agenda item to move the initiatives forward.

But, supposing you are still early in your career path, you can still use what you have learned in your work. It just means narrowing the scope. Look at your next project and evaluate—is there a way to build self-documentation into this pipeline? If you

---

5 Hat tip to Chris Ford (*https://oreil.ly/8NS-q*) for suggesting you approach this topic by asking for PETs, not cattle.

have a chance to evaluate an emerging technology, how can you introduce the subject of PETs?

You'll learn more about looking at real-world problems and evaluating how PETs fit in the next two chapters, including steps toward a new type of governance that is built into systems, rather than bolted on.

Summary

In this chapter, you learned how to read regulations, evaluate the impact of privacy, look at terms of service and privacy policies, and interpret how those texts might affect your work as a data scientist. You also gained empathy for legal professionals and some tools for enabling collaborative conversations. You began to re-evaluate the governance basics you learned in Chapter 1. What does the governance of the future look like? What if PETs were a normal part of daily data workflows and platforms?

In the next chapters, you'll dive directly into addressing these forward-facing questions. This will help transition your learning from academic understanding to a practical one by looking at real-world problems and questions.

## CHAPTER 9

Privacy and Practicality Considerations

Throughout this book, you've learned a number of different technologies and concepts in data privacy. You've used open source libraries and tools to implement some of them right out of the box.

But, as with most interesting problems in technology, data privacy has no one-size-fits-all solution. You'll need to take what you learned in this book and figure out how it fits new use cases and problems you encounter in your work. You need to practice how to actually "see" these problems and how to apply the technologies and concepts for appropriate use cases.

In this chapter, you're going to learn how to do just that. I'll help you walk through several use cases with different privacy risk profiles and show you what a future-thinking solution could be. Walking through these examples will help you learn how to spot privacy risks and opportunities to improve current approaches. This chapter will help you approach use cases with a practical mindset—able to figure out how to tackle a privacy risk problem without veering into unnecessary complexity.

The first step will always require thinking about managing privacy risk in practical ways. Since it is unlikely that you can mitigate all privacy risks for all use cases, especially at organizations that hold personal data or that serve many customers, you need to determine how to communicate clearly about risk and manage it transparently.

Getting Practical: Managing Privacy and Security Risk

As you exercise your new knowledge, you will inevitably be pulled into more conversations around privacy and risk. Your opinion and ideas will be incorporated into a group of security and privacy experts and decision makers across the organization. In these situations, you'll need to communicate what risk appetite[1] you believe is appropriate given the scenario.

If you are new to managing risk, this can be an overwhelming experience. There is a lot of pressure to give the "right" advice or to make the "right" decision. If you have perfectionist tendencies, this can be very stressful. Realizing that these are largely not life-or-death decisions and that the process is iterative can help you navigate these moments and avoid freezing at critical junctures.

To make better decisions and to determine when an issue is truly mission critical, you'll need to use your data knowledge, risk empathy, and practical privacy knowledge. These are the essential skills for the risk modeling evaluation step as covered in Chapter 8. By leveraging these skills, you will offer sage advice for determining next steps and managing the owned risk.

Evaluating and Managing Privacy Risk

Privacy risk will look different at every organization, and it's likely you'll see several different levels of risk appetite if you switch industries. One key factor in determining how to assess privacy risk at an organization is to determine the organization's risk appetite (*https://oreil.ly/mQH-i*). If you work in Europe, for example, or in a highly regulated industry such as finance or healthcare, you will observe much less privacy risk appetite. This is due to the more stringent regulations and larger risks and the culture that those risks engender at the organization.

 When an organizational has strong regulatory pressure, especially for long periods or even from the beginning of the organization, this is reflected in the overall organizational culture. This often means risks are more clearly noticed and understood, which is very helpful! But sometimes this also presents itself as general fear or uncertainty when anything new is suggested. More on managing this in "Embracing Uncertainty While Planning for the Future" on page 236.

---

1 Depending on your organization or use case, there might already be a well-known risk appetite, and you will be evaluating the risk and potential mitigations to fit this risk appetite. Otherwise, you will be asked to determine or collaborate on appropriate risk appetite given the data science value that a certain use case brings to the organization.

In some organizations privacy risk is not seen as risky at all, or it is newly recognized because of increasing controls, consumer backlash, and changes in strategy. If you are at an organization like that, you'll be navigating unstable conversations where the former approaches are clashing with the new reality. In these situations, it's often the case that the former risk appetite was too large, and those in charge of managing risk are clamping down. This might impact products and change data use to fit newer regulations like GDPR. Managing these conversations will require extra empathy. Sharing your new ideas and opportunities to decrease risk with technology can also help open perspectives.

Learning what types of scenarios the legal, compliance, risk, and audit stakeholders are facing will help you decide how to evaluate risk. Becoming familiar with the various scenarios that these stakeholders face will automatically filter the technical landscape. This is part of the collaborative threat modeling process, where everyone shares their understanding of the risk, which helps guide the priorities. For example, if legal is particularly worried about misuse of personal data under GDPR, you know that governance concerns, data access, and anonymization can help reduce and mitigate that risk.

Once you have input from legal stakeholders, it's then important to understand what's top of mind for security leaders at the organization. What are their top priorities and concerns? What types of attacks concern them most? Many security leaders won't fully understand the depth and extent of privacy attacks or privacy risk the way that you do after reading Chapter 4. For this reason, you'll first need to listen and learn what they already have on their plate.

Rather than overwhelming them with a variety of new attacks that they haven't heard of, tailor your message first. See how privacy relates to their top concerns right now. For example, they might worry about sensitive data being used in the public cloud— or even how to transfer sensitive data cross-cloud or within multicloud settings. Depending on your analysis, using a technology like encrypted computation to expand encrypted processing could address these concerns. If this collaboration continues with future top priorities, these conversations will help grow understanding and interest in privacy risk and technologies at a critical place in the organization.

Sometimes your proposed mitigations may be seen as too experimental or radical. These technologies are still quite unknown outside of the field of privacy engineering. Although these technologies are frequently used at larger technology companies and in sectors like finance and healthcare, they are new to many people and industries. Initiate these conversations by introducing mitigation compromises and experiments where better technology can be implemented later. The use cases in this chapter follow this approach and demonstrate ways to navigate the conversations.

If your recommended mitigation is not prioritized, you'll want to ensure people understand the resulting privacy risk. Figuring out how the organization documents security considerations and concerns is a good starting point. Developing privacy risk documentation with similar structure and language builds alignment across large organizations. As mentioned in Chapter 8, the main risk stakeholders should understand their collectively owned risk so they can assess, prioritize, evaluate, and improve their risk approach via iterations. If the risk you see is well documented and understood—especially when suboptimal mitigations are put into place—this positions privacy technologies more clearly as part of the next evaluation or conversation.

Remember that privacy isn't an on-off switch; it's a continuum. If your first mitigation isn't implemented, keep the conversation going. Is there a compromise you can reach along the continuum? Can you have a checkpoint in a few months to see if there are new ways to review the risk now that the product or data flow is working? Helping others see the range of possibilities along with the risk is instrumental in reducing privacy risk across the organization.

Identifying the primary risks, using what you learned in this book, and determining your privacy engineering focus will make ways to raise those concerns more obvious. Even if you currently work at an organization where privacy is not taken seriously, it doesn't mean that you should adopt that mindset. Learn to use your voice, speak up when you see something, and introduce privacy as a normal part of technical conversations; you might be surprised by who participates in the conversation and supports your ideas.

It can be a long road to bring an organization from simple acceptance of privacy risk to documenting it to mitigating it with privacy technologies. One thing that accelerates this conversation is communicating about possibilities in the future landscape. You want to shift the conversation from a "not now" to a "yes, but when." Let's explore how to do that.

Embracing Uncertainty While Planning for the Future

Trends in data protection regulation and shifting consumer expectations of privacy highlight a future where there are more privacy protections and less data collection. But knowing exactly when this will happen and which regulations, consumer industries, and technology companies will move first is impossible.

This type of uncertainty makes conversations and forthcoming decisions difficult. If you are in leadership at your organization, take a proactive approach and use the knowledge in this book to develop new ways of thinking about privacy risk and owning it rather than avoiding it. If you aren't in leadership, you still have influence at the organization. Being a strong voice with a plan will shift attitudes even in the face of uncertainty.

During times of increasing uncertainty, people often become anxious, even afraid. Making decisions out of fear or under the influence of anxiety doesn't result in the best outcomes. Knowledge you have gleaned from this book, plus ongoing study, puts you in a position to shepherd the conversation to one about facts instead of fear.

When people are in states of fear and anxiety, it is hard for them to listen to facts. For this reason, the conversation about feelings needs to happen first. What is it that is making them feel this way? What is scary about shifting to focus more on privacy technology? By listening empathetically and compassionately, you can provide a sounding board for those concerns that also tells you more about what is happening across the organization. As mentioned in Chapter 8, studying nonviolent communication here helps.[2] This is also where the conversation can shift to the nagging feelings of guilt that "we should be doing better." Privacy technologies here open an exciting new possibility, one that not only reduces liability and risk but also makes people feel good about how they manage and work with data.

Once people feel heard and better understood, they will be open to new information. Based on what you learned in previous conversations, you can guide and influence decisions around privacy at an organization with actual knowledge and information. There are many ways to do so—running informational meetings, starting a privacy book club, publishing thought leadership and sharing it, holding workshops, or even demonstrating privacy technology in a hackathon. All these approaches and many others like them nurture more understanding within the organization. They also foster a culture of talking about privacy and develop a group of advocates and champions who want to participate.

Speaking Up and Lifting Up

You can accomplish this type of education and evangelism regardless of your place in an organization, but, of course, your level of influence will vary.

Many times this will depend on privilege, status, and the functionality of the organization's culture. These are things that you cannot change without great effort and leadership support. If you find yourself in a place that is resistant and opposed to this work, know there will be other places that are different.

For those of you with more power and privilege, pay attention when those with less power and privilege are speaking up on these topics and lift up their work and voices. Make space for them at the table (*https://oreil.ly/4OqEg*) and create new opportunities for them to shine.

---

2 If you have the time, I recommend joining the yearlong Compassion Course (*https://www.compassion course.org*) and participating in a study group.

In the world of security and privacy, it is easy to get stuck reacting—making decisions in response to events, news, lawsuits, and so forth. The entire organization must shift its thinking to be more proactive, enjoying well known and documented benefits of this approach. According to the UK's annual cybersecurity study (*https://oreil.ly/vdCmC*), a proactive approach can prevent data breaches and other untoward cyber events.

Shifting to proactive security and privacy means incorporating regular forward- and future-thinking sessions, like threat modeling and risk assessment, and using the output of those sessions for product and business planning. This can help a company get ahead of the game, potentially avoiding compliance issues, fines, and public scorn.

It requires, also, a regular cycle for modeling, simulating, evaluating, and reviewing threats, as shown in Figure 9-1.[3] This cyclical approach and its results teach teams about the actual impacts of threats, rather than keeping them theoretical or "imaginary." When you create a more data-driven and experiment-driven risk assessment process, you can prioritize effective mitigations and move away from somewhat arbitrary expert assessments.

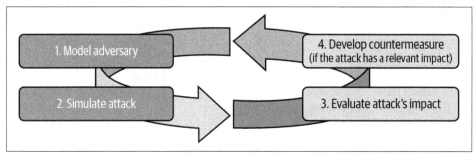

Figure 9-1. Proactive security

One final note: there are business benefits to embracing privacy, including reputation. Companies like Apple have fundamentally shifted the conversation with the public using privacy as a core differentiator in their market messaging. The iOS changes Apple made to allow easy opt-out of undesired data use from applications have already created seismic shifts in how certain business models function, such as microtargeted advertisements. Embracing privacy—and embedding it in your products and business—ensure that you lead these shifts instead of falling victim to them.

You can encourage incorporating these new technologies by leading the conversations, the planning, and the evolution of the internal culture. Another important

---

3 This graphic is inspired by work from Battista Biggio (*https://battistabiggio.github.io*), an important researcher and contributor to the field of security in machine learning.

aspect is recognizing quick wins and "thin slices"[4] to test privacy technology and grow competence and familiarity with these areas. In the following section, you will learn several practical examples from the real world to spot ripe opportunities for privacy technology.

Practical Privacy Technology: Use-Case Analysis

Learning to apply privacy technology will be an ongoing process as you take the knowledge from this book and apply it to your data work. In this section, you'll see real use cases and evaluate how privacy technology can help them. Pay attention to patterns and ways of thinking and compare what you learn here to your own experience in data. Your questions and ideas as you read can signal interesting paths for applying privacy technology at your organization, in your field, and in your career.

 These use cases are based on real-world examples. To preserve confidentiality, certain details have been changed or eliminated. However, the problem and the core decision-making process are preserved.

Federated Marketing: Guiding Marketing Campaigns with Privacy Built In

Marketing is a great area for expanding privacy technology use, as it is often the first place that regulations affect companies. If you work at a marketing company or closely with a marketing team, I'm sure you have already seen how consent, opt-out, and compliance affect the entire business model. Teaching marketing departments how to do marketing differently, with privacy at the core, is an interesting part of privacy technology work.

This use case involves data sharing, marketing, and managing those needs in a safe and privacy-aware way. Let's dive in and learn more!

---

4 Thin slices are small, usable pieces that function like MVP features or proofs of concept and spawn feedback and collaboration between the users and the creators. The idea comes from agile software delivery and lean methodologies, where you want to deliver value quickly. It's better to show the "customer" something that does what they need or want, even if it's not fully functional, than to spend months building what you think they need only to find out it isn't right.

Problem statement and desired outcome

In this use case two companies wanted to combine marketing efforts. One company wanted to see which of its customers also were customers of another company, and the managers wanted to build some interesting product offers that they could advertise based on data that the other company had available.

One of these companies was based in Europe, so it faced more stringent regulation. The notification rights of the GDPR would not allow them to simply exchange customer information. The legal and compliance departments at both companies did not want the customer data and consumption patterns sent directly to the other company. How could they find a fitting solution?

It is marketing departments that have, most often, lost access to data due to new regulations like GDPR. If your organization has a marketing department, you can talk to them about their struggles to see if privacy technology could help provide customers more protection while helping the business find new ways to advertise.

In an ideal world, they would have Trent (a trusted third party) (*https://oreil.ly/Qr59K*), which could look at the data that both companies sent and safely find the intersection. Trent could also analyze the buying patterns and send the the analysis and matched users to the company that wanted to advertise. The company could then use this analysis to advertise new offerings to the (ideally) interested users.

Current solution

The current solution for this problem leverages a trusted execution environment (*https://oreil.ly/Mz8YZ*) and software that runs the comparisons and analysis in the secure enclave. There's a more in-depth review of enclaves in Chapter 10, but briefly, they are a confidential computing tool that obfuscates the data and program execution from the person or company running the hardware.

In this case, the decision makers believed enclaves looked a lot like a Trent. But usually enclaves solve a problem of distributing trust by shifting trust from the hardware provider or cloud service to the execution environment.[5] Enclaves provide security guarantees for running only your specific software on special processing units. To meet the privacy concerns, that software then needs to be designed, coded, understood, and audited by both parties. Enclaves also cost significantly more than normal computing power and have some quirks when optimizing programs due to their special execution, making them sometimes difficult for software engineers to navigate and maintain.

---

5 Ironically, most of the enclave providers are also hardware and cloud providers.

This decision was made in good faith and likely reflects organizations where knowledge about privacy technologies is quite low. This will be the case at most organizations for coming years and is where you can most help. What could be a better solution to the marketing teams' problem?

Privacy-first future solution

You might have read the problem statement and immediately thought of your exercise with Moose and Private ID in Chapter 7. You're exactly right. Let's explore why.

First, the use case essentially is a private set intersection problem. They have customers together, and they want to both find the overlap and do some analysis. This puts you squarely in the encrypted computation world. They also have fairly stringent privacy and secrecy demands, which means you likely want to provide minimal encryption and potentially also differential privacy or other ways of masking or aggregating the output so that it doesn't leak much information for any one user.

 When you see a requirement for a trusted third party, you should immediately consider encrypted computation. Trent is a character from the world of cryptography because they, as a trusted third party, represent properties that cryptography provides. When cryptographic protocols are designed, the characters like Trent represent attributes and methods needed in the actual cryptographic computation. This is part of universal composability (*https://oreil.ly/xNWO-*) and an essential piece of cryptographic proofs.

Migration from the current solution, which does not include any easy guarantees, to one that uses an approach similar to Google's Private Join and Compute ("Private Join and Compute" on page 189) would provide a privacy-first future solution. This could be done using either homomorphic encryption protocols or secure multiparty computation protocols, or a combination of those two. One added benefit of this approach is it's cloud- and hardware-agnostic, meaning it can be run without specific hardware and it can be migrated to new clouds or environments without problem. It's also much more auditable, since it relies on proven cryptographic protocols and you are ideally using a well-audited and maintained implementation. If so, both parties should be able to review the computation plan and ensure it meets their expectations. Depending on implementation software, there may be easy-to-digest graphs and computation plans so all stakeholders can review the computation and understand how to modify it for the desired privacy and secrecy controls.

One neat property of this solution is the ability to also test and combine it with other ideas. For example, you could use encrypted computation to perform the private set intersection and then perform the analysis on the data in a federated manner, where each player runs analysis on their part of the data. The parties could then share small updates with differential privacy (i.e., federated analytics) instead of finishing the analysis in encrypted space. If the analysis requires additional privacy controls, you could add a differential privacy mechanism directly to the encrypted computation before the decryption step. By combining the approaches you've learned in this book, you can figure out exactly where the sweet spot is for providing the appropriate controls that fit the privacy versus utility needs of the use case and the threat model.

You should start with a small proof of concept that lets you model the problem quickly and iterate. Here are some steps that can help you through that start, should it be new to you:

1. Once you have decided to implement a new technology as an experiment, ensure that you have already defined the problem clearly and that all stakeholders are clear on the desired outcome.

2. Choose one or more libraries to experiment with. Outline your approach before starting. Determine how you will set check-in points and identify potential rabbit holes or complexity problems and how to talk about those as a team.

3. Experiment, build, and learn—just as you normally would as part of your data science process. It helps here to have a multidisciplinary team, with added skills like infrastructure, software development, architecture, and even networking experts. When in doubt about a way forward, focus on the product outcomes!

4. At regular intervals, check in on time-sucks and problems. Make quick trials, spikes, and decisions to move through tough learning curves. Sit on a problem for a few days and do something else if you get too stuck.

5. If possible, test with fake data regularly and as part of your proof-of-concept development. Make fake data that looks like your problem, even if it takes a few days to get right. Once your proof of concept works on fake data modeled after your real data, move to real data from at least one party and test a few runs.

6. Evaluate your test runs and real runs. Can this scale? What bugs did you find? What would you do differently if you were operating in production? What are the still open security risks and threats? Use those answers to guide your proof of concept into either further experimentation (back to step 3) or production use.

In this example, you saw a first look at moving from new (but ill-fitting) technology to technology that your team might have never even heard of. Some of these conversations will come in bursts and take a while before you get enough yeses to move to things like a proof of concept or real implementation.

The investment is worth it—both for your career and for the organization's outcomes. Learning how to guide others through these shifts takes time; creating room for experimentation and advocacy can help. If you familiarize your marketing and technology teams with encrypted computation, they will benefit as they look to the future, avoiding vendor lock-in and the unknown cloud costs that come with inappropriate solutions like enclaves.

Let's investigate the next use case, which also involves sharing of data in a private and confidential manner.

Public-Private Partnerships: Sharing Data for Public Health

To get a full view of public health, authorities often need to collaborate with private companies that have different health data and health indicators. For example, whether looking at a problem like cancer or a pandemic, it would be good to have health data from private insurers, private hospitals, and public authorities. This could be to support research initiatives, assist budget planning, or prepare hospital and healthcare capacity.

These types of data partnerships also happen outside of healthcare, like when private-sector partners collaborate on a problem. In this use case, you'll discover ways to facilitate such a collaboration safely, with privacy-preserving methods.

Problem statement and desired outcome

This case aims to assist in planning budgets for healthcare costs across a country where data from health providers, private insurers, and the government were combined to establish a clearer view. The goal is to understand the cost of healthcare at a high level; there is no desire to view this at a patient-by-patient level. Aggregate healthcare costs, broken down with other attributes, could be used to better plan future government healthcare investment and spending.

The desired outcome is to provide the government with these metrics without violating the confidentiality of these patients. The healthcare providers and the insurers want to participate and share their data without leaking private or confidential information about patients, customers, or operations.

Current solution

The current solution uses a privacy-aware hashing algorithm that operates like a Bloom filter to hash the identifiers. These identifiers and the related cost or disease data is then sent along to the government. Both the providers and the insurers use this system to send data to the government servers. The algorithm is a privacy-preserving method from research. The probabilistic nature of the hashing mechanism adds some noise and therefore helps provide better privacy.

As you know from a close reading of this book, this likely meets a strong pseudonymization requirement but not anonymization. Probabilistic hashes can leak quite a bit of extra information, especially if the data attached to them has no protections. Even if they have some probability of returning a different hash, they represent a single individual. This ID number likely has a limited search space. Since the government will know all of the IDs it has issued, it is possible that someone there could, if motivated, track the health of a given individual. This is obviously not ideal if the goal is to use today's leading privacy-preserving technology.[6]

Privacy threats aside, this probabilistic filter also adds unnecessary noise to the dataset. Unlike the probabilistic noise of differential privacy—which is both tuned to the problem and can offer privacy guarantees—the noise from this approach is just noise without protections.

What could be a better way to upgrade this system using today's privacy technology?

Privacy-first future solution

When imagining a privacy-first future solution to this problem that guarantees confidentiality and protects privacy, you have two options. One would leverage secure multiparty computation (MPC), and the other would set up a completely federated system. There are also possibilities to combine these approaches. Let's explore each one first.

In any situation where multiple parties need to share data, MPC is always a possible solution. It makes sense, here, because the parties would like to calculate the overall costs together. With a solution like replicated or additive secret sharing, which you learned in Chapter 7, they could design the collection so the government receives the final shares and then calculates the result. You could automatically formulate the analysis to ask directly for the type of result you want (average cost per user, total cost for a particular type of treatment, number of treatments per month, and so on). Each party could also add their own differential privacy mechanism, adjusting contributions per person, sensitivity, and epsilon, should that be desired. Then, the government could decrypt the answers all together and ensure they were the only ones who can reveal the output. This keeps confidentiality and privacy high. It also means the data and analysis must be agreed upon in advance, with clarity on the outcomes and privacy guarantees you would like to provide.

This could also be designed in a federated manner with or without MPC, like you learned in Chapter 6. In this case the computation would be sent using a federated analytics setup so that each contributor runs the analysis locally without moving any of the data. The result of that aggregation is sent either directly to the government or to an aggregation server run by the government. If extra confidentiality is needed, this could be a secure aggregation, leveraging MPC or HE. Differential privacy could also be added to the aggregation step, providing stronger privacy guarantees.

---

6 The initial implementation is several years old—and homomorphic encryption was ruled out as a possibility because the libraries were not advanced enough at that time to be used.

Each of these possibilities preserves more privacy and is more confidential than the current approach. Ideally, you are starting to notice how you can combine privacy technologies in interesting ways to solve problems. You, together with software and infrastructure teams, will be evaluating these trade-offs to determine which fits best. One role you can now play is to expand the possibility and solution space, while providing solid privacy and data science advice to these teams as they design the solution.

Another common problem is compliance with privacy regulations. Let's analyze a use case related to GDPR to see how you'd build a better future solution.

Anonymized Machine Learning: Looking for GDPR Compliance in Iterative Training Settings

GDPR compliance, as you learned in Chapter 8, is no small task. Companies in Europe and across the world are still adjusting compliance mechanisms today as data collected under older consent policies expires and as case law changes interpretations of consent.

Under GDPR, certain types of person-related data collection and processing are allowed only if consent is freely and unambiguously given. When data is collected, the data controller must outline a retention period for use of that data. If consent is revoked, the data must be deleted within 30 days. Once the retention period expires, the data must be deleted.

As you learned in Chapter 8, anonymization is one method to take data collected under GDPR and move it outside the reach of the regulation. If you can prove that you have properly anonymized data, it is no longer subject to GDPR requirements and, therefore, can be held longer than the retention period.

Problem statement and desired outcome

In this use case, a retail enterprise has collected purchase data as part of normal business operations. They have trained several machine learning models on this data for a variety of critical marketing and business purposes. Since GDPR went into effect, they have to document and add more protections for their data processing, including new policies on data retention and use.

They can retain some of the data regardless of consent or expiration because it falls under "legitimate interest." But some of the additional data they collect falls under the consent and expiration requirements. They will need to delete or anonymize this data should they want to use it without restriction or deletion as part of their training and normal processing.

They want to continue using this extra person-related data for machine learning as it has proven to boost model performance. How can they fulfill GDPR requirements and still have performant models?

Current solution

In their current approach, they implemented k-anonymity as a preprocessing step for their machine learning feature store. As you learned in Chapter 2, k-anonymity involves choosing a k value and grouping people into groups of minimum k persons based on their attributes. If a row or individual doesn't end up in a group, that information gets removed.

For a machine learning pipeline, this means testing the currently valid data, creating the groups, and processing those into features that end up in the feature store. Those features are now "anonymized" and can be used to train compliant models.

However, you might also remember from Chapter 2 that k-anonymity does not provide rigorous privacy guarantees. In this case, it would be a questionable use of anonymization, because it is not combined with l-diversity and t-closeness. k-anonymity unnecessarily destroys information for users in groups smaller than k. Is there a better way to anonymize data for compliance?

Privacy-first future solution

You're already thinking about differential privacy, aren't you? This offers a privacy-first anonymization mechanism for machine learning pipelines, like you explored in Chapter 5. It definitely adds better privacy guarantees and is about as future-proof as you can design GDPR compliance.

But you still need to incorporate differential privacy in your training. If you would like to have differential privacy guarantees for your machine learning, you need to depend on machine learning libraries that implement differential privacy. You also need to compare those models with ones trained on less data, but with no need for privacy guarantees (i.e., only data that is not expired or ready for deletion).

As this means changing the core machine learning operations and pipelines, it is a large investment. As you also know from Chapters 2, 3, and 5, you probably don't want to actually create differentially private features for the feature store, because this would involve local differential privacy instead of global—adding more noise than you want. If you are currently heavily invested in feature stores as the primary way to perform machine learning operations, this would change how you train, test, and compare models.

If this is the best approach, it's certainly manageable, but only with a large investment of time, development, and effort. At some companies, this investment is more costly than the risk of GDPR noncompliance. It might be, therefore, some time before this approach is commonplace for GDPR compliance.

Let's investigate a use case that might be familiar to you, and even a reason you may have picked up this book—long waits or complete blocks for data access.

Business-to-Business Application: Hands-Off Data

In my work on this problem, I've seen countless use cases where no data is allowed to be used or where data scientists wait months to get access. Let's take one example to see how privacy technologies can help.

Problem statement and desired outcome

In this example a company builds tools for other companies that manage those companies' internal data. For privacy and security reasons, each company gets their own secure data storage. The data produced by the application is owned by each of those customers, and the application developer does not access this data in any way, other than to keep the service running.

Current solution

For teams like this, the usual solution is to continue operating as is—without ever using the data for more insights, use cases, or growth. This is, indeed, a very privacy-friendly option. However, in some cases this means the company falls behind other less privacy-friendly business models and has difficulty competing, as they do not have any way to use data to determine which product features are working, what ones could be improved, and how to prioritize new features or offerings. There are also some features, such as offering machine learning products for their customers trained on that data, that are simply impossible to develop without using the data.

Privacy-first future solution

In order to benefit from data science and to create new product offerings using data science, a significant shift in company positioning and stakeholder perspectives needs to occur. It is essential to work closely with the compliance, legal, and privacy teams to determine what fits the current product contracts and customer needs. They should guide the conversations with the customers directly should anything need to contractually change before any privacy technologies are used and tested.

However, there are several options you have learned in this book that can help alleviate the customer concerns around data access and use, particularly if the utility trade-off is clear. For example, is it worth it to them to offer data use if they get an improved search algorithm or a useful machine learning model in return? If you can show them the benefits and protections you can offer, this can shift their mindset and open new opportunities for privacy-first data use.

In these setups, the most common applicable solutions are federated or distributed use cases (Chapter 6), where the data primarily stays in the secure area and only small updates or results are shared with the application provider. For example, the application provider could use federated learning across several customers who are similar to see if a model can be built to optimize search. If necessary, this can be combined with differential privacy and secure computation to add an extra layer of secrecy and privacy.

There could even be use cases where secure multiparty computation (Chapter 7) fits, should several of the customers be willing to solve a problem together and benefit from this collaboration. Take an example where each company would benefit from combining their data with other customers, such as supply-chain or logistics data, which would help all customers if they had a better bird's-eye view of the system. If those customers are willing to compute together but are not willing to do so with plain-text data, then secure computation could be a service the application provider could provide, along with support to build those partnerships.

As you know from reading this book, leveraging privacy technology in new ways and creating standard workflows that apply privacy technology as a normal part of data science and machine learning means shifting ways of thinking. As you learned in Chapter 3, if you aren't designing the systems, platforms, and architecture with these possibilities in mind, it will be difficult to retrofit them. The most effective privacy-preserving systems are systems where privacy is built into the initial design and planning.

Step-by-Step: How to Integrate and Automate Privacy in ML

Let's take a step back from specific use cases and see if there is a more generalized approach to help you build privacy into the systems from the start. This requires using the common methods you experience in machine learning and data science workflows, but ensuring that privacy is an element in each step. Your goal is to make privacy the easy choice when working on machine learning and data science products and their related business goals.

Iterative Discovery

The early stages of a data science or machine learning project often involve figuring out the problem you want to solve. In this stage, you are running iterative discovery—to figure out what use case or context-specific information you need to learn, to see which approaches or methods might work, and to discover what data is already available and what other data you might need.

This is the perfect time to incorporate privacy choices if you are working with person-related or sensitive business process data. Incorporating privacy into the framing of the problem and examination of available data and accompanying considerations for privacy versus information (see Chapter 2). Assessing which privacy-preserving methods can help at this stage influences how the system looks and functions—making potential technical trade-offs quite obvious. Clearly it is ideal for this to happen before any code is written and before architecting the system. A system and architecture that is already in place will limit what is manageable for any given use case.

Additionally, if privacy and legal teams must give approval, it may not be possible to use more data and to test ideas unless you have a plan to better protect that data (see Chapter 8). Navigating the legal conversation early on ensures that your product or service is approved and well understood by the necessary stakeholders. You don't want to be halfway through developing a new machine learning product when you learn that it will not be GDPR compliant or future-proof.

If you decide to actually just use less sensitive data as a result, that is a fine outcome. Data minimization de-risks all experiments and workflows. The best outcome is to have more privacy, even if it means less use of privacy technologies you learned in this book.

When privacy is a frequent part of continuous discovery and teams are confronted with the question often, they are more inclined to make the investment and build privacy directly into their normal data science delivery. This begins an iterative process to explore various technologies, determine what fits best, evaluate which libraries can be leveraged and tested quickly, and then integrate them. Teams will then become familiar with these technologies and how they can change and guide data science decisions.

Once data privacy is a core part of the continuous discovery process, privacy conversations will spawn privacy knowledge sharing and understanding across wider groups of people and teams across the organization. To ensure this knowledge ends up more evenly distributed, document it directly in the product and solution discovery process.

Documenting Privacy Requirements

Like writing software and user requirements, writing privacy requirements can and should be a normal part of the data science and machine learning workflows. This documentation and process can be skipped if the data science project does not touch any person-related or other sensitive data.

Having the conversation for each project, though, greatly increases the knowledge sharing on the team and raises awareness around privacy and associated risk. Like how software engineering introduced new standards and practices into machine learning, making it more test-driven and continuously integrated, choosing privacy as a top-level concern in data projects will shift the culture around how person-related data is handled and managed. Performing regular privacy risk assessments, together with incorporating this conversation into normal workflows, can shift privacy from a nice-to-have to a must-have on teams and data products.

As discussed in Chapter 5, documenting privacy risks of machine learning models and their mitigations are a recommended starting point for machine learning teams or businesses where machine learning is a core value driver. Even just incorporating standard governance into workflows, like what you learned in Chapters 1 and 3, can be enough to raise awareness and change attitudes toward privacy in a data team or organization. Consent-driven documentation and auditable and self-documenting workflows offer privacy by design and ensure that privacy rights are easier to offer and guarantee.

When privacy requirements are formalized, the resulting structure makes the privacy-first solutions obvious. This requires that the entire team have a basic understanding of the potential technologies to ease evaluation. You can start a series of trainings to cover the basics of scientific privacy and the potential technologies, create a knowledge center for sharing this information asynchronously, and utilize internal communities and learning groups to spread the word. Spending time on awareness and making these topics accessible will drive demand for these technologies.

When the knowledge is more evenly distributed, these conversations are part of standard project or product evaluation discussions. Then, documenting privacy feels as normal as documenting experimental results or architecture design records. These discovery and documentation artifacts are valuable not only for that particular use case but also to anyone who looks at it for inspiration when starting a new one.

Taking inspiration from data governance documentation in federated governance systems, like Governance 2.0, and combining ideas like Data Protection Impact Assessments or Privacy Cards for data science projects will guide and inspire what is the right level of documentation for your organization and team. Documentation is not a one-size-fits-all part of data science work, but using the approaches you learned in Chapters 1, 3, 5, and 8 should give you inspiration for what you can test and modify.

Your documentation will include consideration of privacy technology as part of the normal evaluation of approaches and experimentation for your data workflows. How can this work when each workflow is somewhat unique?

Evaluating and Combining Approaches

You will need a knowledgeable team to evaluate privacy technologies as you did in this chapter's use cases. Build ways to share knowledge via conversations and documentation and increase the number of team members who can speak to these subjects. For some teams, it might be enough to have one person who understands the technologies and who can communicate them well to the rest of the team. For other teams, you'll want to expand knowledge via new learning initiatives and grow that understanding before proceeding.

When incorporating new technology with any workflow, it will first largely slow the approach. Taking privacy technologies into consideration and evaluating their impact on the system and the level of effort to integrate them will take practice. This is why documentation is so important, so you can see trends in the privacy requirements at your organization and use them to plan a generalized approach should the same concerns or solutions come up multiple times.

When evaluating one privacy technology, you will want to explore ways to combine approaches. The second use case in this chapter demonstrated that there are times when more than one technology could work, and where combinations of them addressed the entire problem. This evaluation will need to be done with a multidisciplinary team who understands the product and customer needs, regulatory and compliance concerns, and the current solution, software, and architecture. These myriad voices help you determine what fits and when it might fit; it also disseminates awareness and knowledge within the team and throughout the organization. Sometimes these conversations lead directly to a very clear trade-off, making the decision easy.

Creating clear and easy-to-use evaluation criteria speeds this conversation effectively. Estimating effort, just as you would for software features, can help you see if the time and effort are worth investing or if you need to build these options into longer-running experiments, proofs of concept, or platform planning.

As part of this process, you'll work out the necessary steps to first experiment with potential solutions and then determine if they apply for more use cases. At some point usage of these technologies will increase enough until they are considered normal choices as part of the average data science toolbox. When this happens, you have also figured out ways to make these technologies easy to use and automate.

PETs Evaluation Criteria

There is no one way to evaluate PETs or privacy mechanisms, and you will learn methods that work for you as you practice this skill in your work. There are, however, some clear starting points that I can share from my own experience. Take this list and the order and modify it for your organization, processes, and preferences:

1. Use case criteria

> What requirements or hard constraints are outlined in the use case itself? These can be hard facts, such as data size, data type, and task type, or other "softer" requirements such as user preferences, product goals, and business value.

2. External team input

> Gather input from the privacy team and infosec team, should you have them. If not, identify stakeholders who can speak to these topics and gather their input, either one by one and learning as you go or holistically in a group setting. What do they consider the problem space and risk? How would they identify a solution?

3. Threat and privacy risk modeling

> Perform threat modeling to identify privacy and security risk and determine what risks should be addressed. Incorporate likelihood analysis if data is available. Define the setting of this use case specifically, in case this ends up solidifying risk perception and understanding. If possible, prioritize risks with stakeholders from step 2.

4. Identify technical privacy requirements

> Use the knowledge and learnings from this book and your continued learning. Is the problem related to privacy or secrecy? What guidelines do you have on the data processing agreements or requirements from a regulatory point of view? Who owns the data, and what would their privacy requirements be? Begin outlining the requirements from a technological point of view, incorporating everything you have learned up to this point.

5. Determine feasible technologies, experiment, and implement

> Based on the output of step 4, you now should have a clear picture of what technologies would fit and which are unlikely to work. Go back to step 1 and use the product requirements and use case to guide what is feasible. If you are working in a greenfield environment, you might have the flexibility to try several technologies and even build proof of concepts. If your timeline is short and your constraints are quite specific, move onto implementation directly and try to deliver it in small incremental chunks rather than all at once. Stay in touch with your product, data, privacy stakeholders, and customers to ensure your implementation makes sense for everyone. Find compromises and build a roadmap if cutting-edge privacy technologies are a good fit for the problem but cannot be easily retrofitted to the current platform and other constraints.

Shifting to Automation

Machine learning and data science have varying levels of automation across industries and organizations. If you work at a mature data organization, you likely already have large-scale automation for data pipelines, data science workflows, and even machine learning engineering operations, such as CI/CD for machine learning. If you work at an organization that is only now building out data science and ML work, then the landscape is probably a lot less defined.

Regardless of the maturity of your current organization, the industry has shifted to more automation and higher software standards in the past 10 years. Cloud and data platform providers have easy ways to take data science activities, such as data wrangling, transformations, EDA and machine learning training, and plug and play those into real running infrastructure.

This automation brings new possibilities and challenges when deploying privacy technology. If you are at an organization with its own platform team, you can work with that team to gradually build privacy technology and libraries directly into the platform. This allows you and other data scientists to leverage them as a core part of how you develop and deploy workflows. But if you are at a team where you are mainly leveraging cloud provider software and services to paste together processing and training pipelines, you'll need to leverage built-in options from your cloud provider or install open source privacy technology libraries and place them into your workflow without hindering other data processing.

As more open source libraries for these technologies appear, you can also expect that the offerings in the cloud will reflect this shift. If you find that automation is too difficult at this stage, keep the conversation going as technologies become more widely available or easier to use. This will position your team and organization well to embrace these technologies as they reach a wider market.

Part of this shift is making privacy a normal part of all data workflows, but how will this happen?

Making Privacy Normal

Following these steps should help make privacy an integrated part of the data work at your organization. Normalizing this new culture, however, requires frequent practice with ever larger groups within the organization. What might start out as a small piece of exploratory or research work eventually becomes commonly accepted and understood with time and repetition.

Making certain that the benefits of privacy considerations are understood will help standardize them as well. Understanding the "why" of privacy technology is just as important—if not more so—than the "how." Persuading product experts at your organization of the customer and product value spreads understanding across the organization. Talking with marketing and business development stakeholders about benefits for reputation and risk spreads the message further. Demonstrating privacy as a core business value proposition is key.

This might involve talking with key management and business stakeholders to familiarize them with the words, approaches, and purposes of such technology. Expecting them to build unknown solutions into the core systems tomorrow is unreasonable, but taking several months to demonstrate privacy technologies' purpose and promote the value they can provide to a forward-thinking data organization helps reduce the unknowns and paves the path for wider acceptance.

There are few shortcuts. However, if your industry is heavily regulated, key stakeholders may already be seeking options but do not know where to look. The knowledge you've gained from this book, supplemented by ongoing learning, will help you offer ways to step up privacy knowledge and privacy-first use cases.

For some organizations, privacy will probably first be embraced in the research, labs, or innovation hubs rather than in direct business-critical data work. By testing ideas in these safer settings, the organization can learn more about them and reduce uncertainty around their application. Let's investigate how this can be done with both internal and external research teams.

Embracing the Future: Working with Research Libraries and Teams

Throughout this book, technologies have been described that are still evolving and identifying new ways to enable privacy-aware data science and machine learning. That will continue—new books, workshops, research, and ideas will take it further.[7]

To remain cognizant of those forward movements or if you find yourself stuck and your use case or problem is best solved by something you read in research, it makes sense to embrace working with researchers directly. Often this also means you can bake privacy in from the start and design a solution that appropriately fits the risk model and use case. You might ask your organization's research group to expand their capabilities to include privacy work, or you might partner with external researchers already working with these technologies.

Working with External Researchers

When you evaluate open source libraries for use or read research to stay current on privacy-preserving approaches, you might notice a group or researcher who works on a library or approach that interests you. Consider writing them a message of

---

7 I will post regular updates to the notebooks in the GitHub repository and relevant updates, questions, and new thoughts on this topic on the Probably Private newsletter (*https://probablyprivate.com*) and my blog (*https://blog.kjamistan.com/*). I would love to hear and discuss your questions, ideas, and content, so please feel free to reach out anytime via the contact information provided at Probably Private.

appreciation for their work and how you might apply it. Often this is really exciting for you and the researcher; they enjoy the recognition and knowing their work is found useful by the industry.

Regardless of who the researcher is, it can be fruitful to reach out if you have questions about the approach. Make sure you do extra work to see if you can answer the questions yourself. Do your due diligence and see how far you can get on your own. Like everyone, researchers are busy and need to prioritize the backlog of incoming messages, work, and their own research. When you adequately prepare yourself before reaching out, your improved questions are more likely to strike up an interesting conversation.

If the researcher or research group is at an academic institution rather than an industry partner (i.e., Google, OpenAI, etc.), you may be able to see the code they used for the experiments and testing. Despite support for open research and open science, not everyone posts their code and data publicly to allow for easy reproducibility; however, many researchers are happy to share the code if you ask nicely and credit their work.

If you get some experimental code, you might end up having to spend time to decipher it and break it down into something usable. Ask for any documentation with the code, in case that can help. I have received 1,000-line Python files with few or no notes and spent several days sorting through what it does and refactoring it into smaller chunks. Determine how much time and effort you can put into rewriting code for use—and remember, the researcher or research group is doing you a favor by sharing the code with you!

If you actively use open source tools or scripts that are part of research and you improve the tool, you can also improve it for others by contributing it back to the library or by creating a useful fork for your specific use case. Don't forget to follow contribution guidelines, leave useful documentation, and write tests for your contributions.

Even if you don't improve the code, it is kind to simply send a message that you found the library helpful. Promote awareness of the subject by giving a talk at a local meetup group, at work, or at a conference. Write a post about your experience. The positive attention aids researchers in funding their work and growing their open source libraries.

If you often work on research code or use research to help solve interesting challenges in privacy and data science, you might choose to launch an internal research group. If you already have one, read on to see how useful these teams can be.

Investing in Internal Research

If you work at an organization with an internal research team, you may be able to influence research direction by educating them regarding the work you are doing in the data and privacy space. This, of course, is a lot easier if you already have researchers focused on data and is less effective if your organization's research is focused on something equally neat but with less privacy such as plastic-eating algae, green energy, new economic systems, and so forth.

Talking with stakeholders and growing the awareness around privacy technology internally may stimulate your organization to invest in this kind of research as a way to differentiate their product and offering. A research team will be formed or your team might even be asked to do that. Congratulations, this is a huge step!

If you haven't yourself led research or been on a research team, you'll probably be working with this team regularly but not directly on the team. When working with internal research teams, remember they are not on a product life cycle like other teams. They are experiment-driven, so it will be difficult for them to predict what they will discover in a two-week sprint. You are already familiar with this mindset from your data science work, but it is worthwhile to remind your team and other teams working with this group about slower timelines and giving them space to explore as a normal part of their workflow.

Ideally, you want to align research outcomes with data or company outcomes and to ensure that the research is focused on top-priority issues. Learning to talk with researchers in this space using the basics you have learned in this book will help you formulate the problems you are trying to solve into clear and measurable experiments. Contributing to a research backlog by documenting use-case occurrences for easier prioritization or sharing privacy requirements documentation can help orient research teams to organizational priorities. Build a relationship with this team, driven by interaction and experimentation, to ensure not only that their research is being well utilized but also to reach your own team goals.

Just as you do with external researchers, support your teams by contributing useful documentation, more modular code, or other improvements. Foster regular exchanges and provide feedback as their library and tools are adopted by others. Keeping the feedback and conversation iterative and cyclical can help your team better define privacy and technical requirements, which will result in research contributions that move your own team's work forward.

If you end up working on such teams and driving research in this space, I hope you'll reach out and tell me about your work. More research in these areas will benefit the entire data world, and I am a big fan of shifting our industry's focus and attention to recognize this important work.

Summary

In this chapter, you used the knowledge that you picked up from this book and applied it to realistic data science and machine learning problems that you might encounter in the real world. You can ideally start evaluating how to apply the technology you've learned directly to use cases and problems you see regularly.

You've also analyzed how to work pragmatically and practically with privacy risk. You now know new processes to raise awareness and document privacy requirements for data projects. By evaluating and comparing privacy choices, you've envisioned how to combine them to fit the needs of a given use case. And you are prepared to work with external and internal research groups to bring future-oriented work directly into your organization.

In the next chapter, you'll continue this practical approach by diving into frequently asked questions on privacy and privacy technology.

## CHAPTER 10

Frequently Asked Questions (and Their Answers!)

In this chapter, you'll get a taste of commonly asked questions that I hear when I present these topics at conferences or meetings. In case you have an additional question, feel free to ping me on Twitter (*https://twitter.com/kjam*),[1] on LinkedIn (*https://www.linkedin.com/in/katharinejarmul*), or directly via Probably Private; I'll keep a thread going with #PracticalPrivacyFAQs. If you publish your own FAQs or question and solution, please send it along so the community can learn and grow!

It's best to treat this chapter as a handy reference for looking up questions as they surface. The index and table of contents will guide you if you need to reread sections that are relevant to a particular project, idea, or product. Such a list is never complete, but I hope this is comprehensive enough to address burning issues and also point you to additional learning.

The sections of this chapter are organized into topic areas, based on where the questions most often arise. These topics are: secure computation and confidential computing, data governance and data protection mechanisms, GDPR and regulations, and finally personal choices and social privacy.

---

1 During the writing of this book the Twitterverse changed. I haven't found a home yet on Mastodon, but you can always use email or even snail mail—details at Probably Private (*https://probablyprivate.com*).

Encrypted Computation and Confidential Computing

This section covers questions related to encrypted computation (sometimes called *secure computation*) methods and confidential computing, which you read about in Chapter 7.

Is Secure Computation Quantum-Safe?

Questions of quantum security comes up often if you talk with folks about cryptography; I find this interesting as there are many protocols you use every day that are not quantum-secure. The neat thing is, most multiparty computation protocols are information theoretic secure, or "perfectly secure," and they are also quantum-secure. Because of the way they are usually implemented, however, they are only as secure as the systems that run them. When you send data across the internet, you usually use public key cryptography, and most of those protocols rely on the hardness of factoring large primes, making them not quantum-secure. If you want to use MPC in practice, you first need to ensure you are also using quantum-secure networking.

The homomorphic methods presented in Chapter 7 have computationally secure methods that are also believed to be quantum-secure, as they are based on the Learning with Errors problem. This problem has the same hardness assumptions as lattices, which are believed to be quantum-safe. The Paillier cryptosystem, on the other hand, is based on factoring, making it not quantum-safe.

I think sometimes people ask this question because they hear a lot about quantum security but don't recognize that many common protocols and their own computing hardware are not quantum-secure. At some point it will be important for everything to move to quantum-secure methods, but until the core of the internet shifts, I don't waste many cycles worrying about it. As I have said before and I'll say again when this question comes up at data science conferences, "Basically, the entire internet needs to migrate to quantum-secure protocols, but I'm pretty sure folks in this audience need to worry about pressing issues in our own field before that—like how data processing and machine learning can become climate neutral and more privacy-aware."[2]

Researchers are still working on how to better evaluate quantum-safe protocols, but it will take time and significant effort to prove there are not efficient quantum-based algorithms that break protocol security. It is known that some protocols, like RSA and ElGamel, are not quantum-safe because they can be broken using Shor's

---

2 Obviously, if you are developing new cryptographic protocols or determining how to move from not quantum safe to quantum safe methods, then this is extremely necessary, timely, and important work. Please continue!

algorithm to factor primes (*https://oreil.ly/Fl_w_*).[3] But the process is not always so obvious, and the lack of large quantum computers available for researchers means it will take time to identify new attacks that can be developed, should such computers become less costly and easier to maintain and use. Even NIST approved an algorithm as a quantum-safe method only to have it be broken on a traditional PC in less than an hour (*https://oreil.ly/OgEys*). This makes clear the difficulty in properly reviewing quantum-safe methods and protocols in general—when even experts can get it wrong.

Can I Use Enclaves to Solve Data Privacy or Data Secrecy Problems?

Enclaves or trusted execution environments (TEEs) (*https://oreil.ly/Ujw-X*) are specially designed hardware and processing units that fulfill specific confidential computing requirements and can be useful for some security models. I think, however, that the types of guarantees they can provide are oversold. When you choose an enclave, you are protecting yourself against the people running the actual hardware—probably your cloud provider. The goal, therefore, is to make certain that, as data is being processed or code is executing, no one can easily "listen in" and figure out what is happening. This concern is about the cloud provider itself and any "neighbors" who use the same shared hardware within a multitenancy cloud environment.

Let's say, for example, that you are an intelligence agency running covert operations in another part of the world and you are concerned that the cloud provider might be cooperating with other local authorities and passively snooping on your cloud usage. This could be worrisome, especially if this shared compute environment has known vulnerabilities where other virtual machines could access shared memory via leaks or CPU processing. If you can guarantee that TEEs or secure enclaves do not leak the important information you are seeking to protect, then these can provide the isolation that you want for your computation.

That said, there have been many successful attacks against secure enclaves (*https://oreil.ly/FuKqo*). And there is a significant cost increase—both in money and time—when using them for data processing and compute. It also means that you have to figure out how to optimize programs for a very different type of execution environment. Finally, you are essentially shifting your trust from the hardware provider to the enclave provider, which is why some cloud providers have also just started making their own enclaves. To me, it all seems a bit too much effort for too few guarantees, which is why, in this book, I focused on encrypted computation. Secure computation is developed via decades of audited research, has well-defined protocols

---

3 At the writing of this book, this is mainly theoretical and not practical due to memory limitations of available quantum computers.

that behave as expected and are not proprietary, can run on many types of hardware in many clouds, and provides better secrecy guarantees.

To summarize, enclaves are a good fit if you don't trust your hardware provider, cloud neighbors, or cloud compute; however, you must then transfer this trust to your enclave provider. There are very few cases where this would affect privacy, and almost all of them would be cases where governments (and potentially warrants) are involved.

What If I Need to Protect the Privacy of the Client or User Who Sends the Database Query or Request?

Sometimes you want to protect the privacy of the query sender rather than or in addition to the query response. In this case, you are looking at a technology called Private Information Retrieval (PIR) (*https://oreil.ly/51zqN*), or related methods like oblivious transfer (*https://oreil.ly/yRfEc*).

These are encrypted computation protocols that allow a user to send a query or request information while keeping the request itself secret. Based on what you learned in Chapter 7, you can imagine this as encrypting the request and being able to process that request while it remains encrypted. This can also be combined with other techniques to ensure privacy for the response as well, by using measures like differential privacy on encrypted data.

The most common use case for this type of interaction is if a user might want to request something confidential about themselves, such as a laboratory or test result. You can also imagine use cases where the request itself must remain secret due to the high security measures of the source and the people using the source, such as in nation-state-level security scenarios. In the future, these technologies could be combined with distributed identity services to allow federated querying of data sources in an "anonymous" or confidential manner.

If you are interested in learning more, I recommend reading Google's improvement of Private Join and Compute, which uses PIR techniques (*https://oreil.ly/yNGjb*).

Do Clean Rooms or Remote Data Analysis/Access Solve My Privacy Problem?

Sometimes solutions like clean rooms or remote data access are compared with confidential compute environments, despite having numerous security problems in comparison. Often, a clean room is an environment where data is loaded and someone like a data scientist can access the data on a virtual machine. "Clean," here, means that the data owner can decide how the data is loaded and what software is available for the data scientist to use. Sometimes the data owner also reviews what the data scientist can export or they receive a screen recording of what was done during the session. However, the data scientist or analyst has full plain-text view of the data itself, meaning there is absolutely no privacy or secrecy offered for the persons represented in that dataset.

Remote data analysis or access is another tool that is often compared with clean rooms. Typically, this involves using a particular library, software, or tool that allows the data scientist or analyst to manipulate the data remotely. Imagine that you had to perform EDA on data that you could not see completely; this is difficult and sometimes frustrating. Unlike the challenges of federated learning, where this might also be the case, I am not convinced that remote data access provides better privacy guarantees. With remote data access, you might be manipulating data to ready it for some action, such as federated or distributed learning, to prepare it for training should it not be in the required format. Sometimes remote data analysis or access is also used to send back results of this analysis to the data scientist—again as plain text and with zero privacy guarantees.

Both of these solutions have huge security and privacy vulnerabilities. In fact, a clever data scientist could use a tool like remote data access to exfiltrate specific information about the dataset or the data itself by running a singling-out query, as you learned in Chapter 4. In both cases, the data is not protected from the analyst in any meaningful way, which means that privacy guarantees are nowhere to be found. Neither of these techniques provides the secrecy guarantees of an encrypted computation. Additionally, an educated expert must review or audit these solutions, along with the logs, to ensure that the results did not leak too much information. Unlike previewing a secure computation or providing differentially private results, this happens after the fact, when privacy or secrecy is already violated.

I generally avoid these solutions and advise that privacy teams not consider them for privacy guarantees. These companies seem to have very effective marketing because the technical guarantees do not actually exist.

I Want to Provide Perfect Privacy or Perfect Secrecy. Is That Possible?

In our world, perfection is a great goal but is rarely attainable. The book is entitled *Practical Data Privacy* because I want you to learn practical ways to apply the best data privacy standards. I expect you to use the theories and best practices that I have shared and fit them to your needs.

You learned a little about perfect privacy in Chapter 2. The full definition would be as follows, defined in survey research by Damien Desfontaines and Balázs Pejó (*https://oreil.ly/LFe4V*):

> An attacker with perfect background knowledge (B) and unbounded computation power (C) is unable (R) to distinguish (F) anything about an individual (N), uniformly across users (V) even in the worst-case scenario (Q).

In this definition, each of the parameters represented by capital letters can be something you tune or leave out depending on the algorithm, implementation, or extension. This is clearly a lot; should you want to take each one into account, it likely means assembling a team to focus on this problem exclusively.

But if you are simply curious to learn more about perfect privacy, start with reading more literature on differential privacy, including Desfontaines's thesis (*https://oreil.ly/35vY1*), which walks through many definitions to consider. If you use this as guidance, you can tweak your approaches to better fit the intersection of "perfection" with what is practical for your application.

You learned about perfect secrecy, or information theoretic security, in Chapter 7. If you want to dive further into perfect secrecy, take a look at the origin with Claude Shannon's "Communication theory of secrecy systems" (*https://oreil.ly/WOB32*), one of the foundational works on information theory and a core paper in the history of cryptography. I also highly recommend reading more books on cryptography—there are too many good ones to list, so pick one that speaks to you and dive in.

With every step you take toward protecting the data, individuals in that data, and their right to privacy, you make a difference. Prioritizing these needs and communicating them clearly to others in your industry, organization, and team has long-lasting impact and ushers many more along the path toward practical privacy. Maybe one day perfection can then be reached, in part due to your efforts to raise awareness and make privacy more accessible, practical, and hands-on.

How Do I Determine That an Encrypted Computation Is Secure Enough?

Using encrypted computation can be a complex process involving multiple parties—each with their own requirements for privacy and security. This means it's a good idea to evaluate the computation with all of those needs in mind. This might also involve speaking to the legal and compliance teams of all organizations participating in the computation and making sure that the requirements are well understood by all parties.

In general, many secure computations will be a big security and secrecy step forward for the participants as it often replaces buying and selling of data or other contracts where data is shared in plain text. If the secure computation is replacing a normal plain-text one, you are already improving the security and privacy requirements substantially.

It is critical, when evaluating the security and privacy of a computation, to use peer-reviewed and audited libraries and tools. One reason open source is such an important part of cryptography is that the protocols are well-tested, well-understood, and implemented properly. If an encryption protocol is proprietary, it could contain unknown vulnerabilities, as cryptography has long embraced open protocol design, peer review, and knowledge sharing. By open sourcing libraries and encouraging open reviews of protocols and implementations, many security vulnerabilities have been discovered and protocols and systems have improved, due to the breadth and depth of the cryptography and security communities and research.

Evaluating the computation itself is probably the most difficult part of considerations around security and secrecy guarantees. You might want to consider mapping the information flow (*https://oreil.ly/l7sOP*) of the data in the computation. You'll also want to take a look at the math involved in the computation to judge if it is doing what it should. This is why using a library that supports these functionalities is important; it can be daunting for one person to analyze all levels of any given computation. You can even test the computation, using dummy data provided to all participants, to ensure the correctness of the implementation.

As long as these requirements are then met, it should be safe and secure for your needs and the needs of the other participants. Once you have run a few computations, you'll have a better understanding of the process and what you need to move forward. Properly documenting the steps and sharing what you learn is an important part of this process as well and can help build understanding and competence on your team and across the organization.

If I Want to Use Encrypted Computation, How Do I Manage Key Rotation?

Managing keys is a crucial part of key-based encryption methods. Regular rotation is typically recommended, particularly for keys used to protect business-critical data and private data storage and use. If you use key-based techniques for pseudonymization, this is particularly important to keep in mind and plan how to manage key rotation, which will also *correctly* break linkage between older and newer pseudonyms.

But not all encrypted computations use keys for the encryption. As you learned in Chapter 7, there are also methods, such as secret sharing, that allow you to encrypt data without a traditional key. Because these methods of encryption will change with each computation, based on random seeds, there is no need to plan for key rotation.

For homomorphic encryption you will be using keys. The good news is that key rotation should not affect the outcomes and can be done on a computation-by-computation basis. If you hold onto older keys because you want the results to remain encrypted in their original format, then you will need to manage key storage; however, it makes more sense to just use encryption at rest to store old results in encrypted data storage as you would any other sensitive data.

If you want to offer end-to-end encryption for users, please take a look at the Signal protocol (*https://oreil.ly/A-l-8*), and remember: make encryption the default and don't save the shared keys anywhere on your servers!

What Is Google's Privacy Sandbox? Does It Use Encrypted Computation?

The privacy sandbox on Android, and the related new web standards (*https://privacy sandbox.com*) in Chrome, is a proposal from Google to shift the current practices of third-party cookies to more privacy-friendly methods.[4]

The privacy sandbox primarily uses federated data and analysis, pseudonymization, and, in some cases, techniques like differential privacy and k-anonymity to protect individuals. In Android, it will also provide functionality that keeps advertising data processing separate from application processing via sandboxing (*https://oreil.ly/C_9zf*), but the proposals do not suggest encrypted computation. The stated goal is to phase out individually targeted advertisements while still allowing advertisers ways to send targeted advertisements to groups. It will be developed and deployed in phases and is likely to have changes over time (*https://oreil.ly/BwH0c*).

Much of the work is based on the original proposal for federated learning for ads that Google debuted in 2021, using federated analysis to create cohorts (Federated Learning of Cohorts or FLoCs). This approach was widely criticized by advertisers and privacy activists (*https://oreil.ly/N_Hi6*), as it had numerous security and privacy issues. Google then replaced the FLoC idea with one based on *topics* (*https://oreil.ly/UXw1x*), which function like user interests. Topics use a federated approach that classifies user interests locally instead of grouping users in a cohort. In the proposal as of early 2023, these interests are then saved as topics and are refreshed every three weeks. Although there are some improvements for privacy when compared with FLoCs, there are still many privacy issues in the current proposal (*https://oreil.ly/qRYJq*).

Since many of the proposals will change before they are widely used and deployed, I recommend going through each of the proposals (*https://oreil.ly/YKaHs*) and drafts (*https://oreil.ly/bIQ_R*) to understand how each one works, especially if you work in advertising or marketing and would like to better understand what will be available.

---

4 There are several major concerns (*https://oreil.ly/6Xnqk*) brought forward for these proposals on whether they actually help solve privacy in any meaningful way. At the writing of this book, it is unclear whether these concerns will be addressed appropriately.

Data Governance and Protection Mechanisms

This section covers questions related to data governance and data protection mechanisms, including pseudonymization and anonymization, which you read about in Chapters 1, 2, and 3.

Why Isn't k-Anonymity Enough?

As you learned in Chapter 2, k-anonymity is an older but still popular method of providing "anonymization." But what is meant by anonymization? You have learned via your exploration of differential privacy that there is no way to release person-related information without someone learning something.

K-anonymity is based on the idea of security through obscurity. If you can "hide" in a group of k or more people, you are "anonymous." But how many attributes do you have to combine to reach an appropriate grouping? For example, you might need to release information such as postal code, gender, marital status, and age. Now you have four things that you need to align to create the group. As you create those groups you are going to end up losing a lot of information from the start because some individuals will get lost and others will necessarily be obfuscated by broadening the categories (i.e., age range or larger postal grouping).

Suppose you now have your groups where there are at least k people with the same postal code grouping, gender grouping, marital grouping, and age grouping. Is this anonymous?

Probably not! There are probably other attributes that leak information (see Chapter 2). Let's say that 70% of people in your grouping have one thing in common, like their income or their education. This now means that there is a 70% chance that an attacker can learn that information or make an informed guess. If there is another plain-text value where 100% of your group is the same, then the attacker automatically knows that information about you.

As discussed in Chapter 2, you can never be certain what outside information an attacker has. Therefore, trying to understand what pieces of the information are linkable and what pieces are identifiable is a losing battle. Differential privacy was invented to shift thinking. Instead of eyeballing a list of attributes and picking groupings that you *think* might fit but are never sure, differential privacy measures possible information gain via statistical reasoning.

But what about with t-closeness and l-diversity?

You can add t-closeness to ensure that the target variables in the groupings match the overall target variables in the population. You can add l-diversity to ensure that the groupings have enough diversity in the released variables so someone cannot easily infer that 70% of the people have a particular quality. But this is still not enough because, again, if you release information, you cannot guarantee anonymity in the scientific or rigorous sense of the word. You will never know what outside information can be used and how much an attacker already knows or can single out an individual.

Not only that, but you probably have completely thrashed your data. If you have properly applied k-anonymity with t-closeness and l-diversity, you have created groupings that have become extremely generalized. And even then, you are not certain what guarantees you can provide other than that you did your best. The targets and other variables involved are not changed or bounded in any way, like you would do with a differential privacy mechanism. If an attacker knows someone in the dataset, then they immediately know this information, which is extremely risky if that information is in any way sensitive.

This is why differential privacy turns the idea on its head, asking instead if you can measure the workings of an algorithm (differential privacy mechanism) instead of looking at the data. When the focus shifts to a probabilistic algorithm, you can start reasoning scientifically about outcomes and still provide privacy guarantees. If you choose to think rigorously about privacy loss and anonymization, the shift to differential privacy is inevitable.

I Don't Think Differential Privacy Works for My Use Case. What Do I Do?

My first recommendation would be to ensure that it definitely does not work. To do so, explore Desfontaines's advice (*https://oreil.ly/uU1xF*), summarized by walking through these three points.

Differential privacy doesn't work if…

1. …you want to identify outliers.
2. …you need to maintain or create one record for each individual or one output per individual to link with another data source.
3. …small changes will dramatically impact the outcome.

If your use case falls into one of these categories, first take one step back. If you are already designing a solution and trying to retrofit privacy, it might be time to analyze the original problem. Is there another way to solve this problem? Do you really need to link this data at the individual level? Are outliers that important to answer the question at hand? How come the analysis is so sensitive to small changes?

Should you determine there is no way to make the problem and solution more privacy-friendly, you'll need to start analyzing other options, some of which are outlined in Chapters 1, 3, and 5.

Can I Use Synthetic Data to Solve Privacy Problems?

Synthetic data has gained attention since 2018 as one way to offer more user privacy while still having all the benefits of realistic data for developers and data scientists. Synthetic data is also used to extend or enhance existing datasets, when not enough data is available.

There are two methods for producing realistic synthetic data—using statistical properties, deterministic rules or generative machine learning trained on real data to generate realistic synthetic data. In either of these techniques, the synthetic data derives directly from real data inputs. Based on what you learned in Chapter 4 about reverse engineering this information out of the models or results, you need to be careful to define the privacy guarantees and how you plan to enforce them.

If you are going to use synthetic data based on statistical properties or rulesets, consider removing outliers by default and creating the distributions using differential privacy. If certain properties are required, for example, that the postal codes appropriately match the location or that other internal dependencies are met, then you'll want to ensure that these don't link directly to one individual. This involves data investigation and, if the process will be automated, adequate testing and checks.

If you are using machine learning generated synthetic data, you can train your model with differential privacy. There is an interesting blog post on this from Gretel.ai (*https://oreil.ly/aHgGU*), a company that provides synthetic data via machine learning. You can track privacy loss and determine when it makes sense to reset your budgets, based on your model and data usage. As you learned in Chapter 4, if you skip this step, it is highly likely that your model will reproduce examples very similar to outliers or distinct regions in your dataset.

I chose not to include a chapter about synthetic data in this book because I think it is an alluring option that often doesn't meet expectations. Synthetic data without differential privacy has the potential to be even more dangerous than real data because people believe it is safe and use it accordingly. It can also have a noisy impact on the data quality, moving things to averages or generalizations. These trade-offs don't make sense to me for most use cases where using the real data plus some protections might provide more value for less effort. However, I'm certain there are use cases I haven't encountered where synthetic data is a good fit. If you find them, I'd be curious to learn more!

How Should Data Be Shared Ethically or What Are Alternatives to Selling Data?

There have been several interesting trends in ethical data usage since the mid-2010s, moving away from data selling and exchanges between companies to more democratic, user-oriented, and collectively managed data. For example, data trusts (*https://oreil.ly/5hpQ-*) allow people to donate their data to an organization that completely manages the data use. These trusts function like legal trusts—allowing donors to define the types of use cases, activities, or organizations for which their data can be used. Trustees guide the conversation and negotiations in accordance to the donor wishes. You can donate your health data, therefore, for use in research but deny its use by for-profit organizations—even for research purposes. Numerous data trusts are active in Europe, the UK, and North America, which are often partnerships between government and research institutions. I suspect this trend will grow over time.

Data cooperatives (*https://oreil.ly/5hkgx*) have a similar structure but follow the rules of a cooperative. Like trusts, these are defined in a legal contract. In cooperatives, members vote on initiatives or fundamental changes, but there is often a steering committee to make day-to-day decisions. The group decides how the data is used and may even decide, collectively, to build analysis tools and do machine learning cooperatively. This democratic decision process allows adjustments and changes as new data types, data use cases, and data privacy technologies evolve. If you are starting a new data collective, please do reach out so I can share it via my networks as well. I see amazing potential for data use in collective structures.

Both of these structures allow more self-determination than the practice of selling data. In business-to-business data sales, people are not usually asked whether they want their data used or shared. Other than European, Californian, and Brazilian residents, most do not have the right to determine how their data will be used. Collective data ownership and consent allow users to directly manage, control, and opt in or out of particular sharing use cases, and can be combined with privacy technology requirements to enable safer sharing controls guided directly by the data owners.

How Can I Find All the Private Information That I Need to Protect?

As you learned in Chapter 1, the first step in identifying information to protect is to define the data you consider private. For example, you can break down the private data into PII, sensitive data, and more general person-related data with the help of privacy law professionals at your organization. If you don't have this guidance, start with broad categories: PII and other data. Remember that PII data represents data that can be used to determine an individual without advanced techniques or attacks, as you learned in Chapter 4.

But as you also learned in Chapter 1, there is no foolproof, automatic way to find all person-related data or PII. Start by documenting the frequently used datasets. Identify what is PII, what is sensitive person-related data, what is confidential corporate data, and what is person-related but less sensitive data, like a list of orders or music choices. Even for this less-sensitive category, you know that this data is still quite revealing on its own, which is why it is important to treat person-related data differently from other data required to run a business.

If you have significant amounts of semistructured data or document-based data, you can also use tools like Microsoft's Presidio to see if there are automated ways to identify some of the PII. If those tools don't work, you might want to think about buying or building a scanning tool that uses specific pattern-matching or NLP-based machine learning to identify when potential PII or other sensitive data is in a document.

Once identified, use lineage, tagging, and data governance measures to properly categorize, document, and track sensitive data. You need to ensure that this data always has appropriate protections and that any data flows or downstream products that use the sensitive data as a source are also properly protected. Refer to appropriate governance measures in Chapters 1 and 3.

I Dropped the Personal Identifiers, so the Data Is Safe Now, Right?

In attempting to protect private data, one frequent mistake I've seen is the elimination of the identifiers, such as name, date of birth, username, etc. This creates problems because the data still has private information and information leakage is quite likely (see Chapters 2 and 4). Once the identifiers are removed, you cannot easily use a technique like differential privacy because you can't immediately identify which rows belong to one another.

If someone has sent you a dataset like this, it's best to work with them to produce a truly privacy-friendly dataset by assisting them with software that provides differential privacy mechanisms. Dropping identifiers to anonymize data is not a real approach to privacy-preserving data sharing or data usage.

How Do I Reason About Data I Released in the Past?

If you have previously released data without using differential privacy, it is difficult to determine what amount of information was leaked. Ideally you can minimally identify which persons were in that dataset and determine if you'd like to remove them from future datasets to better protect them over time. If that is not possible, as it was not for the US Census, then craft a reasonable set of parameters going forward.

Moving to differential privacy from less secure methods is already a massive step forward. Rather than fixating on what might have been revealed in the past, spend more energy on how to track releases from here into the future. This will benefit your users now and help provide better protections for them moving forward.

If you are using differential privacy, several methods measure and track release of private information over time. Many of the best libraries—like Tumult Analytics—should let you combine techniques to calculate privacy loss. When you use differential privacy regularly, you must determine when you want to reset the privacy budget. To compare your choices with open and published differential privacy releases, take a look at the list of real-world differential privacy releases from Desfontaines (*https:// oreil.ly/B8AW2*).

For many real-world differential privacy use cases, you'll choose a more aggressive privacy budget reset to keep the quality of the data high. But experimenting and determining how to offer longer privacy budget guarantees for people is worth the time and effort, particularly if you are releasing data publicly. Focus on optimizing the amount of privacy protection you can guarantee while still delivering useful data for your releases. Talk with people who use the releases to find this balance and iterate and improve on it with each release.

I'm Working on a BI Dashboard or Visualization. How Do I Make It Privacy-Friendly?

If you are working in data visualization and using personal data, you might be wondering how to ensure that the visualizations are privacy-friendly. You can use and combine techniques to provide the appropriate level for the privacy risk. If you are providing visualizations for the general public based on research data or other company data, use differential privacy to provide appropriate and rigorous protections. For an internal dashboard that guides leadership decisions, ensure the granularity is coarse enough to avoid singling out attacks or displaying PII. Minimize personal data use and find the appropriate techniques by asking your users what data they actually need to make their decisions.

Both interactive and dynamic visualizations should be engineered and tested with this in mind. This probably means integrating privacy technologies into the data access mechanisms. This can be a normal part of development if you are building your own BI or visualization tools. If you are using packaged tools, like Tableau, PowerBI, or others, figure out how to create a data source that you know is appropriately tuned for the visualization.

Review techniques discussed in Chapter 3 to explore how data engineering work can integrate privacy techniques as a normal part of data processing. Maybe this means that only the raw data sources are fully unprotected and that all other databases and data storage have some privacy techniques applied. Or a particular database or data storage holds the processed private data but is accessible to only a few administrators, meaning that most of the internal and external data work uses protected data unless there is a very specific need.

Most visualizations want to visually convey trends, patterns, or changes in the data. At this level, the granularity is often coarse, so you can see much of the data at once. This is a great fit for differential privacy. If, however, you are using visualizations to find anomalies or outliers, make certain to protect them as best you can or that those using the visualization are aware that the data is highly sensitive.

Who Makes Privacy Engineering Decisions? How Do I Fit Privacy Engineering into My Organization?

Often it is the role of data governance at an organization to decide how privacy engineering fits into the current organizational structure. If your organization already has a strong governance process and you'd like to introduce your coworkers to privacy engineering, I recommend using Chapters 1, 3, and 8 to help guide your conversations and approach them in their own language and ways of working.

If your organization doesn't yet have a strong governance decision-making process, you'll want to support building that first. Privacy engineering should be implemented when, where, and how it makes sense for an organization. If an organization doesn't yet have a clear way of making these decisions, you'll end up with privacy technology clutter or scattered approaches. While I strongly believe in federated experimentation (see "Data Governance 2.0" on page 226 in Chapter 8), you need a guiding decision from a multidisciplinary group of experts based on business needs, regulatory landscape, and risk. This group should also help set the tone for decisions on the privacy versus information continuum and produce guidelines for using privacy technologies, in coordination with infosec and technology stakeholders.

If you are a technical leader in an organization and believe privacy engineering could benefit your platform, software, and data work, you are in a position to create privacy engineering and test how it could work. At the time of this writing, there is no one path for deploying privacy engineering teams; I anticipate this won't change in the coming years. This is because the privacy risk landscape and changing technological advances benefit from an agile approach. Use your own organizational and team knowledge to determine how to start, and be prepared to shift approaches regularly until you find an effective way to keep both the privacy engineers active and engaged as well as the teams working with them. Just like any other specialists in the organization, these folks work well in multiple advisory roles or when focusing on a particular difficult use case and moving along to the next priority.

If you want to be a privacy engineer and would like to advocate for this role at your organization, use the stakeholder management skills you've learned in discussing privacy and risk to start a conversation with the appropriate people at your organization (see "GDPR's Data Protection Impact Assessment: Agile and Iterative Risk Assessments" on page 209, "Working with Data Engineering Team and Leadership" on page 80, and "Data Security" on page 102). Even if you convince just one of them to take a chance on a proof of concept or even a series of awareness workshops, you are making progress. Keep up advocacy internally and ensure that you are bringing their attention to relevant use cases, business goals, and engineering challenges that prove how privacy technology and privacy engineering would help. Remember, they have many competing priorities and demands, so try to meet them where they are and distill what you are seeing from where you sit.

Regardless of your role at this moment, it is bound to change! If you stay up-to-date on privacy engineering by joining communities, conferences, and conversations, you're bound to find new pathways into this growing field.

What Skills or Background Do I Need to Become a Privacy Engineer?

Privacy engineering is a fairly new discipline, and the demands will change over time. Part of the reason I wrote this book is to expand the definition of a privacy engineer. Let's walk through where the field is now and where it could go.

Currently, most people who work as privacy engineers have advanced degrees in one of the technologies you learned in this book. They are cryptographers or differential privacy and/or distributed systems experts, having dedicated many years to understanding these fields in depth. They are capable of taking a blinking cursor and turning it into a new differential privacy mechanism, a cryptographic protocol, or a federated analysis system. If you are one of those people, I am honored you are reading this book. These roles are incredibly important and will grow, but they require years of study, mastery, and expertise—which you may not currently have.

When I analyze the needs of the current technical landscape, I see that the industry and field need people that can use these technologies without creating them from scratch. How can the field shift to have data engineers, data scientists, and software and platform engineers who can confidently use these technologies? As you have learned in this book, most of these tools require some specialized knowledge and a willingness to learn more when the problem presents complexity.

Just as there was a need for machine learning engineering, for DevSecOps, for platform engineering, I see a current need for a broader definition of privacy engineering. And this means expanding the definition of privacy engineers to those who have taken time to learn more about the problem and use the skill set they already have to apply privacy technologies to real-world problems.

Taking my definition further, this means you can help determine what skills you have, what skills you might need, and how you can contribute to privacy engineering. You could also decide it's worth entering an advanced study to focus on one of these technologies. Or you could decide to self-study, to engineer open source libraries into problems you are working on, and to continue learning.

My advice if you are just starting your career or if many of these concepts were new to you is to pick a focus. What chapter inspired you the most? What chapter made you want to read every paper linked or mentioned? Focus on that one and don't worry about the others for now. Read the literature, study with a book, or attend an online or in-person university course. Keep learning and talking with others in the field. Try applying it to a use case that you find. Learn from people with more experience or knowledge. You will make mistakes, and you will learn from them.

As you grow your knowledge and skills, there will be a point where you notice that you don't have to look up as many things, where you can analyze the problem more easily, where the solution becomes obvious, and where you can explain it to others and teach them. Perhaps this is the point where you are willing and able to call yourself a privacy engineer.

Eventually this field will have stronger definitions and clearer job expectations. One day there will be a list of questions to ace the privacy engineering interview. But that point is not right now, when privacy technologies are first being integrated and used daily at a growing number of companies. Be willing to live in the ambiguity of job descriptions right now, and be willing to do this work even if you don't call yourself a privacy engineer. Your early and avid involvement will open up new opportunities for you and others and help expand today's definitions to larger and more inclusive groups.

Why Didn't You Mention (Insert Technology or Company Here)? How Do I Learn More? Help!

Should any new technologies, cool companies, or open source libraries come up that either I didn't include or that might have not been available as of early 2023, please always feel free to reach out and start a conversation (*https://probablyprivate.com*). As I have mentioned, I will continue a thread on FAQs to help inform and update as the field grows and develops.

That said, you also now have a base theoretical understanding and numerous practical examples. I hope that you can use this book to continue thinking critically about the space and evaluate how new technologies fit into your use cases and needs as they emerge.

There is also a growing global and many local communities around privacy technologies, privacy regulation, and interpretations of privacy. Sometimes all it takes is a post asking for help or advice. Choose platforms you enjoy using and connect with others who care about these topics. If you are stuck, ask publicly or contact folks privately. When you figure something out, write a blog post or give a short video about what you found. You can and should participate in this conversation and help others along the way. Sometimes by synthesizing what you have learned, you will also solidify your understanding and, via your research, learn new technologies, approaches, or interpretations.

GDPR and Data Protection Regulations

This section covers questions related to GDPR and data protection regulations that you read about in Chapter 8.

Do I Really Need to Use Differential Privacy to Remove Data from GDPR/CPRA/LGPD/etc. Requirements?

I cannot give you legal advice, because I am not a privacy lawyer. I can share, however, that I have never met a privacy lawyer who said that differential privacy would not work to meet these regulations requirements for anonymization.

But I have also spoken with many privacy lawyers who say that other techniques also work, such as redacting all PII or applying k-anonymity or other less secure and privacy-preserving methods. If you choose to avoid using a technique like differential privacy—for whatever reason—it would be best to consult a lawyer.

It's also important to note that newer regulations will have new requirements. Ones based on GDPR will have clauses similar to what you reviewed in Chapter 8, asking for techniques that apply current state-of-the-art guarantees. This means that definitions like differential privacy are more future-proof than weaker and older techniques.

When collaborating with lawyers who want your input, look at the various approaches explored in this book and dive in on those you find appropriate. You can use Chapter 8 for advice on working with lawyers on legal requirements and look at Chapter 9 for thinking through use cases, should you need inspiration.

I Heard That I Can Use Personal Data Under GDPR for Legitimate Interest. Is That Correct?

You might have heard about legitimate interest, either from a lawyer or from seeing the legitimate interest sections of cookies or other trackers. What does legitimate interest mean?

Under GDPR you can use personal data for legitimate interest without explicitly obtaining user consent for that processing. This is outlined directly in the regulation as follows:

> Processing shall be lawful only if and to the extent that … processing is necessary for the purposes of the legitimate interests pursued by the controller or by a third party, except where such interests are overridden by the interests or fundamental rights and freedoms of the data subject which require protection of personal data, in particular where the data subject is a child.

But how does one prove legitimate interest? And what exactly is covered under it? The ICO provided some useful advice on this (*https://oreil.ly/9VCEZ*), outlining a three-part test based on prior regulatory advice when managing sensitive data. The test has the following steps:

Purpose test
Is there a legitimate interest behind the processing?

Necessity test
Is the processing necessary for that purpose?

Balancing test
Is the legitimate interest overridden by the individual's interests, rights, or freedoms?

The ICO goes on to give several examples of possible legitimate interest, like fraud detection or direct processing related to serving the customer's requests. The article also addresses how direct marketing can be covered by legitimate interest if it is balanced with an individual's rights and interests.

But there have been occasions when the courts have ruled that legitimate interest does not cover the processing. In 2020, the ICO issued a notice and fine for Experian due to data brokerage activities, which Experian qualified under legitimate interest (*https://oreil.ly/Kd-OP*) and a follow-up report on data broker compliance for those who collect and broker data via legitimate interest (*https://oreil.ly/v5hX7*). In another example, the French authorities fined Clearview AI €20 million (*https://oreil.ly/EO8Aj*), rejecting its claim that scraping images of people online to provide facial detection systems was legitimate interest.[5]

If you are collecting data directly from persons for a specific use and then using it for a secondary purpose, you will need to determine with your privacy professionals if this is acceptable. If you didn't collect the data directly, you should evaluate how to notify individuals of the processing and use and ensure you follow Article 14 requirements (*https://oreil.ly/X7nXS*).

---

5 The company shortly thereafter raised cash via another funding round—plausibly to finance the payment.

In data collection and processing work, you will need to speak to a lawyer to best understand what falls under legitimate interest for your use case. If this is your primary purpose for processing data, stay abreast of news about fines and regulatory intervention. Asking for consent is always the more secure way to make certain the data complies with GDPR's recommendations.

I Want to Comply with Schrems II and Transatlantic Data Flows. What Are Possible Solutions?

The current practices for dealing with Schrems II (*https://oreil.ly/4SYfs*) are unlikely to remain; they are, basically, an extension of the old practices. This means the core issue, NSA snooping on data flows, is not truly alleviated by these interventions or responses. If you want to be future-thinking, shift your approach to transatlantic data flows toward a longer time frame. Cloud providers such as Microsoft and Amazon are already evolving their infrastructure to allow some larger European customers more choice and autonomy for preventing data flow into the US.

If you are unfamiliar, Schrems II was a European court ruling that outlawed the prior processes used to protect European residents under transatlantic data flows, previously covered under the EU-US Privacy Shield (*https://oreil.ly/QTSpI*). The legal argument was that non-US Citizens and European residents should be able to use services without US intelligence agencies snooping on those activities. After the Snowden revelations regarding PRISM and other NSA surveillance programs (*https://oreil.ly/RdFEg*), it is clear that this means that data flowing into the United States is not guaranteed to remain secret even if it is encrypted via SSL and TLS. Also important to understand here is that data stored in the US or any other jurisdiction is always subject to warrants, making it critical that companies continue publishing transparency reports (*https://oreil.ly/kEhtM*) and that you read them to review what services you would like to use at your organization.

This lawsuit was a follow-up to a previous ruling (Schrems I) that invalidated Privacy Shield but was ambiguous about its replacement. These lawsuits were brought forth by Max Schrems, a lawyer and privacy activist based in Austria who founded noyb, which stands for "My Data is None of Your Business," a nonprofit data rights organization (*https://noyb.eu/en*). Lawsuits like these will probably continue because current practices have changed very little.

Several interesting technologies described in this book could help protect data from snooping and, therefore, better future-proof transatlantic data flows. Consider federated data analysis (Chapter 6) and distributed encrypted computations (Chapter 7). Personally, I could see a future in which these technologies are used to meet more stringent standards, put forward by the European Court, to protect its citizens and residents from US government snooping.

Personal Choices and Social Privacy

This section covers personal choices around privacy and privacy's social aspects. I find these questions very interesting and get them frequently when I speak about data privacy. I included these in hopes it will inspire you to discuss privacy with colleagues, friends, and family.

What Email Provider, Browser, and Application Should I Use if I Care About My Privacy?

As privacy awareness grows, so does the availability of privacy-friendly services. There are now so many that I couldn't provide a comprehensive list of all options here. But, as you learned in Chapter 8, reading through the privacy policy and terms of service can tell you how your data is handled. Here are a few points to help you come to your own decision:

Data collection
> What data is collected? This should be apparent in the privacy policy text. Investigate ways to turn off optional data collection. For example, most browsers allow you to choose whether debugging data can be sent to the browser provider. You can also install extra plug-ins that protect your privacy or that block extra data collection. If you are curious, you can also watch your own network traffic via Wireshark or even reverse engineer your applications to determine what data is being sent where. If you have the time and energy, a closer look can be fascinating.[6]

Data storage and location
> Where and how is the data stored? If you live in the EU, you might decide to keep your data inside EU borders.[7] If so, there are a few services that offer to keep your data within the EU or the EU plus several other countries, like Switzerland. This ensures the data is not easily available to authorities outside of the EU. There are also services that allow you to determine your storage location—for example, to set up your own cloud or backup storage location or to choose local-first or local-only storage. As discussed in Chapter 6, local-first data is a new and exciting trend that I expect to grow over time.

---

6 If you find something new or interesting, please publish it and share!

7 EU authorities have also tried the NSA methods of snooping on internet traffic, including the BND demanding access to DE-CIX, a major networking interchange in Frankfurt. DE-CIX sued BND and won (*https://oreil.ly/YEWyW*), making the access illegal.

Data retention and portability

How long is the data held, and can you move your data at will? To discover the retention period, read through the privacy policies or directly ask if they are not listed. Usually you can write a company via their privacy contact address to ask such questions. For portability, keep your own backup of your data. Nearly every service has a way to export your data thanks to GDPR and other regulations aimed at avoiding data lock-in. It makes sense to take a look at what data you can export and to decide if you'd like to regularly export data and delete it from the service.[8]

Data sharing and third-party usage

Who are third parties that can use or access the data or who receive shared data? This is not always obvious and might not be listed in the privacy policy, but look for a section on third parties and what services they provide. You can also contact the company directly to ask, but it might not be shared with you. If you find a privacy policy or company that clearly describes how data is shared and what third parties are involved, that company is probably more transparent than most.

Encryption and keys

How is data encryption used, and who has the keys? As you learned in Chapter 7, data can now be used while remaining encrypted. There are many services that provide end-to-end encryption without ever needing to decrypt the data, like messaging applications or browsers. To evaluate if the application does so, this is normally described not only in the privacy policy but also in the marketing of the product itself. You should find out where the encryption keys are stored and how often they are rotated. If they are stored *only* with you or on-device, then this means the company cannot and will not decrypt your messages. You might be interested to learn how the Signal protocol works and how to turn it on for messaging applications, like WhatsApp (*https://oreil.ly/gVw-d*). In contrast, when keys are stored on the service itself, they can be used by the service to decrypt the data.

---

8 I'll be personally sharing several of my home data creations via my blog and sharing them on the Probably Private newsletter (*https://probablyprivate.com*), if you want inspiration!

There are a few organizations that regularly review services based on privacy considerations. I recommend Mozilla foundation's privacy not included (*https://oreil.ly/A0KVi*) to folks who ask me for product recommendations, because it is a good starting point for questions. There is also a fairly comprehensive curated awesome-privacy list (*https://oreil.ly/Xv15u*) with plenty of great recommendations. If you use iOS, take a look at the application privacy details (*https://oreil.ly/7EUeC*) for an idea of what data is used and how, and to investigate if there are ways to turn off collection.

Using the previous criteria will aid you in coming to your own decision about your comfort level with various applications, browsers, and services. If you've done this research, make sure to share it to help others make informed decisions.

My Friend Has an Automated Home or Phone Assistant. I Don't Want It Listening to Me. What Should I Do?

It can be difficult to navigate privacy boundaries with friends and family; it is often a hard conversation for everyone involved. The best advice I can give is to approach all conversations with empathy and be clear about your own needs. There is nothing worse than a conversation that goes sideways because there is an early misunderstanding or defensiveness that triggers an emotional reaction; then the other person can no longer hear what you are trying to say.

Start by being straightforward about your needs and your boundaries. Tell them what you would like, but without judgment. Perhaps you say something like, "Hey, I know you use Alexa and it works well for you but, personally, I feel uncomfortable. Could you turn it off when I am visiting? That would help me feel more secure and be able to enjoy our time." Obviously, this is easier if you are guest. If you are living with someone, it will require a longer discussion and willingness to compromise.

This conversation goes more smoothly if they are interested in learning more about your concerns. Apply the knowledge you've gained through this book, and you can be the privacy champion and educator within your family or circle of friends. Again, the more you approach these conversations with openness, without judgment, and with questions and information, the better they will go. Along the way, you'll learn what works for you. Each conversation and well-set boundary will add to your own knowledge, understanding, practice, and skills, giving you confidence to move forward.

This is a good time to remind you: many online and technology choices end up affecting the privacy of people close to you such as when installing applications that look in your contacts or connect with your address book. Being social is part of the joy of these online connections, sometimes even the entire point! In an ideal future, these applications would provide the necessary privacy and opt-out options so that people can keep connecting, talking, and living without fear. In this future, the responsibility of providing and enforcing privacy lies on the company or organization providing the service, not the individual.

I Gave Up on Privacy a Long Time Ago. I Have Nothing to Hide. Why Should I Change?

When I talk about privacy in larger groups and more general settings, I often get a question asking why I am working on privacy. Inevitably, there is someone who has decided that "privacy is dead" and that everyone should just give up and just submit to unlimited surveillance and data collection without consent. Usually, there is also someone who claims the only people who want privacy are criminals or terrorists. Since everyone else has "nothing to hide," society should kill all privacy in the name of "security."[9]

In case you come across individuals like this, here are some ways to reason with these extremist opinions. For those who argue that privacy is dead or that everyone should give up, I ask them if they have ever been a victim of something like revenge porn, where revealing or sexually explicit images or videos of a person are posted on the internet without their consent to cause them distress or embarrassment. The common response I hear is no, but this example helps them understand the impact of privacy on people who are not like them. It usually also jolts them out of their assumptions around privacy, which is useful because these assumptions are often incorrect. If this example works for you, you can ask them to imagine that such a violation happened to them. How would they feel? How would they react? Every human can get tunnel vision and assume that others have experiences like theirs. For people who argue that privacy is dead, I've noticed that they haven't used empathy to better understand why others might need privacy and why it is worth the fight.[10]

Choose examples that work for you, of course. Some examples that show the importance of privacy are police surveillance in particular neighborhoods, state surveillance of immigrants or dissidents, price gouging based on personalized advertising, or even search result tampering. These are all examples where unequal access to privacy and information create problematic relationships of power, control, and oppression. If better privacy were provided for everyone, especially those who need it most, many of these issues would cease to exist.

---

9 Perhaps there is also a pessimistic view here, where they feel resigned to this fate. If so, I hope you can cheer them up and give them some hope!

10 If revenge porn doesn't work for you, you can try several other examples, such as unlawful arrest (*https://oreil.ly/eDAJ7*), targeted misinformation (*https://oreil.ly/6r9AO*), or political protest (*https://oreil.ly/pkzNU*).

For those who argue that privacy is not required because they have nothing to hide, you can point out that they cannot speak for everyone else. For example, if their data does not hurt them and they directly benefit from more data collection, then you can remind them that not everyone benefits from more data collection. I sometimes describe how their own data can single out other groups in harmful ways. If they are benefiting from a model outcome, there is probably another group—unlike them—in another decision boundary where the outcome is not as favorable, like with credit scoring algorithms. It's important to remember that privacy and benefits from privacy are not evenly distributed—like other forms of privilege in our world.[11] This distinction is not always obvious to those with the most privilege in a given society.

The privacy versus security argument is one that will continue for many years to come. I personally have never been able to sway someone who believes that privacy is detrimental to security. Maybe you will have better luck; if so, please feel free to write me on how the conversation went as I am curious! This debate is important even when the people in the discussion don't agree. Sharing how privacy violations and surveillance affects many humans worldwide makes the fight for privacy rights stronger. I encourage you to keep speaking truth and fighting for privacy with empathy and compassion—despite the odds and counterarguments.

There are plenty of talented security professionals who also see the fields as supportive, rather than combative. If you follow legislative debates around topics like building "backdoors" into cryptographic systems (*https://oreil.ly/0lsqL*) or creating key escrows (*https://oreil.ly/AWG6F*), so others can get access to decryption keys without consent, you will also see the strong pushback from security and cryptographic efforts against insecure and privacy-leaking systems.

Can I Just Sell My Own Data to Companies?

I've had numerous conversations with folks working on ways to empower users to directly sell their data. I'm not a big fan of this idea because it could incentivize the industry's same privacy problems and possibly exacerbate other problems, such as algorithmic bias and unequal treatment of people and their data.[12] Despite that, there is a burgeoning interest in allowing users to directly sell their data for usage.

---

11 To learn more about this, I recommend reading *Race after Technology* by Ruha Benjamin (2019) and *Dark Matters* by Simone Browne (2015) and following Professor Chris Gilliard's work (*https://oreil.ly/WP5jm*).

12 I gave a talk on these and related problems in 2019 at the Chaos Communication Camp (*https://oreil.ly/w6LvN*).

There are numerous startups and platforms that have built data ecosystems, but no single marketplace has won significant traction. There are, of course, successful user research and survey-based marketplaces, but there you also need to spend time answering questions about yourself or participating in surveys or research work.

There will need to be a significant shift in the ways companies collect and use data before these marketplaces succeed. If it becomes harder for companies to offer products for free in exchange for massive amounts of data collection, then these companies would be incentivized to change their business model. If companies cannot collect enough data, this would open opportunities for users to directly sell their data.

What does excite me is the concept of users with locally controlled data. Access could be given or revoked at any time. This concept, combined with technologies like federated learning, encrypted computation, and differential privacy, would protect the data being used. If people, regulators, and communities got together to collectively manage their data, this achieves stronger bargaining power and produces better outcomes for everyone involved. This potential future is exciting and could support research and government initiatives to solve problems using insights from data.[13]

I Like Personalized Ads. Why Don't You?

I have been in numerous conversations where people are offended or feel personally attacked when I explain that I do not like personalized advertising. This can be a touchy subject.[14]

Since this is clearly provocative for some people, it's worthwhile to determine what benefit they get from personalized ads. One response I have often heard is that people find out about interesting products they didn't know existed. This is a great example of personalized ads working well for them!

Personalized ads do not, however, always work that way. You've probably experienced buying a gift and being shown similar products for weeks, even though you are not actually interested in them. Or you view a product and decide not to buy it, but it continues to follow you around. Or you experience a tragic moment (*https://oreil.ly/MqDdV*), which then follows you as a sad reminder and toxic spiral. There is a reason why some of the most popular browser extensions are those that block ads. They can be annoying and unhelpful in many cases.

---

13 Nimisha Asthagiri and I gave a talk on this at Strangeloop 2022 (*https://oreil.ly/M-MP_*).

14 If someone is very reactive when discussing personalized ads or any topics from this chapter, it's a good idea to just back away from the conversation completely. When someone is deeply triggered or defensive, the conversation is unlikely to go anyplace productive.

There are also times when personalized ads can be malicious. In *Weapons of Math Destruction*, Cathy O'Neill reports how lower income groups received targeted advertisements for profit-based colleges that offer little actual education. Professor Latanya Sweeney discovered that criminal records ads were being shown when her name was searched (*https://oreil.ly/A-T8f*), likely because those ads were targeting searches for names more common in US Black communities. In *Algorithms of Oppression*, Professor Safiya Noble exposed sexualization and objectification of BIPoC people and communities via targeted ads and search results, which I also found via my own NLP research (*https://oreil.ly/_DBPv*). These examples are just a few of many that show how personalized ads can do actual harm to individuals—and why many privacy activists including myself want personalized ads to be an opt-in and explicit decision rather than a default.

There are better approaches when thinking about recommendations and intention-based search. Within the field of recommendations, there is now more experimentation with session-based recommendations, where the actions of the user for a short period guides the recommendations rather than anything personalized (i.e., PII-based or long user-history based). I anticipate some exciting possibilities to make ads and recommendations more useful by removing the personalization and, instead, focusing on intention. Regardless of my age, gender, race, class, and job, if I am looking for a good thriller to watch, that is what I want to see ads for right now. And, if two hours later I'm searching for a pizza joint, then there is no need to correlate the two or anything else about me to provide me with that recommendation.

Is (Fill in the Blank) Listening to Me? What Should I Do About It?

Powerful algorithms, patterns, and trends—and related privacy leakage—make people believe they are being listened to via applications because of how that leaked information can be connected. Although it has been shown that there are discrepancies in wake words (*https://oreil.ly/keTKx*) as well as meeting software that listens for noise all the time (*https://oreil.ly/Ml7Yo*), it is unlikely your application is listening to you without your knowledge unless it is specifically designed to do so (i.e., home assistants, security cameras, etc.).[15]

---

15 If your threat model involves a real threat of state surveillance, please ignore this advice and assume that your devices and online communications cannot be trusted.

In general, applications should not be trusted until you have thoroughly reviewed the terms and privacy policy. If something seems suspicious or if you fear that an application does have spyware or adware on it, the best idea is to disable and uninstall it immediately. There are many examples (*https://oreil.ly/7FOuC*) of malicious applications (*https://oreil.ly/zzO11*) hidden as helpful free applications—like for weather, games, or other utility functions. Reading the reviews and looking up the application developer is a good idea!

Applications seem to be listening because of the vast array of data available to them. It could be that people close to you end up searching what you told them about using your home WiFi. It could be that you searched something related yourself or recently purchased something related to the topic. It could be that there is a trend or other pattern that is highly correlated and making it seem that—just as you hear about something—it is following you. This can be via either ads or algorithmic recommendation systems that will use vast datasets and trends to determine how to make you "engage." These scenarios are real examples of ways that data is collected today and used to link people across disparate datasets in targeted advertising and content.[16]

Even though these applications are not actively listening to you, transcribing your words and then feeding it back to you in algorithmic form, they are still violating basic privacy by failing to ask for consent to link these disparate data sources. If you feel as though your privacy has been violated or that something is listening to you, communicate that to the privacy team at that company. It might not change their business model or approach, but the more they hear it, the better.

When possible, review more privacy-friendly applications. Unfortunately, this often means paying for privacy, which is not possible for all persons. Sometimes this means paying for an application where privacy is built in, or it could be that you have to do more things for yourself or with more effort, like building your own system for sharing photos. This is a useful reminder that privacy and privilege are deeply intertwined.

This shows how privacy inequalities are perpetuated and how users are punished for choosing privacy, making it less accessible and easy for everyone and violating the principles of Privacy by Design. In a privacy-respecting potential future, users can and should safely install applications and use software with secure and privacy-first defaults that support respectful and consensual data use—regardless of the amount of money they have or time they invest.

---

16 Cracked Labs issued a very telling report on corporate surveillance (*https://oreil.ly/3mLjE*) if you'd like an in-depth view of some of the larger data vendors that collect and link data for companies.

Summary

In this chapter, you reviewed commonly asked questions related to many of the topics covered in this book. As stated in the introduction, this wasn't meant to be read from start to finish but instead used as a handy reference should these questions come up in your work and life. As you apply what you have learned, you will develop your own opinions and approaches that are different from mine. This is not only fine, it is encouraged!

I'll keep exploring these questions via my newsletter, Probably Private (*https://proba blyprivate.com*), so subscribe and send questions to keep the conversation going.

## CHAPTER 11

Go Forth and Engineer Privacy!

You've learned so much in this book thus far! I hope you are inspired to do data science differently. You've learned a variety of new skills, theories, and technologies that can help you steer your team and the entire industry in new directions. To wrap up, I'd like to discuss the impact that data has on the world and how you can make choices that affect not only your daily work but also the lives of others.

I'm going to walk through several alarming phenomenon that machine learning and its related data analysis and collection have created or expedited in the world. Then I'll go through ways communities are fighting back and using techniques you've learned in this book to have more control of their life and work.

Surveillance Capitalism and Data Science

You may have heard the term *surveillance capitalism* (*https://oreil.ly/zVb4q*) before; perhaps you've even read the book by Shoshana Zuboff of the same title.

Surveillance capitalism describes an economic system where personal data is used as a form of capital. The phrase "If it's free, you are the product" exactly explains what surveillance capitalism is and how it functions. The idea of collecting data by providing free or discounted services is not new, but the ability to turn that data into massive value is fairly recent. Advances in data collection, analysis, and machine learning open new possibilities where data brings value to a company and therefore has become a form of capital.

But why should you care? Presumably, you work in data science and benefit from the fact that data is more valuable. It would be hard to imagine getting paid to work solely with data if it was not valuable. The work that you do as a data scientist, data engineer, and/or machine learning engineer means that you take data and make it more valuable. You are compensated based on that increased value, and, therefore, you benefit directly from the same forces that created surveillance capitalism.

Of course, this is exactly why you, and all data scientists, should care. If you don't analyze the systems you directly benefit from, it is difficult to properly see them and their effects on the world. This is normal and expected and directly related to how power and privilege function in societies. Until you examine surveillance capitalism and come to your own conclusions about how it impacts humans, society, and the world separate from your own benefits, you won't be able to clearly speak about it.

In this section, I'll walk through several things I have observed regarding surveillance capitalism, but I encourage you to further explore it on your own.

Gig Workers and Surveillance at Work

The impact of surveillance capitalism on human work is readily apparent in the rise of gig workers. *Gig worker* is a term that describes someone who works as an independent contractor on a part-time basis. Essentially, these workers are freelancers, but often they find their jobs via platforms or marketplaces that have sprung up in recent years, offering small jobs of varying levels of time and attention. The word is derived from the concept of a "gig" for musicians playing in exchange for money that was often variable—dependent on the audience, the venue, and the other musicians.

The promise to gig workers is a more flexible lifestyle—but that is not how it has worked out for many gig workers. Companies that created the gig economy use massive amounts of data collection from their workers and their customers to optimize profits. Workers are enticed to work longer hours when demand is high and disincentivized through lower margins when demand is low. Unfortunately, rather than offering a flexible schedule, gig work becomes part-time shift work without the benefits of healthcare, stability, minimum wage requirements, or paid vacations because the workers are "independent contractors."

And it doesn't actually end there for most gig workers. Continual rating and management of their activities with algorithms adds an extra level of pressure that most of us will never experience in our work life. Being evaluated at every interaction, sometimes by people who you cannot see because they are using a doorbell camera to watch you, is truly a dystopian future taken directly out of *Black Mirror* episodes. This behavior is the focus of Data and Society's report on gig workers and digital cameras used at doors to surveil them (*https://oreil.ly/Vx4-9*). This algorithmic management has extended into other areas of the economy and world—now influencing and affecting the working life of many shift workers, factory workers, and an increasing number of other jobs.

Surveillance for "Security"

When evaluating surveillance capitalism, you will immediately come into contact with surveillance systems deemed as ways to enhance security. Similar to using door cameras to "manage" gig workers and surveil their activities in order to "feel safe," these systems are then extended and deployed at scale by both residents and federal, state, and local authorities.

This poses the question, does surveillance actually reduce crime? As you might expect, answering this question is not only difficult, it also ignores many reasons why crime occurs. This, however, has not stopped many US cities from expanding surveillance machinery and systems (*https://oreil.ly/3Dgb5*) paid by taxpayers, whether they are successful or not. This occurs not only in the US, of course. Witness the rise of CCTV and facial recognition systems in the UK (*https://oreil.ly/tGByZ*), massive surveillance in China (*https://oreil.ly/pyofp*), and increased private surveillance in South Africa (*https://oreil.ly/5gGu7*)—all in the name of security.

Predictive policing systems reinforce biased policing and strengthen it via feedback loops (*https://oreil.ly/jhhgA*). If police are already targeting BIPoC, poor, or immigrant communities, the shift toward algorithmic systems increases the chances of this behavior and creates a feedback loop that will mean police are exclusively deployed to these neighborhoods. What crime is happening elsewhere that is not being addressed? What other safety measures could police provide if they were not being instructed by an algorithm? Finally, are policing and surveillance systems the answer to the root causes of crime in today's world?

But it doesn't stop there—surveillance of political dissent has a long history in the realm of "security." This is easy to see in systems like China's Great Firewall, but also clear in systems like Palantir, Clearview AI, and technology used by many governments to monitor internet traffic and social media content, extending to local authorities and universities as well (*https://oreil.ly/j8CB_*).

Luxury Surveillance

Very nearly the opposite of gig worker style surveillance, the concept of luxury surveillance is perfectly articulated by Professor Chris Gilliard in the Atlantic (*https://oreil.ly/mRQ06*). The idea? You pay, essentially, to be surveilled by private companies due to small conveniences and "luxuries" you receive from the algorithmic use of your data and that of others. Examples here range and expand daily—from intelligent home devices and smart watches to self-driving cars that record data and send it back for centralized training.

This may describe several people you know, fitting well in the "I have nothing to hide" category outlined in "Personal Choices and Social Privacy" on page 279. But the use of this data should make us wonder if anyone is being harmed by this type of luxury. You need look no further than this chapter or ask what else your data might be used for (*https://oreil.ly/QqFyc*) and who it might be used against (*https://oreil.ly/blqoN*).

When you contribute your data directly to systems without ability to retract that data, you have almost no say in how that data is used. What is currently a luxury for you could be a surveillance nightmare for someone else. You know from your data work that when you encode data into multidimensional space, there are also unmapped or unknown regions of that feature and decision space. What happens to the people who live in those "regions"? What happens to people who don't have the same life or lifestyle as you? Is your data used to push other people further into another decision area or out of all decisions whatsoever (*https://oreil.ly/oUX6S*)? Is your data used to target them for different types of systems?

Finally, what benefits you today may not benefit you forever. Companies will change how they use data, with whom they share it, and where it is stored and processed without asking for your consent. Protecting your own and others' data now is the only way to avoid future scenarios where that data is used against you or in ways you do not condone.

Vast Data Collection and Society

The current practice of collecting vast amounts of data as a potential asset affects our society because it fundamentally changes how people control public information about them. A good read on the philosophy of privacy is Helen Nissenbaum's *Privacy as Contextual Integrity*, in which she outlines how privacy is inherently contextual. This context is easy to lose or miss when real-world interactions are translated into online or software interactions.

This shift is also seen in the way that younger people have needed to respond to create identity online. danah boyd's work *It's Complicated: The Social Lives of Networked Teens* illuminated this 10 years ago. These are ongoing trends in social media, clear in user choices like "Finstas" (fake Instagram accounts used to to interact with profiles when you want to pseudonymize your identity) and ephemeral media choices (i.e., disappearing messages) on messaging applications.

I'll outline two areas where I see troubling shifts happening in the current landscape: generative machine learning as a form of data laundering and the rise and spread of targeted disinformation and misinformation.

Machine Learning as Data Laundering

The rise of generative machine learning has been evident since the arrival of GANs, and the size and use of these models as well as other generative architectures have vastly increased in recent years. Models such as DALL-E, GPT-3, and Stable

Diffusion make it easy for anyone, anywhere, to generate new text, images, audio, and video in seconds. Projects like GitLab's Copilot could be used, one day, to write whole swaths of programs based on prompts. Becoming a "prompt engineer" is now a new potential career path.

This all sounds like great advances in machine learning, right? Shouldn't I be excited to see the field reaching new heights? Frankly, the rise of the massive models means fairly poor outcomes for privacy and control of your own information. You probably already know that these models are trained with terabytes of data, scraped directly from the internet and further refined by the daily user interactions, often without clear notification. There is no attention paid to copyright notices, the context of the content, or permission from site creators or maintainers. This has led to cases like ISIS executions and nonconsensual porn that can be directly found in Stable Diffusion models (*https://oreil.ly/YTEVN*) or journalists finding their writing in GPT-3 (*https://oreil.ly/FTuFC*). Should these trends continue, who will be able to control their own face, their own voice, their own words, and the use of them?

When data is released online, it is with the assumption that a human will find that content, review it in its full form, and, potentially, interact with the author or creator. Data scraping to feed large models ignores and subverts this context. It takes data, stripped of its context and intention, to train massive algorithmic models, which essentially stores fragments of that data for later use in often very different contexts. It destroys not only the contextual integrity of that data but also any semblance of privacy and consent. This is also the case with using daily user interactions, which many users believe are private, to further refine reinforcement learning in systems like ChatGPT-3+.

I have argued that these systems look a lot like data laundering, and I am not alone (*https://oreil.ly/-LYRy*). Taking others' work, words, faces, and voices and using an algorithm to "wash" them of attribution rights and consent rights is like taking money and washing its origin to claim it is "clean." The use of "AI" as a way to deflect blame and remove accountability is a trend that has been happening for many years, apparent in deaths caused by self-driving cars (*https://oreil.ly/Uv-tF*). It removes the responsibility of the people and companies making those algorithms and places blame on the model itself or the humans interacting with the model.

These models have taken data from all over the internet, including artists' work from profiles, content from educators and influencers, and paid content from hardworking journalists, programmers, and authors, and used it as their own capital.[1] Unsurprisingly, these models can now mimic humans who were not asked whether they

---

[1] For those who were paid for their work on labeling, writing and interacting to build larger training datasets, they were often severely underpaid (*https://oreil.ly/PvH-c*).

wanted their data or their content used. Those creators are unlikely to ever see remuneration or get credit for their contributions.

Disinformation and Misinformation

The rise of online disinformation and misinformation has been fueled by the gaming of algorithms for financial benefit. "Falling down a *(insert social media or online content platform)* hole" is a common phrase because of the ways that recommendation algorithms work and how they optimize nudges toward more "engaging" content, where people will like, click, reply, dislike, or otherwise interact with the content. This "engagement" could also be called *enragement*, because these algorithmic optimization systems find shortcuts via polarized and outraging content.

There have been numerous studies on this phenomenon (*https://oreil.ly/47yq_*) on a variety of platforms; it is a clear outcome of engagement metrics and the near real-time optimization of these metrics via recommendation engines. Regardless of the algorithm you choose—reinforcement learning, multi-armed bandits, or other more simplistic models—this is the effect of optimizing for clicks, views, comments, likes/dislikes, and time on site.

The Cambridge Analytica scandal also demonstrated that patterns in private data can reveal other private attributes, such as how or even if someone will vote. Personalized advertising makes it easy to then target these voters based on something as simple as a handful of online likes to persuade them to vote, not vote, or vote a particular way. Data analysts can trivialize this danger as a "fun" data insight (*https://oreil.ly/IxCPw*), but campaign managers are well aware that this type of targeting is very effective in mobilizing, demobilizing, and influencing voters.

Writing misinformation and disinformation is now a fruitful way to make money online, given the amount of money platforms pay to advertisers and platform participants who produce engaging content. A study by MIT Technology Review (*https://oreil.ly/XPczL*) revealed the expanse of the problem, showing that one could make a fairly decent income by just producing clickbait articles full of misinformation. The growth and reach of this type of misinformation—and, sometimes, disinformation (*https://oreil.ly/gU-o3*)—is assisted by recommendation algorithms that make it more "valuable" for everyone to produce and rapidly increasing the number of humans affected.

Being able to easily, quickly, and automatically target and influence people based on their income, gender, race, family, and political preferences at massive scale is a new phenomena. The effect it has on societies over time is not completely understood. Studies have shown that it facilitates the spread of conspiracy theories and mistrust, eroding social systems and political goodwill. This undermines political systems and social values and polarizes political and social topics, which is antithetical to democratic and socialist values.

Fighting Back

Change is the only constant in the world. The way things are right now does not have to be the way they are forever. I have decided to focus my time, passion, energy, and work on privacy because I strongly believe that shifting this in the data industry is a way to influence the problems described thus far in the chapter.

With the knowledge you have from your own work and what you have learned from this book, you can decide to have an impact on your team, on your product, and on larger societal problems and questions. Privacy technology will not solve all these problems, but awareness of the issues and a critical eye regarding the use of private data, along with this knowledge, can contribute to changing the current state.

In this section, I want to share what I think can help our societies and world. There is nothing more inspiring than groups of people working together on problems—find other like-minded folks and communities and stay in touch.

Researching, Documenting, Hacking, Learning

This book has included hundreds of citations from researchers, journalists, hackers, and thinkers. None of the knowledge I have gained in my career, and now shared with you, would be possible without the number of people who have worked, are working, and will work on data privacy.

Work by activists, researchers, and hackers shows that even companies such as Apple, which has teams dedicated to differential privacy, have vast privacy leaks (*https://oreil.ly/e9Xqx*). Embrace the hacker mindset of looking deeper and checking to see if things really work as they say they do. This research can reveal new attacks, spread new understanding, and unearth untoward practices.

So, keep learning! Keep researching! Keep hacking! These methods build a better understanding of privacy problems and inspire new ways to address them.

Collectivizing Data

Working directly with people affected daily by surveillance capitalism and algorithmic oppression is one way not only to learn more about the real effects of vast data collection systems but also to empower people with their own data. There have been numerous successful protests and actions against mistreatment and exploitation of gig workers; data skills can assist these actions in the future.

Organizations like Driver's Seat (*https://driversseat.co*) help gig workers see their own data and earnings, allowing them to come to their own conclusions about when and how they would like to work. As you may know from your own work, data can empower people to make better decisions. Some organizations also work with local governments like the Worker Observatory (*https://workersobservatory.org*); if you are interested in this work, see if there are any local initiatives in your area.

Beyond gig workers, there are, in fact, many other opportunities to collectivize data and fundamentally shift power in the current data trends. For example, what if you and your neighbors optimized deliveries together instead of individually? What if you and a group of friends tailored your search results to better reflect what you actually wanted to find on the internet? What if you collaborated with your peers to create a fine-tuned GPT model that didn't have the toxic text or problems of an internet-trained large language model? What if a region in the world with strong surveillance could optimize, randomize, and collectivize their DNS queries? What if a city could optimize energy usage and distribution via cooperatives rather than private companies?

Each of these possibilities opens up new practical privacy challenges and opportunities, which is why this book exists. Exploring new ideas for data sharing, data usage, data ownership, and collectivization becomes possible when more data scientists, engineers, and architects understand how systems like this might look, function, be practically tested, and run. If there is a particular community-based initiative, a burning problem or a product idea that helps people collectivize rather than centralize their data, I hope this book has given you some tools for making that a reality.

Regulation Fining Back

Regulatory authorities are, themselves, responding to the expansion of corporate data collection, control, and usage by issuing larger fines and penalties for egregious privacy regulation violations. In November 2022, Google settled a record-breaking privacy violation for nearly $392 million (*https://oreil.ly/hv1v2*) for unlawfully collecting location data after users explicitly turned off location tracking. In that same month, Meta was hit with a $277 million GDPR fine (*https://oreil.ly/VD7Nm*) for illegally exposing users' data online. The year before, Luxembourg fined Amazon a €746 million GDPR fine (*https://oreil.ly/P88Ud*) based on nonconsensual data collection and usage, though this was later overturned in appeals. And Meta agreed to pay a $725 million settlement for a class-action lawsuit based on privacy rights related to Cambridge Analytica (*https://oreil.ly/_Z85D*).

These lawsuits illustrate that egregious data collection and privacy violations by large tech companies will no longer be tolerated in the present or the future. As more privacy regulations come online—such as California's privacy law and several laws that are being proposed around the world at the time of this book publication—you can expect these decisions to continue and increase. GDPR went into effect in 2018. Only since 2020 is it clear that regulatory authorities are preparing to fully enforce the law and expand enforcement over time. Regulations like these have slow starts but long-lasting impact.

Outside of the reach of GDPR, there is also growing dissent among data owners around the world—and legal action to work against usage of data without consent. The GitHub Copilot lawsuit (*https://oreil.ly/sUok6*) opens the door for data ownership and rights battles against generative models, which will focus on how these massive models are trained and who benefits and who is harmed from this vast data collection. If successful, that lawsuit will create new options for data owners and producers such as musicians, authors, artists, writers, and coders to defend their own data from the reach of generative algorithms.[2]

Supporting Community Work

Working with communities affected by data collection and surveillance promotes reflection of the current vast collection and surveillance environment and spawns ideas and action for different paths forward. Empowering communities with more data and privacy know-how can create potential alternatives to the status quo.

When I first began to focus on privacy and ethical machine learning, I was inspired by community projects, like the Amazon Workers movements worldwide and striking Deliveroo drivers, that organized against unfair pay and working hours. Another movement stirred me, in particular: Stop LAPD Spying (*https://stoplapdspying.org*). Their countersurveillance work is, literally, a life-or-death question for many Black and Chicano/a Angelenos. Their methods for organizing are fundamentally grounded in community-first solidarity. They have not only created their own data collection, analysis, and studies of LAPD policing, and successfully countered predictive policing initiatives, but also continue to work on education, protest, and action against police surveillance systems, driving toward an abolitionist future.

I'm sure you will have your own sense of the kind of community work that piques your interests and how that intersects with systems of data collection and power. If you don't yet know of any community groups, take the time to research those in your city, state, or nation, focusing on folks directly impacted by data collection, surveillance, and vast usage of data. Getting involved in these groups means bringing a beginner's mindset to your work—learning and listening first and then finding ways to leverage what you know in support of the hard organizing work that is already happening. Trust me when I say this work is what you'll remember for many years in the future—as it can be so transformative, inspiring, and beneficial for everyone involved.

---

2 There are already groups of artists working on this by developing sites like Have I Been Trained? (*https://oreil.ly/BG1k4*) where artists seek to identify if their work has been trained to create models like DALL-E and send a request if they would like to opt out.

Privacy Champions

The skills you have learned in this book will help you determine what areas of privacy engineering, data science, and machine learning are the right mix for you. Start with the knowledge you now have and continue to learn and grow, engaging in ways that fit your beliefs, career, and priorities.

If you decide to focus on a particular technology or issue you found enticing, talk publicly about it, write about it, and spread your knowledge, thinking, and motivations. This awareness encourages others to question vast data collection and surveillance systems. Being a privacy champion at your work and in the industry is not always easy, but it is extremely important.

I wrote this book, in part, as a way to change the current data trends that support systems of inequality and oppression. This quest is a lifetime of work and something I have engaged with as long as I can remember. If just one person is inspired by this book and continues work like this, then I have achieved my goal. It takes collective action and community to achieve foundational change. I hope this book is one small contribution.

Your Privacy-Aware Multitool

You have accumulated new skills and knowledge via this book and can now go on to use these to solve problems and imagine new ways of doing data work. Let's take a look at what your privacy-aware multitool looks like (Figure 11-1).

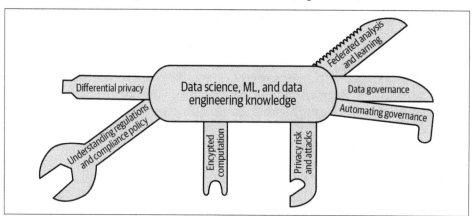

Figure 11-1. Privacy multitool

In Figure 11-1, you can see all of the topics and skills you've learned in this book. To expand your knowledge of data science, machine learning, and data engineering, you can now reason about data governance and automate it. You can now understand and see privacy risk and attacks. You know when you might want to apply technologies such as differential privacy, encrypted computation, and federated learning or analysis. You can understand regulations and read compliance policy, assisting your work as a technical expert in this space. Pretty neat, right?

The use cases in Chapter 9 demonstrated how many of these tools can be combined to solve real-world problems. Identifying what tool fits which use case is something you'll get better at, with practice. Experiment, keep learning, and keep your multitool close at hand.

To conclude, I want to take you through how the skills you've learned fit frameworks that are well regarded in privacy and machine learning. You'll see how your new skills can help you take a theory and turn it into an application.

Building Trustworthy Machine Learning Systems

You might have already heard about the EU's so-called AI Act (*https://oreil.ly/wJcm_*), which was finalized on December 6, 2022 (*https://oreil.ly/iR_mG*), and will go into effect within the next year or two. As part of preparation for that legislation, the EU assembled a group of researchers, practitioners, and policy makers to discuss how AI systems should work if they are going to be more ethical, trustworthy, and based in human rights.

What came out first was a variety of documents, studies, and recommendations that later helped shape the law. One artifact of this process was the EU Trustworthy AI Guidelines (*https://oreil.ly/PvJjs*), which are outlined in Table 11-1.

Table 11-1. EU trustworthy AI guidelines

Topic	Shortened description
Human agency and oversight	AI systems should empower human beings, allowing them to make informed decisions and fostering their fundamental rights. Human-in-the-loop, human-on-the-loop, and human-in-command approaches can help provide necessary oversight.
Technical robustness and safety	AI systems need to be resilient, secure, and safe, ensuring a fallback plan in case something goes wrong. They should also be accurate, reliable, and reproducible.
Privacy and data governance	Ensure privacy and data protection and adequate data governance mechanisms exist. Validate access to data.
Transparency	The data, system, and AI business models should be transparent. Decisions should be explained in a manner adapted to the stakeholder concerned. AI systems should identify themselves as such along with their capabilities and limitations.
Diversity, non-discrimination, and fairness	Unfair bias must be avoided. Fostering diversity, AI systems should be accessible to all, regardless of any disability, and involve relevant stakeholders throughout their entire life cycle.

Topic	Shortened description
Societal and environmental well-being	AI systems should benefit all human beings, including future generations. It must hence be ensured that they are sustainable, environmentally friendly, and socially beneficial.
Accountability	Ensure responsibility and accountability for AI systems and their outcomes. Auditability plays a key role therein, especially in critical applications. Accessible redress should be ensured.

It's likely that you immediately notice that privacy and data governance are explicitly called out in these guidelines and that they touch on several other topics from this book. In Chapter 1 you learned about human oversight of data systems, in general, and how solid documentation builds clear and auditable data workflows and systems. In Chapter 5 you learned about the intersection of fairness and privacy. Chapter 4 explored societal and personal harms related to privacy violations. Chapter 3 taught you how to build transparency into data collection and create audit trails for data governance, while helping you understand consent and responsible data usage. In Chapter 8 you thought through understanding and outlining the impact of data collection and usage on people, documenting potential harms caused by data collection or processing, and then explored ways to mitigate those harms.

You can see that privacy and the topics covered in this book are woven into the fabric of trustworthy AI systems. There are, of course, other factors at play and important work that privacy does not cover such as testing robustness against other types of attacks on AI systems and creating documentation for AI systems beyond the privacy aspects. Many of these topics link, organically, to one another. As you pay close attention to privacy and use knowledge gained from this book, you will notice how privacy supports these other topics. This is why privacy and the importance of human consent are fundamental concepts when considering trustworthiness and human rights within data systems.

Privacy by Design

In this book, I've referenced "Privacy by Design" several times, and you may have heard about this list of guiding principles before you picked up this book. Ann Cavoukian's principles on how to build technology systems with privacy awareness was first published in 2009 and has since been referenced in many guidelines, frameworks, policies, and regulations. Let's take a minute to review a summary of the original text, outlined in Table 11-2.

Table 11-2. Privacy by Design principles

Principle	Shortened description
Proactive not reactive; preventative not remedial	Anticipate and prevent privacy invasive events before they happen. Do not wait for privacy risks to materialize; instead, aim to prevent them from occurring. Privacy by Design comes before the fact, not after.
Privacy as the default setting	Deliver the maximum degree of privacy by ensuring that personal data are automatically protected in any given IT system or business practice. If an individual does nothing, their privacy still remains intact. Privacy is built into the system, by default.
Privacy embedded into design	Privacy by Design is embedded into the design and architecture of IT systems and business practices. It is not bolted on as an add-on, after the fact. Privacy is integral to the system, without diminishing functionality.
Full functionality—positive-sum, not zero-sum	Privacy by Design is a positive-sum "win-win" game, not a dated, zero-sum approach. Avoid false dichotomies, such as privacy versus security; demonstrate that it is possible to have both.
End-to-end security—full lifecycle protection	Embed privacy into the entire lifecycle of the data involved. Ensure that all data are securely retained, and then securely destroyed, at the end of the process, in a timely fashion.
Visibility and transparency—keep it open	Systems and processes can be checked and viewed to ensure they are operating according to the stated promises and objectives. Parts and operations remain visible and transparent, to users and providers alike. Remember, trust but verify.
Respect for user privacy—keep it user-centric	Above all, Privacy by Design requires architects and operators to keep the interests of the individual uppermost by offering strong defaults, appropriate notice, and user-friendly options. Keep it user-centric.

This list makes clear the purpose of this book and the topics it covers. You've learned how to implement privacy in a proactive way as a default and embedded directly into data collection systems and the systems they feed—machine learning, analytics, and other data use. You've explored new ways to architect and design data systems where consent, data protection, and privacy fundamentals dramatically shift how data flows work. You've investigated how to offer full system functionality while protecting privacy—finding that balance between privacy and utility—and making sure the user is in control and able to opt out at any time. You've learned about false dichotomies between privacy and security and considered privacy risk and attacks, learning how to build both data security and privacy into workflows. You now know how to discuss these topics with stakeholders, how to create awareness in the organization, and the importance of documentation. All this is meant to provide the user with a better experience and to increase the current privacy options.

Even though Privacy by Design was formulated in the mid-90s based on research in which Cavoukian was involved, the principles still hold today, some 30 years later. Many of the technologies and applications you've learned in this book allow you to build fundamentally new systems, which are private by design.

Privacy and Power

Privacy can also be analyzed in relation to systems of power and oppression in society and the world (*https://oreil.ly/sShiw*). These systems operate when biases and prejudices are institutionalized and operate on a systemic level—solidifying power for some while others are oppressed by that systemic injustice.

Figure 11-2 outlines a basic view of systems of power and oppression, showing how the combination of injustice and bias intersect with institutional structure and control that creates and maintains these systems.

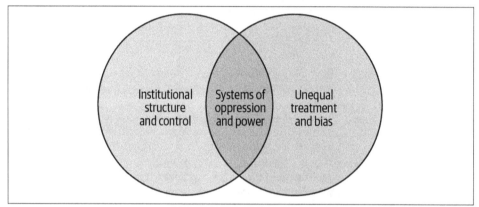

Figure 11-2. Systems of power and oppression

These systems exist in many (if not all) societies and differ based on the political and societal history of a particular place. Some systems of power—like white supremacy and colonialism—have expanded and crossed regions, shaping entire new societies that use these systems as a basis for their structure.

How does this relate to privacy? Well, it's complicated. As outlined in a long read from the *New Yorker* (*https://oreil.ly/IqQFo*), privacy regulation and the right to privacy in the US was, initially, rooted in basic systems of power. Powerful persons, namely, wealthy white men, wanted to guarantee their own privacy to control their personal narratives and hide their oppression of others. They understood that privacy was related to power and it could be used to grant them additional privileges.

If you look at privacy through the lens of power, it's clear how it can work. Fundamental access to privacy can help a person control what is known about them and how they can present themselves. It can help shape how they are perceived by the world and what information they use in what context. It allows them to start fresh, change their mind, change who they are, and decide who they would like to be and where. It has tremendous power—for both the individual and society.

In my life, I've worked to fight against systems of oppression, knowing that despite the benefits I receive from many systems, they hurt me and others by controlling the possibilities of everyone involved. When I benefit from a system of power, it cannot be disentangled from the person who is directly harmed. It hurts me as it hurts them, because we are both stuck in a harmful cycle of pain, guilt, and anger—with no control and no solution.

Change happens when you can recognize systems of oppression from which you benefit and use your power to disengage, speaking and acting directly against that system. This could be via your work, your words, your relationships, and your privileges. When large groups of people do this together, it creates revolutionary change. It can take systems of oppression that have existed for decades and fundamentally shift them in new directions.

Privacy can be used as a liberating tool: a way to change access to privacy from being unequally distributed to privacy for everyone. It can be used to speak about systems of power and oppression and point out unequal access to data, to information, and to consent. It can be weaponized to destroy systems of surveillance capitalism and the tyranny of unwarranted data collection. Privacy as power can leverage the things you've learned in this book, making them tools for creating a new relationship between data and power in society.

When people can control their own identity, their own data, and their own contexts; when people can communally organize using their collective data to shift outcomes and relationships to power systems; and when people can build new data systems based on human rights instead of company profits, the data world will have fundamentally shifted, moving away from the current state of oppression and into a more egalitarian and social future.

Tschüss

This book has been a work of passion for me—a resource I wished existed when I first started learning about these problems. It was created in many early mornings and late nights. I hope it inspires you to do data science differently and to teach others what you know and have learned. Only via collective efforts and awareness will the current trends change and allow for a more democratic, privacy-aware, and consensual data future. I hope to see those shifts during my career and see society benefit from data when incentives are aligned with human rights and equality.

You have the skills, the knowledge, and the power—so go forth and engineer privacy!

Index

Netflix Prize attack, 85-88
New York City taxi dataset, 90
Nissenbaum, Helen, xviii, 292
Noble, Safiya, 285
noise (see Laplace mechanism)
noise reduction, 52
noyb, 203, 278

O

O'Neill, Cathy, 285
oblivious transfer, 262
Opacus, 121-124
open source libraries, 159-161
Open Web Application Security Project
   (OWASP), 110
oppression, privacy and, 302
outliers
   memorization and, 98
   monitoring, 135
OWASP (Open Web Application Security
   Project), 110

P

Paillier encryption, 180-182
Papernot, Nicolas, 118
partially homomorphic encryption (PHE), 179
PATE architecture, 118
peer review, 178, 264
Pejó, Balázs, 263
perfect privacy, 263
perfect secrecy, 264
perfect security, 168
person-related data
   defined, 5
   sensitive data as, 7
personal choices
   FAQs, 279-286
   friends with automated home/phone assis-
     tant, 281
   leaked information via applications,
     285-286
   personalized ads, 284-285
   "privacy is dead" argument, 282-283
   privacy-friendly services, 279-281
   selling one's own data to companies, 283
personal identifiers, removal of, 271
Personal Information Protection Law (PIPL),
   216
personalized ads, 284-285

personally identifiable information (PII), 5
   defined, 5
   finding/identifying, 270
   identifying, 8
PETs (see privacy-enhancing technologies)
PHE (partially homomorphic encryption), 179
phone assistant, automated, 281
PII (see personally identifiable information)
PIMO (Private Input Masked Output), 25
PipelineDP, 63, 74
pipelines (see data pipelines)
PIPL (Personal Information Protection Law),
   216
PIR (Private Information Retrieval), 262
plausible deniability, 34, 78
political dissent, surveillance of, 291
post-processing, 101
power, privacy and, 302
PPML (see privacy-preserving machine learning)
PPRL (Privacy-Preserving Record Linkage), 23
practicality considerations, 233-257
   embracing uncertainty while planning for
     the future, 236-239
   evaluating and managing privacy risk,
     234-236
   integrating and automating privacy in ML,
     248-254
   managing privacy and security risk, 234-239
   privacy technology: use-case analysis,
     239-248
   working with research libraries and teams,
     254-256
predictive policing, 291
Presidio, 25, 271
privacy (generally)
   as core value proposition, 82, 238
   fighting back against incursions on, 295-297
   legal issues, 201-231
   perfect, 263
   practicality considerations (see practicality
     considerations)
   secrecy versus, 166
Privacy as Contextual Integrity (Nissenbaum),
   292
privacy attacks, 85-112
   analyzing common attack vectors, 85-102
   attacks against privacy protocols, 101-102
   data security and, 102-106

About the Author

Katharine Jarmul is a privacy activist and data scientist whose work and research focuses on privacy and security in data science workflows. She has held numerous leadership and independent contributor roles at large companies and startups in the US and Germany—implementing data processing and machine learning systems with privacy and security built in and developing forward-looking, privacy-first data strategy. She is a passionate and internationally recognized data scientist, programmer, and lecturer.

Colophon

The animal on the cover of *Practical Data Privacy* is a species of morid cod called *Eretmophorus kleinenbergi*. Not much is known about this fish, and some scientists believe it may not be a unique animal at all but rather the juvenile stage of another morid species. It is found in the Mediterranean Sea as well as parts of the Atlantic Ocean, and grows to be about 3.5 inches long.

Morid cods, of the family *Moridae*, are also known as codlings, hakelings, or moras. They are small- to medium-sized fishes, generally with large eyes, a chin barbell, two dorsal fins (one short and triangular, the other long), and an elongated body tapering to a narrow tail. Their diet is made up of a variety of plankton, invertebrates, smaller fish, and crustaceans. They have been found at depths up to 8,200 feet but tend to live in shallower water.

Morid cods are classified in the same taxonomic order as cods. While they share some external similarities, morids differ in skeletal structure and the shape of their swim bladder (an internal organ filled with gas that allows fish to adjust their buoyancy and remain at their current depth without the effort of swimming).

Many of the animals on O'Reilly covers are endangered; all of them are important to the world.

The cover illustration is by Karen Montgomery, based on an antique line engraving from a loose plate, origin unknown. The cover fonts are Gilroy Semibold and Guardian Sans. The text font is Adobe Minion Pro; the heading font is Adobe Myriad Condensed; and the code font is Dalton Maag's Ubuntu Mono.

O'REILLY®

Learn from experts.
Become one yourself.

Books | Live online courses
Instant Answers | Virtual events
Videos | Interactive learning

Get started at oreilly.com.

CPSIA information can be obtained
at www.ICGtesting.com
Printed in the USA
JSHW062121020523
41158JS00001B/1